YWES 1999

CW01096289

HENRY JAMES AND THE
LANGUAGE OF EXPERIENCE

In *Henry James and the Language of Experience*, Collin Meissner examines the political dimension to the representation of experience as it unfolds throughout James's work. Meissner argues that, for James, experience was a private and public event, a dialectical process that registered and expressed his consciousness of the external world. Adapting recent work in hermeneutics and phenomenology, Meissner shows how James's understanding of the process of consciousness is not simply an aspect of literary form; it is in fact inherently political, as it requires an active engagement with the full complexity of social reality. For James, the civic value of art resided in this interactive process, one in which the reader becomes aware of the aesthetic experience as immediate and engaged. This wide-ranging study combines literary theory and close readings of James's work to argue for a redefiniton of the aesthetic as it operates in James's work.

Collin Meissner is Assistant Provost of the University of Notre Dame and lecturer in the University's English Department. He has published essays in *Genre, Studies in the Novel, The Henry James Review,* and the *Colby Quarterly*.

HENRY JAMES
AND THE LANGUAGE
OF EXPERIENCE

COLLIN MEISSNER

CAMBRIDGE
UNIVERSITY PRESS

PUBLISHED BY THE PRESS SYNDICATE OF THE UNIVERSITY OF CAMBRIDGE
The Pitt Building, Trumpington Street, Cambridge CB2 1RP, United Kingdom

CAMBRIDGE UNIVERSITY PRESS
The Edinburgh Building, Cambridge CB2 2RU, UK http://www.cup.cam.ac.uk
40 West 20th Street, New York, NY 10011–4211, USA http://www.cup.org
10 Stamford Road, Oakleigh, Melbourne 3166, Australia

First published 1999

Printed in the United Kingdom at the University Press, Cambridge

Typeset in Baskerville 10½/12pt   [CE]

A catalogue record for this book is available from the British Library

Library of Congress Cataloguing-in-Publication Data
Meissner, Collin.
Henry James and the language of experience / Collin Meissner.
p.   cm.
Includes bibliographical references and index
ISBN 0 521 62398 7 (hardback)
1. James, Henry, 1843–1916 – Political and social views.
2. Language and languages – Political aspects. 3. James, Henry, 1843–1916 – Language.
4. Aesthetics – Political aspects.
5. Consciousness in literature. 6. Experience in literature.
I. Title.
PS2127.P6M45   1999
813′.4–dc21   98–39565 CIP

ISBN 0 521 62398 7 hardback

For Mary Rose, Emma, Hannah, and Dea.
For filling my life with so much joy.

Contents

Acknowledgments

I would like to pay thanks to a good number of people who contributed directly and indirectly to this book. First, my parents, Horst and Gudrun Meissner, know more than I how well they encouraged me to "try to be one of the people on whom nothing is lost." Gerald Bruns and James Walton both know how much this book originated in and is the final result of the numerous conversations we have had about Henry James in particular and literature in general over the last several years. Gerald Bruns shared his thoughts about James with me over many lunches, a pleasantness I continue to enjoy as we return again and again to the wonder of James's vision. I am particularly thankful for his patience in letting me find my way through this project, for the precision of his commentary, and for his uncanny knack of asking exactly the right question at exactly the right time. Jerry's vision is always expansive, his approach to literature always honest, and it has been one of the great benefits of my intellectual development to have him as such a patient, selfless, and energetic teacher. I might as well say the same of Jay Walton. Jay's generosity is equaled only by his keen insight, his special ability to listen with active attention, and his remarkable facility for recalling and applying everything he has ever read. This project was improved immeasurably as a result of Jay's careful reading and incisive remarks. Many times along the way in our struggles with James, both Jerry Bruns and I have sought out and received Jay's insightful commentary. I can easily say Jay Walton remains, simply put, the finest reader of literature I have ever known. He is a mentor and friend about whom I cannot say enough.

I would also like to pay special thanks to Paul Armstrong, whose book *The Challenge of Bewilderment* struck that nice balance of explanation and provocation. His comments on several chapters of this book and his encouragement about the whole were always gracious and wise. In addition, I would like to thank the two readers who vetted this project for Cambridge; their criticisms and suggestions brought many improvements I would have been unable to accomplish on my own. In this line, Andrew Taylor merits high praise. He proved himself a most gracious copy-editor whose indefatigable capacity to root out and change all contractions brought this book a tone it lacked. Joni Gibley's work on the index was an inexpressible benefit. Some parts of chapter one appeared in a different form as "*The Princess Casamassima*: A Dirty Intellectual Fog," *The Henry James Review* 19, no. 1 (Winter, 1998), 53–71; a section of chapter four under the same title, "Lambert Strether and the Negativity of Experience," first appeared in *Studies in the Novel* 29, no. 1 (1997), 40–60; and chapter five appeared in *Genre* 19, no. 1 (1996), 473–94. I am grateful for permission to reprint this copyrighted material.

I would fall short of honesty if I did not acknowledge the important role Emma played in reminding me of the need to get away and play now and then. At her insistence I broke free of the computer and worked out many a confusing issue in James's work while she and I played frisbee.

More importantly, I owe a tremendous debt of gratitude to my wife Mary Rose whose support and commitment to this project included her willingness not only to read James along with me, but an unfailing patience for listening to me work out my ideas. She has been a searching critic of these pages. Throughout the composition of this book her insightful suggestions about James, her insistence that I write with greater clarity, and her genuine interest in James's work make this book as much her's as it is mine. Of course whatever shortcomings there are remain mine alone.

CHAPTER I

The experience of Jamesian hermeneutics

An old story goes that Cimabue was struck with admiration when he saw the shepherd-boy, Giotto, sketching sheep. But, according to true biographies, it is never the sheep that inspire such a man as Giotto with the love of painting; but rather, his first sight of the paintings of such a man as Cimabue. What makes the artist is the circumstance that in his youth he was more deeply moved by his first sight of works of art than by that of the things which they portray.

Andre Malraux, *The Psychology of Art*

I

I should say right away that my purpose in this book is not to construct an argument about hermeneutics as a general theory, but rather to give an account of James's hermeneutics in his own terms. To this extent, then, my goal throughout has been to try as much as I can to foreground James's own language while making secondary criticism an important "secondary" partner. My focus has been to try and clarify what is perhaps the most elusive concept in James's writings – his idea of experience.[1] I will argue that James's hermeneutics is a hermeneutics of experience, but "experience" in what sense? If we consult James's Prefaces, we find a heterogeneous array of usages: experience as a general term, a formative concept in art, as something from which we are disconnected, as a fine flower, a germ, something which we lack, or which comprises "human communities," or as something by which we are assaulted. But perhaps most of all, for James "experience" is "our apprehension and our measure of what happens to us as social creatures," as he says in his Preface to *The Princess Casamassima*.[2] To be sure, experience in James is an affair of consciousness, but it is also intersubjec-

I

tive and social. Indeed, it is something James's readers as well as his characters undergo.

In the empiricist tradition experience is characterized in terms of sensations and impressions. It is principally an occupation of the eyes. James's work is rooted in and enriches this tradition, but it is not confined to it. For him, experience is rather something one lives through or suffers. I find it useful to think of this process dialectically as a movement of bewilderment and enlightenment, where experience is something one acquires, but chiefly through loss or failure or the breakdown of things. Indeed, Jamesian experience reveals itself to be a fundamentally negative process in that typically James's narratives dramatize a collision between competing "fields of knowledge, types of normativity, and forms of subjectivity."[3] Throughout his writings James consistently exposes nativist conventions and conscious or unconscious transfigurations of reality as constructs whose aim is to allow the interpreting or experiencing subject to exert some measure of control over external circumstances. The extent to which these manipulations are successful is the extent to which these individuals are ultimately unaware. James's fiction directly challenges individuals like Mrs. Newsome, *The American*'s Madame de Bellegarde, or *The Turn of the Screw*'s Mrs. Costello who profess objective standards of ethical behavior while actually hiding behind what Paul Armstrong has referred to as "culturally contingent customs that organize experience along particular lines and that owe their existence to the agreement of the community to practice them" (*Phenomenology*, 5). Jamesian hermeneutics puts under scrutiny this question of codified ways of knowing and modes of behavior we take so much for granted that we have become not only unaware but the unwitting victims of their manipulative effect on our daily lives.

By focusing on experience with a hermeneutical–phenomenological understanding of what that entails I can correct misconceptions about James's aesthetics and politics which are now widely circulating. Notions of the political which neglect its rootedness in experience misrepresent James and misconceive the problems of power, of subjectivity, and of understanding as he develops them in his work. If my argument is correct, my analysis of the consequences of experience should offer a way of reading literature which first foregrounds the danger of taking experience as the origin of knowledge, and then enables literature to contest directly the hegemony of ideological systems which base their ascendency on the subtle manipulation of the subject's (meaning, again, character's and reader's) consciousness. The reason I use the vocabulary of hermeneutics and phenomenology instead of that more closely associated with cultural criticism is that hermeneutics offers a way of looking at experience that highlights the important dialectic between the subject's private consciousness and his or her social construction. For this reason I claim that a hermeneutic–phenomenological politics of experience and subjectivity offers a more provocative understanding of culture and identity in James than the Foucauldian and New Historicist social theories which now hold sway. Often these latter theories depend upon essentializing interpretive categories and neglect the powerful dialectic which takes place within and without the subject's consciousness as a private and public arena wherein the most compelling principles of political and cultural life are dramatized – an experience, I argue, the James text inevitably makes the reader encounter as well. To this extent my argument attempts to correct theories of the political in James which are not based on experience and to point out that *any* adequate theory of culture, society, and history needs to be experientially based. James's work, from his first stories and early novels, his travel sketches, through his discovery of a distinct voice in his middle phase, including his disastrous venture as a dramatist, and on into the late masterpieces and critical commentaries consistently reveals a writer finely attuned to the way in which our conditioned experience of "experience" shapes our perception of all that we come into contact with, including our perception of self.

While I deal throughout this book with texts that cover the full range of James's career, I concentrate on three major novels in particular detail: *The American* (1877), *The Portrait of a Lady* (1881), and *The Ambassadors* (1903). These texts cover the trajectory of James's career and reveal, in concentrated detail, his response to Europe and how the development of an international theme offered him the opportunity to produce a form of art which would provoke engagement (*The American*). In writing *The Portrait of a Lady*, James experiences a moment of insight, an epiphany that reveals the power of art in sharp detail, in constructing Isabel's night vigil of chapter forty-two, and comes to see how the novel can function as a vehicle of self-discovery for its audience, not through didacticism, but through a manner of autodidacticism or autogenesis wherein the reader comes to enjoy the double privilege of being both the subject and object of the text. James came to call this discovery his center of consciousness technique, the full narrative power of which is perhaps best displayed in *The Ambassadors*. This text returns to *The American* and absorbs the more external nature of that text into Lambert Strether's intense investigations into his own subjectivity as it is opened before him by what we could say is an extended vigil of the sort Isabel Archer experiences. In *The Ambassadors* James's persistent investigations into foreignness, cultural and personal, into subjectivity, public and private, and into how our ability to experience these conditions is itself a production all come together in a hermeneutic method whose revelatory force is stunning, even to himself, as his autobiographical works make apparent. These texts show the poignant refinements of James's aesthetics and reveal, in the developments one can trace along the trajectory of James's career, the growth of a distinctly Jamesian hermeneutics rooted in the belief that asking how and why we have particular experiences and how and what they mean to us is the only way an individual or a culture can break free of the manipulative forces that forever threaten one's interpretive sover-eignty. It is for this reason James adjured his audience to cultivate perception as a form of understanding, adjured his audience to be open to experience since in one's openness lay the potential for growth and development as well as freedom from confinement. James formulates the basic structure of this injunction in the Preface to *The Portrait of a Lady* when he attests to the "high price of the novel" being rooted in its "power" to range freely over "all the varieties of outlook on life ... created by conditions that are never the same from man to man" (1074–75).

It is perhaps here, in James's documentation of the process through which one's understanding of experience and of one's self is, as Ross Posnock has argued, "itself dependent on the production of narratives derived from cultural imagery," that the subtle power of Jamesian hermeneutics gains its full force and reveals its deeply political consequences for the individual (*Trial of Curiosity*, 67). One can look to *The Ambassadors* as an explanatory example, but almost any James text would be similarly exemplary. We recall how in *The Ambassadors*'s outline James tells us that the story will be of a man who comes out on the other side of his experience changed. But in what way is he changed? How does the change register itself on Strether and on James's audience? The answer, the text shows, is that Strether has finally become himself and America is exposed in such a way that it can never again be for him, and for readers of his experience, what it once was. In effect, Strether's embassy overthrows the self-aggrandizing certitude which had come to characterize American cultural and political ideology in the late nineteenth and early twentieth century. Paris relentlessly contests and challenges Strether's imported notions of behavior and systematically exposes Mrs. Newsome's Woollett as a land of genteel hypocrisy characterized by a deceitful moral prudery. Rather than enable self-development, Woollett, and by extension, America, James suggests, undermines the country's celebrated freedom to self-determination by consistently reminding the individual that things must be done "by the book," to paraphrase Mrs. Newsome. This unflinching rigidity is behind Daisy Miller's death, entombs Catherine Sloper, and all but exterminates Lambert Strether. In remarking on this aspect of James's politics, Robert Dawidoff argues that "Strether's experience speaks to the feelings of dislocation from the inside out," and that these experiences reveal James's deeply held belief that the "prevailing American genteel moralism was degenerate morality," whose goal, he felt "had to do with keeping the enterprise of American business culture going behind a veneer of professed ideals" (*Genteel Tradition*, 135, 97).

Capturing, exposing, and taking one through the process of recovery from the inscription of a cultural hegemony is the project of Jamesian hermeneutics. For this reason the language of hermeneutics, which always has as its goal an explanation of how understanding and interpretation occur and why they occur as they do, is particularly suited to reading James. In exposing the hidden conditions of belonging to a culture and the inherent disenfranchisement belonging demands, James's fiction cultivates a politics of individuality whose ultimate consequence is the arming of its readers with a new vision of the expenses and requirements of membership. "In political terms," as Posnock explains, James's fiction allows one to see a culture's power structures, to see how a culture operates via "the rigid identification with one role or place" and how freedom depends upon "a dynamic of shifting involvements that resist finitude and definition" (*Trial of Curiosity*, 76). In being armed through awareness, readers of James achieve a heightened and potentially threatening level of emancipation, not because they will put down a text like *The Ambassadors* and erect barricades, but because they will not again be such easy and unwitting participants in their own production and control. Think again of Strether, "he begins as a failure and ends liberated from success," as Dawidoff puts it. *The Ambassadors* "records his piercing of the ideology that imprisons him" and shows a way beyond the singularity produced and promoted by America's mercantile culture (*Genteel Tradition*, 135).

So, by examining the hermeneutic and phenomenological aspects of experience, viewing experience as an event which is individually lived and socially mediated, my analysis challenges the prevailing analyses of James which follow a Foucauldian line of inquiry. The most powerful example of this line of thought remains Mark Seltzer's *Henry James and the Art of Power*. Seltzer's critique of James's blindness to the epistemological coerciveness of power offers a powerful reading of James's conception of knowledge and experience. Seltzer rightly points out that Jamesian criticism has steadfastly assumed a "radical opposition between aesthetics and politics" in James's work, and has persisted in reading him as "the very exemplar of an aesthetic outside the circuit of power" (156, 147). And to the extent that Seltzer exposes "the ruses that have maintained an opposition between the art of the novel and the subject of power," he has successfully "changed the rules by which we speak of the politics of the novel," at least insofar as James is a participant in the forum (24). But Seltzer's argument depends upon a slight misreading of James, one produced by the very aesthetic power structure Seltzer claims has unjustly imprisoned James. For Seltzer's argument to work, James *must* be the genteel aesthete who "tries to protect the aesthetic by displacing the reality of power with an artful illusion" (134–35). Thus, Seltzer describes what he calls the "double discourse of the Jamesian text," a discursive practice "that at once represses and acknowledges a discreet continuity between literary and political practices" and shows how the end product of this double discourse reveals James's "complicity and rigorous continuity with the larger social regimes of mastery and control" embodied throughout his work (148, 15, 13). In short, Seltzer's argument turns James into a version of Mrs. Newsome, Woollett's doyenne, who governs everything through a strict management of reality.

Seltzer's assessment of the (James) novel as a "relay of mechanisms of social control" which "engages in an aesthetic rewriting of power" is largely accurate, but Seltzer ultimately avoids a crucial aspect of James's texts, and the novel in general. James would agree with Seltzer that "[a]rt and power are not at odds in the novel"

(149). But James would say the important discovery in that under-lying architecture is not that art and power interanimate each other, but what one does with both art and power. Rather than artfully reinscribing the status quo's power structures, James's work frees the subject by making that subject aware of the economies of power which exert influence at culture's visible and invisible levels. And while that awareness which I will show is the purpose behind James's writing may itself be a form of power, that power is enabling rather than imprisoning. What Seltzer's account neglects to consider is the personal nature of experience in one's political, social, and historical transactions. Any account of James and the novel in general must consider another double discourse, that between a subject's private reflections on any given event and the social discourse which inscribes that event. This dialectic is perhaps the only means available for one to escape the pressures of the external world, while at the same time coming to understand how those pressures have acted like an invisible hand which has shaped the way one comes to understand experiences in the first place.

In marking the radical split between the privately understood or desired and publicly constructed or contained notions of self, James puts his finger on the rift he saw as specifically produced by modern culture's unswerving attention to the acquisition of material goods. His fiction and criticism relentlessly approach, embrace, and expose commercialism's multifold influences on the individual subject's daily life, as well as its impact on the culture's day-to-day and historical activities. James's fiction registers these tensions by setting virtually all the events within an advanced capitalist economy which forms the super-structural backdrop against which the events, and the characters' experience and understanding of those events, are undergone, interpreted, and, eventually, by way of reading, pressed upon the reader's consciousness. One could say the coercive force of capital is the politics of experience in James's texts, that the political content discovered in reading James is the manipulative force of capital which begins as an emancipating tool of consumption and winds up imprisoning the individual and culture in a world where consumption becomes the only form of meaning and meaning itself is divested of any higher significance than commodity exchange. It is perhaps this aspect of James's narratives that has led Peggy McCor-mack to conclude that "James's novels depict recognizably, even aggressively, capitalist societies," whose characters are frighteningly reduced to "respond[ing] to this setting as if it were an exchange economy in which they survive and hope to prosper by practicing whatever form of commodities transaction they can afford." One such practice, McCormack argues, consists in the characters "displaying their human assets as cultural commodities valuable only when made public or exchanged in interaction" (*Rule of Money*, 2). James's concerns with the intellectual and artistic astringencies produced by such a culture can be felt at every stage of his work and include even his own conception of himself as an artist whose public success remained by and large unattained. In fact, we can see James negotiating the terrain of the exchange economy McCormack describes in his remarks about Isabel Archer from the Preface to *The Portrait of a Lady*. James likens himself to a "dealer" in rare goods who has a "precious object" he may choose not to " 'realise' " by keeping it "locked up indefinitely rather than commit it, at no matter what price, to vulgar hands" (1076). James's refusal strikes me as a direct remark upon the subjective divestiture required by a commercial culture, which is how he understood America to be singularly organized, a point he makes bluntly in one of his travel essays for *The Nation* in 1878 when he explains America's defining characteristic as being composed of a people that is "exclusively commercial" ("Americans Abroad," 209). In 1900 the German philosopher Georg Simmel published a lengthy study, *The Philosophy of Money*, that captures exactly the sense of the age which permeates James's work and provides some important background to the social psychology as well as the practical politics at play in James's fiction. The central point of Simmel's work is that a money culture produces a radical split between the objective and subjective sides of human beings, with a powerful predominance of the one over the other – and where the one (the objective) is defined by the intellect and the other (the subjective) by feeling. Simmel's thesis helps us understand James's concentration in his fiction on the way consciousness works to understand experience since, as Simmel says, "Money has provided us with the sole possibility for uniting people while excluding everything personal and specific" from the business of living (345).

In a way, Simmel's text draws out the background of James's novels and helps us to understand better the super-structural framework James is operating with. What Simmel's argument foregrounds is the extent to which not only interpersonal relations and public transactions are conceived of as value-added instances of communication, what James refers to as the "perpetual passionate pecuniary purpose" embodied in New York (*American Scene*, 111), but the extent to which money has skewed the intellect and converted it into an essentially featureless, faceless, impersonal, and generally disinterested faculty, an "indifferent mirror of reality" whose sole practical purpose is entirely absorbed in the relation of ends and means, where money is the end and everything else is the means (*Philosophy of Money*, 432). It is against this backdrop that James stages his interactive investigation into the function of perception and experience in understanding. James understood with remarkable clarity the economic basis of the aesthetic as well as the integral relationship between avarice and art. While his fiction is full of instances which illuminate this point, perhaps the letter Hyacinth Robinson writes from Venice, a Renaissance mercantile capital, most directly acknowledges the material circumstances of aesthetic production. We recall how at this point in *The Princess Casamassima* Hyacinth is caught between his commitment to revolutionary upheaval and the "inestimably precious and beautiful" art he finds throughout Europe. Torn, he realizes the lukewarm feelings he has for Hoffendahl's plot in comparison with his passionate commitment to the aesthetic which now seems worth whatever price civilization pays.

The monuments and treasures of art, the great palaces and properties, the conquests of learning and taste, the general fabric of civilisation as we know it, based if you will upon all the despotisms, the cruelties, the exclusions, the monopolies and the rapacities of the past, but thanks to which, all the same, the world is less of a "bloody sell" and life more of a lark.[4]

At this point Hyacinth is articulating James's understanding of what the full compass of aesthetic production looks like. But James also understood that the audience for his works was one produced by a money culture which had reduced value to its purely commercial and material elements and was, as a result, generally suspicious of art's unquantifiability. Think here of the vague but ubiquitous commercial enterprises which govern *The Ambassadors*'s Woollett, or of James's voiced dismay at the pecuniary motives behind the establishment of New York's Metropolitan Museum where the focus of attention rested on the "money in the air, ever so much money, grossly expressed" for "acquisition," rather than the works of art the museum would hold (*American Scene*, 192). To bridge this gap between the crass economic conditions his audience understood and the aesthetic values it beheld with suspicion, James embodied both within his fiction, showing them to be alternate sides of the same mobile. The mobile analogy is apt because for James the aesthetic and the material were not specifically distinct but often flowed into one another, as he saw was the case with the Metropolitan Museum which he understood was "going to be great" and which would carry out an "Education" that "was to be exclusively that of the sense of beauty" (193, 192). It is for this reason that throughout his work James keeps turning the mobile around, now revealing its crass economic imprint, now its illustration of the beauty of form. In this way James's work gives precedence to the aesthetic while still acknowledging the material conditions of its production. This is not to say that James educated his audience to see art in acquisitive and monetary terms, like an Adam Verver; rather, by showing art as extending the economic and even making its own value-added contribution to one's ability to understand and live a more per-ceptive and engaging life, James began a process of recovery in which the subject's consciousness could be freed from the impri-soning and manipulative economic influences that go with what Simmel calls the relentless "broadening of consumption" that characterizes a money culture (*Philosophy of Money*, 455). In other words, what James's novels do is aggressively educate and shape their reader's understanding first that he is being manipulated to be one way and not another by cultural forces beyond his control, and then, in identifying this coercive process, allow the reader to take over the business of becoming individual which, in James's mind, meant becoming responsive and perceptive, something art was particularly good at fostering.

Not surprisingly, the language of hermeneutics and phenomen-ology especially focuses on just this interpretive revelation and for this reason is particularly suited to developing a methodology for reading James, especially given that James constructed his narrative method specifically so as to provoke an epistemological crisis in his reading audience, a crisis whose primary event is to make the reader aware of how much interpretation is always already a product of interpretation. So James actually does change the politics of the novel, as Seltzer rightly argues. Only he does so not through a "reinscription of power within the ostensibly 'powerless' discourse of the novel," but by making the novel a marketplace in which the economies of power are displayed. In reading a James text the reader is made aware of power's presence, and in being made aware made free insofar as freedom is possible and desirable.[5] So rather than being blind to the epistemological coerciveness of power, James is potently aware of power's multifold discourses and his representation of experience seeks to make visible those invisible power structures in such a way that the reading audience can find in his novels the ultimate escape, not into a fantasy world, but into a world that is suddenly made clear and a self that is finally one's own. What I suggest is that James makes this emancipation available to his audience through an unavoidable and subtle lesson about the nature of experience, rather than removing the potentially liberating capacity of the novel by forging a "criminal continuity between art and power," as Seltzer asserts (*Henry James and the Art of Power*, 170).

Students of James will recognize the debt my study owes to Paul Armstrong's *The Phenomenology of Henry James*, but they will also recognize how this study departs in significant ways, primarily through its more specific focus on how the hermeneutics of experience, particularly in light of Hans-Georg Gadamer's claim that experience has a liberating, reorientating negativity about it, offers a way of reading James that can help us get past the opposition between formalism and historicism which has placed contemporary criticism in a state of semi-paralysis. Since Armstrong's study follows a more purely phenomenological path, he omits Gadamer's hermeneutical branch of phenomenology. And while Gadamer comes out of the phenomenological tradition, namely that of Schleiermacher, Dilthey, Husserl, Heidegger, and Wittgenstein, he sees understanding as less an act of transcendental consciousness (Husserl), and more as an event in which we come to understand how we stand in relation to other people, to ourselves, and to our immediate historical situation. For Gadamer understanding presupposes belonging to a tradition and is always of a subject matter. Gadamer continually forces us to ask what light a text throws on what matters to us. In addition, understanding always entails application; it cannot be the solitary act of a disengaged ego because understanding a text entails understanding the claim it has upon you. According to Gadamer's hermeneutics, one is always exposed to the text one seeks to understand and understanding itself always takes the form of action. The applicability of Gadamer's hermeneutics, his analysis of herme-

neutical situations and how one comes to understand them, is thus
directly relevant to the hermeneutic struggle James's characters
experience. For while Husserl's phenomenology or Foucauldian
methodologies can help explain the larger social texts or "discourses" which determine meaning in, say, Woollett and, to some
extent, in Paris, Gadamer's hermeneutics is much more able to
capture the subtleties behind the epistemological crises that not only
characters such as Strether, or Christopher Newman, or Isabel
Archer, but readers too experience through the course of experiencing a James novel. And by clarifying how we come to understand
the subtleties of James's text, Gadamer helps us to appreciate not
just the vital and actively engaged quality of Jamesian aesthetics, but
also to understand how James allows us to return terms like
"consciousness," "subjectivity," and "experience" to critical discourse without either essentializing, reifying, or psychologizing
them.

II

As I have mentioned, for James experience is "our apprehension and
our measure of what happens to us as social creatures"(1091). But
this understanding is complicated. Within James's work two rival
and incompatible theories of experience exist. On the one hand
there is a cumulative theory which understands experience as something to be acquired. The fundamental flaw in this view is that it
privileges the immediacy of experience without offering any ground
on which to question the primary nature of the subject's disposition
toward it. To this extent subjects find in the experience a reflection
of all they bring to it, a vision ultimately secured by the particular
experience. In other words, by focusing on experience as a purely
external phenomenon, the subject – whether character or reader –
wanders endlessly in a hermeneutic circle. In *The Princess Casamassima*
James refers to this self-ratifying interpretive quandary, at its worst,
as a wandering "blindly, obstructedly, in a kind of eternal dirty
intellectual fog" (5:340). What James seems to be referring to here is
our willingness, as "social creatures," to resign, for convenience, our
"apprehension" to the authority of interpretive hegemonies precisely
because we mistakenly limit our notion of experience to a purely
external encounter and never ask why we are disposed either to have
or understand a particular experience. As Joan Scott shows of

experience in general, the "evidence of experience," as an eviden-
tiary and interpretive concept, has traditionally been naturalized as
evidence which "reproduces rather than contests given ideological
systems" ("Experience," 25). Scott's argument about the need to
historicize "the notion of experience" is directly relevant to the
conception of experience as it functions in James's hermeneutics
(34). As Scott points out, by accepting experience as "the origin of
knowledge" we ineluctably accept the "vision of the individual
subject" as the "bedrock of evidence upon which explanation is
built." But this interpretive move has grave consequences, not the
least of which is that we leave unasked "[q]uestions about the nature
of experience," about the diverse constitutions of subjects, "about
how one's vision is structured – about language (or discourse) and
history" (25). One is reminded of James's characterization of Mrs.
Newsome as "all cold thought," as an agent who operates via an
understanding which simply "doesn't admit surprises" (22:220).

Here too, in the way we fall prey to the manipulative ordering and
validation of experience Scott speaks of, we find James's attention to
the subtle manipulations by which a money culture shapes the way
we see and understand. In explaining the historical connection
between money and value, Simmel addresses a point James's novels
consistently investigate and which Scott foregrounds as the dubious
claim to objective veracity inherent in asserting "the evidence of
experience" as the foundation upon which "explanation is built"
(25). As Simmel points out, the value of "objects, thoughts and
events can never be inferred from their mere natural existence and
content" since their value has nothing to do with their "natural
ordering" and everything to do with the constructed valuation we
place on them. And when we speak of valuation conceptually we
mean "the whole world viewed from a particular vantage point." In
a conclusion James and Scott would share, Simmel explains how we
"are rarely aware of the fact that our whole life, from the point of
view of consciousness, consists in experiencing and judging values,"
and that our life "acquires meaning and significance," from values
which are socially produced (*Philosophy of Money*, 59, 60). Not surprisingly, in James's novels value is more often than not produced by
individuals whose commercial success has elevated them to the
status of bearer of meaning and allows them to shape the direction
and interpretation of both the culture at large and the understanding
of individual experiences within that hegemony. The latter half of

this power is what James found particularly disturbing. Another way of saying this would be that Mrs. Newsome has the financial power to determine what constitutes an experience and how that experience is understood in Woollett, and her power to carry this out comes both from the mercantile influence she wields and the community's willing compliance with those values.

Mrs. Newsome and her Woollett hermeneutics constitute a conceptual framework which authorizes experience and reality for everyone and everything within the shadow of her influence. The suggestion in *The Ambassadors* is not just that Woollett is incapable of dealing with the particularity of experience, or that its attitude precludes the present moment, but that it has succeeded in displacing time completely. The past, the present, the future of Woollett have already been, so to speak; they are predetermined by the textual restriction of its reigning matriarch. (To this extent Mrs. Newsome resembles Madame de Bellegarde, *The American*'s preserver of the *ancien régime*.) It is just this sense of prosaic detachment in Mrs. Newsome's manner that has led Martha Nussbaum to remark that people like Mrs. Newsome "triumph over life, they don't *live*" ("Perceptive Equilibrium," 69). The sense of safety a constructed past offers as a way of mediating between experience of the world as such and the illusion of experiencing the world is a characteristic Madame de Bellegarde and Mrs. Newsome share. James presents the ramifications of this manipulation of life by suggesting, via Mrs. Newsome, that Woollett cannot "live in the present moment" (68). In her own way Mrs. Newsome is an example of Walter Benjamin's angel of history. For like Benjamin's angel whose "face is turned toward the past," Mrs. Newsome too can only encounter the future when it has been filtered through and edited by what she knows to have already been accounted for in her understanding of experience (*Illuminations*, 258). Thus Strether's dilemma as an ambassadorial representative. His experience is already produced before he even sets sail: "I was booked," he says "by her vision" to find things according to "her book" (22:224). Woollett, as Strether eventually comes to realize, refuses to accept the fact that subjects, that truths, are multiple, and that given the differences between Paris and Woollett, the whole notion of containing categories is revealed to be an act of interpretive desperation or aggression whose goal is more readily understood as a denial of the claim experience makes and, as such, a denial of life itself. In Scott's formulation, like Simmel's, Mrs.

Newsome is a manifestation of the subject who, because she is so constituted, finds in the visible component of experience the ratification of her particular epistemological disposition. Again the point here is that these characters retreat into an almost holographic reality – one where illusion and insubstantiality stand in the place of the real thing and are accepted as such. If nothing else, James's texts, like *The Ambassadors*, work their way toward giving the lie to and exposing the dangers of treating experience as though it were a simple event one can verify visibly but whose challenge one can refuse to accept – a challenge which includes allowing experience to enter, upset, and perhaps overthrow the very nature of one's subjective construction.

III

In James's fiction *The Spoils of Poynton* can be seen as an objectification of the merely acquisitive view of experience. Here the spoils, Mrs. Gereth's collection of artifacts housed at Poynton, represent the sum total of her lived experiences. Upon visiting, Fleda Vetch sees that "Poynton was the record of a life," and that for Mrs. Gereth, "the sum of the world was rare French furniture and oriental china"(10:22, 24). For Mrs. Gereth, the spoils "were our religion, they were our life, they were *us!*" (10:30–31). Again, this mode of experience's limitations inheres in the very conception of experience itself. By classifying experience as something empirically verifiable, collectable, Mrs. Gereth creates herself in the spoils and consequently not only reifies her subjectivity – leaving her identity fixed in connection with the spoils – but seals off any possibility of growth outside her artificially circumscribed boundary. In Jamesian hermeneutics the drawbacks of this cumulative view become evident when one encounters something that cannot be contained within one's collective experiences, or when one is deprived of the artificial security this view offers and is required to make one's way through the world naked. Since experiences in the cumulative view form a bounded territory, not a general responsiveness to the world, the interpreting subject suddenly called to act appropriately in a unique situation will inevitably fail. *The Spoils of Poynton* dramatizes this probability when Poynton goes up in smoke. Deprived of her collection, Mrs. Gereth resigns herself to the oblivion of a non-productive mind. As she remarks to Fleda Vetch toward the novel's end: "action's over, for me, for ever, and you'll have the great merit of knowing when I'm brutally silent what I shall be thinking about" (10:245). This vision of Mrs. Gereth's mental sterility, of her inability to engage in productive action, is, for James, the result of the cumulative attitude toward experience.

What James objectifies about experience in *The Spoils of Poynton* he also dramatizes in many of his Europeans who also collect experiences. These Europeans are experienced in a worldly sense, suggesting an attitude which holds that quantity of experience confers moral authority. Think, for instance, how Madame de Bellegarde or Prince Amerigo meet the requirements of this identity. Madame de Bellegarde, we recall, sets herself up as the measure of what constitutes acceptable national and personal action and declares "the Bellegardes have been used to set the example, not to wait for it" (252). As for *The Golden Bowl*, James makes the limitations of the cumulative view a main focus of the novel. When asked by Maggie how he will react to his developing knowledge of the Ververs, the Prince casually admits "I know enough, I feel, never to be surprised," only much later to complain to Charlotte Stant that "the difficulty is, and will always be, that I don't understand them" (23:8–9, 309). The Prince explains his subjective and cultural construction in language which matches James's characterization of the "experienced" European.

There are two parts of me ... One is made up of history, the doings, the marriages, the crimes, the follies, the boundless *bêtises* of other people ... Those things are written – literally in rows of volumes, in libraries; are as public as they're abominable ... (23:9)

The second part, of course, makes *The Golden Bowl* an intensely difficult novel and dramatizes the impossibility of understanding the particular merely by referring it back to one's knowledge of a type. This second part, "very much smaller," as Amerigo explains, "represents my single self, the unknown, unimportant ... personal quantity" which exceeds Maggie's capacity to understand it and leads the narrative eventually to destabilize if not destroy all sense of empirical certitudes in human affairs (23:9).

The cumulative view's limitations consist in artificially sealing the subject off from the world and wrongfully elevating it as a self-ratifying authority that passes judgment according to submerged and often unrecognizably self-serving certitudes. James challenges these epistemological assumptions throughout his fiction by orchestrating his characters' deeply involved participation in alien worlds whose cultures and language force the visitor into a radical self-examination.[6] In the juxtaposition of cultures James brings about a multidimensional revelation. The individual is suddenly made alien and forced to understand his cultural and personal beliefs in the context of an alien and refractory world. And the foreign world also finds its public and private assumptions suddenly called into question by an alien who simply *sees* things differently. The structure of this collision in James's texts points up the interpretive limitations and ethnocentric dangers associated with a self-serving, cumulative view of experience, and calls attention to the need to develop a subjectivity which is permeable and welcomes that which is alien as an opportunity to enlarge one's consciousness and understanding. In provoking this epistemological revelation James demystifies or diffuses the coerciveness of power rather than, as Seltzer argues, subtly reinforces the "criminal continuity between art and power" (*Henry James and the Art of Power*, 170). By stripping away what appear as interpretive or epistemological certitudes, James's hermeneutics strips away the ground on which the subject has been nurtured. Focusing on the experiential basis of this interpretive event in James's novels and the effect it has on his reading audience reveals how theories of reading James which neglect to consider the hermeneutic–phenomenological politics of experience limit the incredibly complicated nature of culture, identity, and aesthetics in his work. In the collision between what one thought and what is, between one's conception of self and that which says no to you, James's fictions open a conceptual rift which forces interpretive revision and engagement in a way that makes his novels not just live and active, but lived, empowering experiences. To this extent, James's understanding of the need to cultivate a vigilant and undogmatic openness to experience so as to bring about an understanding of the multifoldness of reality parallels Gadamer's assessment of experience in *Truth and Method*. Where James sees the goal of experience to be an inclination toward new experiences, Gadamer sees the "truth of experience" as containing "an orientation towards new experiences." The experienced person, in Gadamer's understanding, is not someone who "knows everything and knows better than anyone else," like Madame de Bellegarde or, interestingly, Mrs. Newsome, but someone who is "open to new experiences," someone

who "is radically undogmatic; who because of the many experiences
he has had and the knowledge he has drawn from them is
particularly well equipped to have new experiences and to learn
from them." As Gadamer goes on to explain, the "dialectic of
experience has its own fulfillment not in definitive knowledge," as
though experience aimed at finality James would say, "but in that
openness to experience that is encouraged by experience itself"
(319). The difficulty, James and Gadamer would say, is in realizing
the difference between an open inclination to experience and merely
operating under an illusion of openness that covers up rigorous
efforts at controlling, imposing, and determining meaning.

We can see this distinction at work in *The Sacred Fount*, which stands
out as James's most problematic venture into the confusing realm of
interpretation. In this text the nameless narrator occupies the
position of Jamesian observer watching a group of people assembled
at a country estate called "Newmarch." Much to the narrator's
alarm, he believes he is witnessing vampiristic behavior among the
couples present and eventually builds an interpretive house of cards
in order to support his observations. Individuals who at first appeared
aged have become remarkably young, while their more youthful
counterparts have seemingly aged at an accelerated pace; the same
holds for the intelligence of others, for the more dull have become
keen and the keen more dull. At a loss to explain these transforma-
tions the narrator comes up with the analogy of a sacred fount which
each of the rejuvenated guests must somehow be visiting. For
Jamesians, *The Sacred Fount* foregrounds in a way none of his other
texts do the inherently tenuous and compositional nature of understanding. Yet while this text challenges the very nature of understanding, questioning whether such a thing is even possible beyond the
various interpretive and epistemological high jinks we perform, it
ultimately delivers a specific message about the hermeneutic trap the
process of interpretation is always waiting to spring. The narrator's
first sentence both initiates the potential dangers James saw in the act
of interpretation and, in its use of the word "ambiguities," highlights
the vagaries of understanding which characterize James's fiction: "It
was an occasion, I felt – the prospect of a large party – to look out at
the station for others, possible friends and even possible enemies, who
might be going. Such premonitions, it was true, bred fears when they
failed to breed hopes, though it was to be added that there were
sometimes, in the case, rather happy ambiguities" (*Sacred Fount*, 1). It

is the narrator's "premonitions" and how they lead to "ambiguities" James wants us to be wary of here. Like Gadamerian foreconceptions and prejudices, premonitions are manipulative interpretive devices that mediate between the reality of an event and one's interpretation of it. Time and again throughout the course of this narrator's efforts at detection James betrays the dangers of the hermeneutic circle. For instance, with each new seeming "discovery," the narrator assumes he has found another piece of what is actually his own puzzle: "the next moment I was in all but full enjoyment of the piece wanted to make all my other pieces right – right because of that special beauty in my scheme through which the whole depended so on each part and each part so guaranteed the whole" (223). Readers of *The Sacred Fount* find "ambiguities" at the turn of every sentence and find in each sentence reasons why they should doubt the whole proceedings, agreeing with Mrs. Brissenden that the narrator is "crazy," just as much as they find reasons why Mrs. Briss is wrong and the narrator alarmingly astute (318). James complicates the hermeneutic challenge in *The Sacred Fount* by allowing the narrator to make a proactive gesture against simply being wrong. In ceding the possibility of "happy ambiguities," James's narrator finds shelter behind an admitted possibility that his interpretation may not be wholly accurate, even that he himself might be subject to error. In other words, one thing *The Sacred Fount* offers in this early sentence is a key to the incredibly complicated and celebrated notion of ambiguity in James. Jamesian ambiguity, like all ambiguity, is always under subjective control and, as such, can never really be refuted. Mrs. Briss is right and wrong. The narrator may and may not be "crazy." The resolution of the ambiguity here rests on the reader's comfort in discerning what is what. And the ability to reach that understanding depends on the reader's ability to avoid acting on "premonitions" or foreconceptions, which include being wary of the traps the text lays, such as Mrs. Briss's attempt to interject the "Truth," which is her truth masquerading as something larger. In Jamesian terms, real understanding will depend on the reader's ability to become "one of the people on whom nothing is lost" ("Art of Fiction," *Literary Criticism*, I, 53). This is what James means when he speaks of experience as being "never limited," of "reality" as having "a myriad forms," and a "measure" that is "very difficult to fix" (52, 51, 52).

In a most interesting way then, *The Sacred Fount* represents the attenuated extreme of the cumulative notion of understanding. The narrator's detective enterprise relies on his ability not only to accumulate impressions or evidence, but then to piece that evidence into a plausible picture of what is taking place at Newmarch. The irony James never lets his readers escape, though, is that the created picture is not really a response to what is going on, but something more like an image that emerges when one follows a paint-by-number template. The narrator's "premonitions" produce the template, all the evidence he discovers is subsequently shaped by and made to fit the overarching design. To this extent then, the narrator's behavior, while more pathological, is really no different than Mrs. Gereth's, Mrs. Newsome's, Madame de Bellegarde's, or the Governess's in *The Turn of the Screw*. Paul Armstrong provides a strong argument that *The Sacred Fount*'s "experiments with representation" dramatize the "vicissitudes of understanding" in James's texts and that this text ultimately "shows how the late style offers the reader an ongoing challenge to reflect about hermeneutic processes that traditional fiction relies on for its mimetic effects" (*Challenge*, 31). In being continually forced to reassess the narrator's interpretive accuracy as well as the basic premonitions which lead him to see things as one way rather than another, the reader is called upon to make his or her own interpretive judgments and in that process made aware not only of being invited into the events of the text, but in being invited to offer challenge to the authorized interpretation, made to think about what role his or her own "premonitions" play in the final interpretive product.

It is not by accident then that in forcing interpretive engagement on his readers James subtly and significantly changes the reading event from a passive enterprise to an active process in which the reader is initiated into the very processes of artistic production which lead to a heightened ability to understand. In his testimonial to the artist's power in "The Art of Fiction," James praises this ability as the "power to guess the unseen from the seen, to trace the implication of things, to judge the whole piece by the pattern" (53). The idea of interpretive product is central. What *The Sacred Fount* eventually forces one to admit is that interpretations are produced which inevitably differ according to the individual viewer's perspective, or, in the language of the text, "premonitions." By calling attention to the role "premonitions" and "ambiguities" (however "happy") play in our conception of reality, James mirrors his brother William's similar concerns as described in his *Pragmatism*. Like

Henry, William was alarmed at the sloppy ways in which "reality" and "truth" were treated as somehow simultaneous and self-ratifying. "Truth," as both William and Henry explained, was really nothing more than the knowing subject's idiosyncratic interpretation of "reality," whereas "reality" was something far more elusive and always already mediated by human understanding, as William scornfully pointed out: "If so vulgar an expression were allowed us, we might say that wherever we find it, it has already been *faked*" (*Pragmatism*, 119–20). And as William held a commitment to the public role of philosophy, Henry also understood the public responsibilities of the artist and saw as part of his role the need to divest his audience of its unknown interpretive constraints. Thus, in recognizing the mediated nature of understanding, readers come to see our inevitable attempts to fix interpretation within systems produced by the interpreting subject either with or without his or her knowledge. In Jamesian hermeneutics, the exposure of this scheme is the first step toward understanding, is what allows one to step away from the self-generated holographic reality that has been masquerading as the real thing and adopt a more novelistic perspective through which we come to recognize the machinery of interpretation as much as we do interpretation's final product.

James contrasts this cumulative view with a conception of experience which not only conditions one to be open to the possibility of experience but brings about an understanding, as James says in the Preface to *The American*, that "the real represents ... the things we cannot possibly *not* know, sooner or later, in one way or another" (1062–63). James goes on in this Preface to explain how a cumulative view of experience is insufficient because "one of the accidents of our hampered state" is that "particular instances" which cannot be contained within any closed system "have not yet come our way" (1063). James's most recognized testament to the need to cultivate a receptiveness to experience is in "The Art of Fiction" where his injunctions to the artist are also injunctions to the audience. When he advises the artist to become "'one of the people on whom nothing is lost'" (53), his comments are also directed at readers who should recognize that "the novel," when "regarded as something more than a simple *jeu d'esprit*, ... treats of life at large and helps us to *know*" ("Nana," *Literary Criticism*, II, 869). To this end, James makes an elaborate connection between art and life, between openness and experience, and between experience and knowledge, suggesting that these forces continually interanimate each other as they play their role in an individual's developing understanding of self and world. To be sure, this is how James intends his description of "experience" in "The Art of Fiction" be read. Experience is not of this or that thing, rather "experience is never limited, and it is never complete; it is an immense sensibility, a kind of huge spider web of the finest silken threads suspended in the chamber of consciousness, and catching every airborne particle in its tissue" (52). James's conviction that experience can never be limited or enclosed is repeated throughout his prefaces. For instance, in the Preface to *Roderick Hudson* James explains that one of the major difficulties with "representation" is that "experience" spreads "round us in a widening, not in a narrowing circle" (1039). Also, in his Preface to *The Awkward Age*, James explains that experience does not offer some "final lesson," which "would, if operative, surely provide some law for the recognition, the determination in advance, of the just limits and the just extent of the situation, *any* situation" (1122). And in the Preface to *The Reverberator*, James says no one can tell where "the chapter of experience shall absolutely fade and stop," because experience is not "a chessboard of sharp black-and-white squares" (1194). In every case, James remarks on the open-endedness of experience and the impossibility of enclosing it within artificial boundaries.

IV

The point of experience then for James is that it is transformative, not affirmative; and to this extent one can find in Gadamer's examination of experience in *Truth and Method* an analytical method which can help provide Jamesians and readers of the novel some conceptual clarification with regard to "experience" as a determining and determined discursive process. In viewing "experience" as transformative both James and Gadamer foreground what they consider the fundamental negativity of experience. As Gadamer explains, "[e]very experience worthy of the name runs counter to our expectations" and brings with it a challenge to our accepted interpretation of the world (319). An experience which merely reaffirms our understanding of self and other cannot really be considered an experience in either James's or Gadamer's hermeneutics since it brings with it nothing new and leaves the experiencing subject unchanged. Here, in their understanding of the interpretive consequences associated with one's ability to grasp the full connection between experience and understanding, Scott, Gadamer, James, and, as I will show, Foucault are all in agreement. Gadamer is perhaps most direct when he explains how if "we look at experience ... in terms of its result [i.e. knowledge], its real character as a process is overlooked. This process is," Gadamer explains, "essentially a negative one ... This is seen linguistically in the fact that we use the word 'experience' in two different senses: to refer to the experiences that fit in with our expectation and confirm it, and to the experience we have. This latter, 'experience' in the real sense, is always negative" (317). The negativity of experience is what James has in mind when he suggests that experience is "our apprehension and our measure of what happens to us as social creatures"; and is why James's fiction must be read as active and able inevitably to break down one's conceptual framework and ultimately lead one to an emancipation from the constraints of a cultural and subjective history (Preface, *Princess Casamassima*, 1091).

Subjective liberation is achieved in James's fiction primarily because he sees experience as an event of deprivation. Readers of James recognize this position in the closing stages of "The Beast in the Jungle." Frozen in anagnorisis before May Bartram's tombstone, Marcher undergoes his first genuine experience with his realization not only that he "had seen *outside* of his life, not learned it within," but that May Bartram "was what he had missed" (*Complete Tales*, 11: 400, 401). In examining this scene in his prefatory comments on the story, James explains that Marcher's career "resolves itself into a great negative adventure," but that the "final picture leaves him overwhelmed – at last he has understood" (1251). It's not surprising then that James's understanding of experience required the development of an aesthetics which forced the reader's involvement and which would be read in terms of suffering and action. Marcher's monumental insight into the constitution of his subjectivity is a truly negative experience whose outcome offers a general release from the subjective constraints which had held him captive his entire life. His final epiphany dramatizes this potentiality through the essential negativity of his experience and the devastating but liberating knowledge it brings.

This horror of waking – *this* was knowledge, knowledge under the breath of which the very tears in his eyes seemed to freeze. Through them, none the less, he tried to fix it and hold it; he kept it there before him so that he might feel the pain. That at least, belated and bitter, had something of the taste of life. But the bitterness suddenly sickened him, and it was as if, horribly, he saw, in the truth, in the cruelty of his image, what had been appointed and done. (*Complete Tales*, 11: 402)

We see this movement from subjective constraint to reversal of consciousness to understanding to freedom throughout James's fiction. For instance, like Marcher's, Strether's developing understanding of the impossibility of cultural and personal approbative certitudes frees him from the confines of his Woollett persona and allows him to envision a larger, more expanded sense of self. Similarly, Maggie's and Amerigo's final embrace, Amerigo's last words to his wife – " 'I see nothing but *you*' " – marks the culmination of an experience which brought all the certitudes of each partner crashing down and leaves them essentially naked with respect to each other (24:369). Freed of the various constraints which had made their marriage a miserable affair, Maggie and Amerigo are given a second chance, are left to begin again their relationship, but with a greater understanding of who they are, who their partner is, and what they would like to become. In each of these examples, experience is transformative and brings about a release from subjective and cultural imprisonment, an event James promotes and readers can appreciate by focusing on the hermeneutic structure of Jamesian experience as opposed to confining these experiences within a scheme such as Seltzer's that treats the novel as a system for reinforcing established "regulative and disciplinary practices" (*Henry James and the Art of Power*, 194). The difference between the approaches is measured in the freedom of the former and the fixedness of the latter. Again, the point for James is not just to draw attention to the discursive power structures at work in the "micro-histories and micropolitics of the body and the social body," but to offer an understanding of those manipulative effects that eventually allows one to break free of their paralyzing hold and escape into an understanding of self, other, and culture which is more correctly understood as self-generating (24). And James would grant that this too is power, but a power more accurately described as productive.[7]

It is in bringing the individual up against the unexpected, forcing the individual to confront what is strange and often refractory that experience demonstrates its connection with bewilderment in Jamesian hermeneutics and how it plays its role in the process of understanding. In forcing the subject to confront the limits of his or her understanding experience leads one to insight. Here, Gadamer's analysis of insight provides a helpful way of understanding James's own method. According to Gadamer, insight

is more than knowledge of this or that situation. It always involves an escape from something that had deceived us and held us captive. Thus insight always involves an element of self-knowledge and constitutes a necessary side of what we called experience in the proper sense. (*Truth and Method*, 319–20)

For Gadamer, as for James, experience brings knowledge and understanding of "what is," where what is "is not this or that thing, but 'what cannot be done away with'" (320). In James's novels insight comes through the eventual upending of culture-bound interpretive orthodoxies. In *The American*, for instance, Christopher Newman undergoes a self-exposure in which his divestiture becomes part of what he experiences. This is an essential feature of Jamesian hermeneutics and is what James believes leads one to recognize the need to cultivate a subjective flexibility and, in Gadamer's words, to recognize the "limitedness of all prediction and the uncertainty of all plans" as a principal step toward understanding (320).

James's theoretical project is perhaps more evident in the scene between Newman and Madame d'Outreville, as through the sequence the reader witnesses Newman's developing ability to understand and respond to an interpretive situation in a way qualitatively different from his earlier grasp of things. Where Newman's former mode of observation was structured around detached observation and, often, deference to a Bädeker, he now has recourse to his own experience of the Parisian social text and converts that experience into useful knowledge. The duchess forces Newman back upon himself by constructing a "brilliant monologue" which prevents Newman from carrying out his intended exposure of the Bellegardes' murderous past. With action made impossible, Newman is reduced to observing her monologue and "admiring the duchess for her fine manners".[8] But in being forced to observe Newman is returned to a reading position where if he is to understand at all he needs to understand himself in front of the duchess's text. This is what happens. "Finding no ready-made opportunity to tell his story, Newman pondered these things more dispassionately than might have been expected" Rather than impose a subjective understanding on the situation, or revert to a guidebook, Newman allows the experience to speak to him, in the sense that he allows himself access to the cultural information which suffuses the duchess's behavior and the internal motivations which have brought him before the duchess. Newman marks his expanded understanding when he asks himself "had it come to that – that he was asking favours of conceited people, and appealing for sympathy where he had no sympathy to give? ... he had come very near being an ass" (346).

The dynamic of Newman's enlarged ability to read the situation and derive a more worldly understanding of his experience follows the pattern of interpretive vigil James exploits throughout his fiction. In this particular scene, when the duchess subtly forces Newman to reflect on his intentions Newman gets the moment of insight that enables him to gain a better understanding of his experience. In the course of *The American*, this sudden inward flight constitutes the second appeal Newman makes to thought. The first comes in the novel's early pages where Newman recounts an important stock-market battle he went to New York to fight. In explaining that event, Newman tells Tom Tristram that "though I was excited with my errand, I felt the want of sleep. At all events I woke up suddenly, from a sleep or from a kind of reverie, with the most extraordinary feeling in the world – a mortal disgust for the thing I was going to do" (22). Newman reacts to this understanding by boarding a steamer for Europe. In both examples Newman's insight comes upon him during moments when for some reason or other his determining narrative is interrupted by forces which exceed his control. This private space or moment of time becomes an opening through which Newman is able to retreat from his performing self and allow for a more direct and involved interpretation of the situation at hand. What is interesting in *The American* is that both of Newman's moments of insight lead him to act, and that his actions bring him into contact with the historical forces which have shaped, are shaping, and are intending to shape his perception of reality. For Newman, the interval of time allows him to become, in a word, an agent in his own destiny. James points out Newman's development by calling the reader's attention to the change in Newman's internal motivation. Where the first act brings about a course of action that takes place, as Newman admits, "quite independently of my will," the second is qualitatively different and entirely the result of Newman overcoming his will. The latter experience in particular can be characterized as an example of the negativity of experience. For while Newman's intentions are thwarted, he emerges from the experience with an enlarged understanding of his situation and the world in general. For James such an enlargement of experience is the principal power of the novel.

From beginning to end of his career, James dramatizes the consequences of experience by highlighting the tension between an understanding of the self as permeable and open to change and the requirements of expected social behavior. One of those consequences is a radical estrangement from one's prior self and former world. I want to underscore the idea that Jamesian hermeneutics accentuates the fundamental tension or dialectic between private and public versions of the self, between a subject's private consciousness and social construction, between bewilderment and enlightenment. Several recent readings of James, Ross Posnock's *The Trial of Curiosity* and Priscilla Walton's *The Disruption of the Feminine in Henry James* for example, erase this tension and find in James an open-ended, permeable subject without paying heed to the absolute requirements of this dialectic as a means for generating understanding of self and world.[9] Neither Posnock nor Walton acknowledges that a completely open-ended, non-referential conception of identity which measures itself and its understanding against nothing leaves one open to manipulation by the modes of power these authors want James's texts to escape.[10] In addition, such a theory of James misses another crucial point, that the generation of meaning and understanding, of identity and politics, takes place in James through an elaborate process of continual revision whereby the interpreting subject is always revising his or her conception of self and world precisely because of that subject's confrontations with things that either say no to or simply challenge interpretation by their very presence. Revision, of course, leads to understanding in Jamesian hermeneutics, and revision, too, is one of the consequences of experience. For James's characters, as for himself, these consequences lead one to a worldly displacement, to a position of living in between worlds, to an understanding that resolution is always premature. It is for this reason that James's fictions all end *"en l'air"* (*Notebooks*, 18). The understanding we see Newman, or Marcher, or Strether, or Maggie and Amerigo reach in the above examples, brings about an insight which, in a real sense, allows them to transcend the boundaries of fiction and find their beginnings in the texts' end.

v

It is not without some irony that I turn to Michel Foucault for help in explaining how the hermeneutical structure of Jamesian experience offers a more accurate and insightful method of reading than those methodologies which take either a more direct Foucauldian approach such as Seltzer's, or those like Posnock's and Walton's which see James as straightforwardly celebrating open-endedness. Foucault becomes exactly Jamesian when, in his "Introduction" to *The Use of Pleasure*, he gives an analysis of his own scholarly method. Foucault's explanation of his work as a project bent upon freeing thought from traditional lines of inquiry, as going beyond the "simplistic appropriation of others," fits Strether's experience particularly well (9). "The object," Foucault points out, is "to learn to what extent the effort to think one's own history can free thought from what it silently thinks, and so enable it to think differently." True inquiry, Foucault goes on to say, must be understood as an "'ascesis', an exercise of oneself in the activity of thought" (9). "After all," Foucault says,

what would be the passion for knowledge if it resulted only in a certain amount of knowledgeableness and not, in one way or another and to the extent possible, in the knower's straying afield of himself? There are times in life when the question of knowing if one can think differently than one thinks, and perceive differently than one sees, is absolutely necessary if one is to go on looking and reflecting at all. (8)

The connection here between James and Foucault is in their attempt to reach a position of interpretive acuity which enables the interpreting subject to recognize, dismantle, and then escape the imprisoning structures of power which society invariably constructs in order to govern and control. Foucault's remark about bringing one to a position from which an escape into a new realm of thought is possible is exactly James's point and is, perhaps, made most available to an interpreting subject through an examination of experience as an event which is both private and public, active and passive, open and subject to social constraints. It is in working through such paradoxes that the knower can be led astray of oneself and come to see that self and the world as though for the first time. Both James and Foucault recognize the importance of this interpretive freedom, and it forms the experience of James's subjects. Strether's forays into his past and his attempt to conceptualize the present are exactly the "ascesis" Foucault speaks of. Strether's insight allows him to dissociate his past from his present reality, to move from imposing an understanding to being engaged in the active process of living through situations, and to emerge on the other side of those experiences with an understanding that reflects one's own conscious attempt *to come* to understanding. That Strether can accept Chad's and Marie de Vionnet's relationship without Woollett's moralizing, despite enormous pressure to do so,[11] demonstrates James's idea that understanding and interpretation, if they are to occur at all, demand action, in the sense that Strether is given a choice between falling back on Woollett's narrowly correct interpretation and his recent, more ambiguous and indeterminable understanding of the affair. James makes this point explicitly in his essay "The New Novel," where he says the whole purpose of any critical engagement is to "make the mind as aware of itself as possible" and to have as its goal "the very education of our imaginative life" ("The New Novel," *Literary Criticism*, I, 124).

This attitude is perhaps best expressed through the basic structure of James's narrative technique. James's narrative form, his use of a center of consciousness, is dependent upon a notion of a flexible self receptive to experience and the opportunity for liberation which experience offers. Furthermore, the center of consciousness operates as a vehicle of transference with which James is able to draw the reader into the events of the text. It is for this reason James refused to confine fiction within the artificial constraints of omniscient narration. Such fiction, he complained, never let the reader forget that one was reading fiction.[12] Rather, a novel, James believed, should give the "air of reality" ("Art of Fiction," 53). Such an atmosphere required the absence of overt authorial control, and that absence allowed the reader to step into the text and join the character in the active process of coming to understand the various experiences included in the novel. It may not be going too far here to apply the language of modern technology as a way of describing an encounter with a Jamesian text, for in many ways reading James is like an experience of virtual reality. This, for James, was the essential power of fiction, this is what made fiction an agent in the

world. Through James's narrative technique the novel offers readers
an image of themselves and an opportunity better to understand not
only themselves in the reflected image, but exactly how it is they
understand at all. As "long as life retains its power of projecting itself
upon man's imagination," James believed, "he will find the novel
work off the impression better than anything he knows," and until
"the world is an unpeopled void there will be an image in the
mirror" ("The Future of the Novel," *Literary Criticism*, I, 109–10).[13]

James consistently returned to this concept of knowing through
experience, to the idea that fiction offered a first-hand opportunity
for encountering multiple experiences and encountering oneself in
the act of coming to understand the fictional experience. James
believed encountering this diversity of experiences was the only way
one could approach an understanding of reality. Indeed, in commenting on "The Point of View" James explains that his story was
"to commemorate" his "perverse and incurable disposition to
interest himself less in his own ... experiences, under certain sorts of
pressure, than in that of conceivable fellow mortals, which might be
mysteriously and refreshingly different" (Preface, *Lady Barbarina*,
122). It seems clear then, that James developed the center of
consciousness technique so as to unite character, reader, and author
in the active process of mapping the social and psychological texts
encountered in the novels, and, by extension, in the reader's own
world. James was convinced that his development of the center of
consciousness technique converted the act of reading from a passive
event to one in which a deep fusion took place between the reader,
the text, and the author, a fusion which allowed the reader to enjoy
the double privilege of becoming both subject and object of the
events contained within the text. Any account of James which
neglects to consider the essential releasement his novels produce on
the centers within and the reader without undermines the explora-
tory power James sought to produce in his works and extend to his
readers by way of his hermeneutics of experience.

For example, Sheila Teahan's recent study *The Rhetorical Logic of
Henry James* seeks to undertake a "detailed rhetorical investigation of
the center of consciousness" so as to correct the phenomenological
and political readings of James which have "reinscribed rather than
challenged" the "prevailing visual model, with its accompanying
subordination of language to perception" (13). Teahan challenges
the "hypostasis of the center of consciousness as a stable and

stabilizing construct" by arguing that the center of consciousness is incapable of accounting for "the incalculable ramifications of figure in the text whose epistemological and metaphysical center he or she embodies" (14, 7). In the result of this collision between the claims of "figuration and causality," Teahan argues that "the Jamesian reflector is effaced and sacrificed in the interest of narrative closure" (7). But this strikes me as exactly contrary to what all James texts seek and finally accomplish. Narrative closure is the last thing one can accuse James of seeking. In fact, no James novel leaves one with a clear sense of closure, and to accuse James of sacrificing his characters so as to effect closure is to suggest James is one of those subjects who view experience as cumulative and eventually complete. These individuals often have enormous worldly power, but power based on ignorance as opposed to insight, on rigidity as opposed to fluidity. It seems a more complete reading of James recognizes how, by uniting the internal dynamics of the text with the internal dynamics of the reader's conceptual framework, his novels accentuate the correlation between experience, knowledge, and subjectivity. To do so is to recognize how, in a very real way, every James text becomes to a certain extent the reader's own in that the reader finds his or her own consciousness undergoing as much an examination and reversal as does the fictional character's.[14] In this way James succeeds in "historicizing the notion of experience" and in making the reader aware of how much any experience is "always already an interpretation *and* in need of interpretation" ("Experience," 34, 37). In doing so, James's texts seek to expose not just the social construction of knowledge and forms of subjectivity by making visible competing versions of understanding, but to pursue the dynamic of estrangement and release produced by the consequences of experience. For James experience exposes the existence of various repressive mechanisms and forces the perceiving subject to reconceptualize his or her understanding of self and world. In this way James's narratives play upon the notion of life as a condition of retroactive enlightenment, a process of living forward and understanding backward, and foreground the author's belief that the act of living is hermeneutics. The logical extension of understanding life as hermeneutics was to make art a species of hermeneutics.

There is a sense in which one can see all of these aspects of Jamesian hermeneutics at work in the famous Galerie d'Apollon memory and dream sequence James characterizes as a nightmare in his auto-biographical study *A Small Boy and Others*. One can find the whole focus of James's artistic life, the development of his hermeneutics, and the refinements of his aesthetics captured in the description of his "admirable nightmare" (*Autobiography*, 196). Indeed, it would not be too much to say that James's description of this event contains the basic dialectical structure of bewilderment and enlightenment, where the one is the condition of the other's possibility. It may seem paradoxical to say that the failure of understanding becomes the medium of understanding, but Jamesian hermeneutics, as the Galerie episode reveals, comes down to something *like* that.[15] James's representation of the Galerie nightmare dramatizes the full measure of James's understanding of experience, or what constitutes an experience. When James describes this "most appalling yet most admirable nightmare," his narrated memory of the event follows the dialectic that I suggest is a formal feature of Jamesian hermeneutics and a central aspect of all James fiction.

The climax of this extraordinary experience ... was the sudden pursuit, through an open door, along a huge saloon, of a just dimly-descried figure that retreated in terror before my rush and dash ... out of the room I had a moment before been desperately, and all the more abjectly, defending by the push of my shoulder against hard pressure on lock and bar from the other side. The lucidity, not to say the sublimity, of the crisis had consisted of the great thought that I, in my appalled state, was probably still more appalling than the awful agent, creature or presence, whatever he was, whom I had guessed, in the suddenest wild start from sleep, the sleep within my sleep, to be making for my place of rest. The triumph of my impulse, perceived in a flash as I acted on it myself at a bound, forcing the door outward, was the grand thing, but the great point of the whole was the wonder of my final recognition. Routed, dismayed, the tables turned upon him by my so surpassing him for straight aggression and dire intention, my visitant was already but a diminished spot in the long perspective, the tremendous, glorious hall, as I say, over the far-gleaming floor of which, cleared for the occasion of its great line of priceless vitrines down the middle, he sped for *his* life, while a great storm of thunder and lightning played through the deep embrasures of high windows at the right. The lightning that revealed the retreat revealed also the wondrous place and, by the same amazing play, my young imaginative life in it of long before, the sense of which, deep within me, had kept it whole, preserved it to this thrilling use; for what in the world were the deep embrasures and the so polished floor but those of the Galerie d'Apollon of my childhood? The "scene of something" I had vaguely then felt it? Well I might, since it was to be the scene of that immense hallucination. (196–97)

Readers of James have noted the essential releasement this dream represents. In his biography of James, Leon Edel suggests the nightmare may have "resolved [James's] long weeks of depression" which followed the news of his New York Edition's failure. Edel conjectures "[s]ince the dream contained a vigorous moment of self-assertion and putting to flight of a frightening other-self (or brother) it may have helped to restore to James that confidence and faith in himself which had crumbled in his life when he received the news of the failure of the Edition" (*The Master*, 445). But if we look through the more direct autobiographical references and examine the narrative dynamics in James's representation of the dream sequence, what we find is the same liberating estrangement which characterizes what we could call the hermeneutic epiphanies James's characters experience at crucial moments in their stories. In his texts, James dramatizes a particular interpretive moment brought on by a sudden anomaly, by the unexpected appearance of, say, Isabel Archer's husband "sitting while Madame Merle stood" (*Portrait of a Lady*, 4:164). These experiences initiate an interpretive vigil in which the interpreting subject is brought up against the limits of his or her understanding and forced to recognize its compositional aspect. By so doing James's fiction succeeds in making " 'visible the assignment of subject-positions', not in the sense of capturing the reality of the objects seen, but of trying to understand the operations of the complex and changing discursive processes by which identities are ascribed, resisted, or embraced and which processes themselves are unremarked, indeed achieve their effect because they aren't noticed" (Spivak qtd. in Scott, "Experience," 33). In a way, James's novels work toward this experience which initiates first a powerful bewilderment and then brings about a process of attunement in which the character's subjectivity divests itself of the constraints which had, up until the moment of divestiture, held it captive.[16]

Immediately preceding the Galerie nightmare, James tells us he imagined himself and his brother William characterized by the Parisian art world as " 'little gaping pilgrims' " enjoined to understand aesthetics: " 'Art, art, art, don't you see? Learn ... what *that* is!'" (*Autobiography*, 191). And though "not yet aware of style," he readily admits he was "on the way to become so," for the Louvre's exhibitions "simply overwhelmed and bewildered" him (195). Years later, in recounting his nightmare, James explains how he made the transition not only to an awareness of style, but to the development of a personal style which would take its place along side those which initially overwhelmed and bewildered him. The dream-memory presents a number of events which appear over and over in James's fiction, most importantly perhaps the initial resistance followed by aggressive assertion, and a sudden, "final recognition" which brings about a tremendous expansion of understanding. Thus the dream can be seen as depicting a figure "abjectly ... defending" himself "by the push of my shoulder against hard pressure on lock and bar from the other side," struggling to maintain the safety of its closure against outside influences. But through what James claims was the "clearest act of cogitation ..., [an] act indeed of life-saving energy" and "aggression," he overcomes his defensive posture, thrusts open the door, and routs his "visitant" (196, 197). Ironically, it is by opening the door, by opening himself to the experience of what he had been resisting, that James attains his "final recognition" (197). In this way, James is led to awareness only after having actively and aggressively engaged himself in the situation at hand. It is by similarly taking an active role in coming to understand his experi-ence of the European social text as embodied in the Bellegardes that Christopher Newman is finally able to escape from the constraints of his native interpretive framework. That understanding always takes the form of action in James's hermeneutics is implicit in James's rendering of the Galerie encounter and is consistently demonstrated in the various interpretive vigils his characters experience and the active role they subsequently take in coming to understand their respective situations.

What James recognizes in the remainder of his nightmare is a truly negative experience whose product is insight. The "far-gleaming floor ..., cleared for the occasion of its great line of priceless vitrines" allows James simultaneously to overcome his fear and to assert his own style in the formerly occupied "glorious hall" (197). In making a place for himself in the Pantheon of art, James also recognizes the need to develop an aesthetics that will cultivate a "finely aware and richly responsible" discrimination which will not only satisfy his quest for style and overcome his anxiety of authorship but empower him by extending through the reading act the full measure of Jamesian consciousness to his audience (Preface, *Princess Casamassima*, 1088). In this way, the Galerie episode dramatizes the change in James from passive, small boy to master novelist whose aesthetics to a great extent succeeded in reforming the novel as a genre. It is no surprise then to find that what James sees as "the general sense of *glory*" in the Galerie d'Apollon's works is a reflection of his own hoped-for reputation: "The glory meant ever so many things at once, not only beauty and art and supreme design, but history and fame and power, the world in fine raised to the richest and noblest expression" (*Autobiography*, 196). In opening himself to the possibilities of experience in the Galerie d'Apollon, James allows himself to absorb what the Galerie offers and in absorbing that atmosphere not only to become a part of all the Galerie is, but to add to that collection his own style. This expanded understanding is the goal of Jamesian hermeneutics, and its empowering capacity, as I show, is an "experience" made available to the reader simply by reading James.

CHAPTER 2

The experience of divestiture: toward an understanding of the self in 'The American'

[F]or Napoleon Egypt was a project that acquired a reality in his mind, and later in his preparations for its conquest, through experiences that belonged to the realm of ideas and myths culled from texts, not empirical reality.

Edward Said, *Orientalism*

I

In *The American*, Henry James's Christopher Newman is characterized as a Bädeker-toting "great Western Barbarian stepping forth in his might, gazing a while at this poor effete Old World" (32). Self-made, self-schooled, and self-mannered, Newman confesses to neither cultivation, education, nor any knowledge about "history, or art, or foreign tongues, or any learned matters" (32). Instead, he quantifies all of Europe as if it were an entity his opening question *"Combien?"* can answer (4). Not surprisingly, Newman learns at the close of his European experience how inadequate his mercantile American discourse is in negotiating the European text he had heretofore understood by guidebook alone. Though markedly changed at the close of his experience, Newman is unable to find the language with which to articulate what he has experienced, either for his own conceptual satisfaction or for the enlightenment of curious others. As the narrator explains, Newman "told his friends that he had brought home no 'new ideas' from Europe" (360). And that is just James's point in *The American*, a novel in which Newman's (in)ability to understand his experiences introduces the basic structure of Jamesian hermeneutics. What James shows in this early novel is how Newman's experience of European culture only becomes intelligible to him when he experiences its power of excluding him, which includes its power of exceeding his capacity for understanding.

36

For James, the central conflict in *The American* revolves around a competition between the acquisitive and the open and revisionary modes of experience. We recall that the acquisitive mode privileges the primacy of empiricism and holds that being experienced means having accumulated a lot of impressions, as if experience were a mode of consumption. The novel's protagonist, Christopher Newman, clearly follows this theory. He wants to experience Europe by "taking it in." James makes Newman's conception of experience as accumulation explicit in the opening stages of the novel, drawing an interesting connection between experience and capital in the process. As the product of a purely commercial culture, which was how James saw America, Newman bears the stamp of money and of money's ruthless objectivity. The minting metaphor here is purposeful, since in Simmel's argument, the connection between capital and a cumulative relationship to experience holds a rather central spot. As Simmel argues, whatever object or person is "sold for money goes to the buyer who offers most for it, quite regardless of what or who he is." Bank notes, we recall, bear a "statement to the effect that their value is paid to the bearer 'without proof of identity'" (*Philosophy of Money*, 436). In *The American*, the seeming "absolute objectivity with which money transactions operate" facilitates Newman's acquisitive attitude toward life and is a means with which James highlights the darker underside of America's commercial culture. Since the climate produced by a money culture promotes an intellectual disposition in which "money" becomes "the breeding ground for economic individualism and egotism" at the expense of any subjective or inter-subjective sympathies, money, Simmel and James agree, "places the actions and relations of men quite outside of men as human subjects" (436–37, 436). This link between Newman's calculative business sense and his (in)ability to make sense of what happens to him becomes increasingly important, we shall see, as *The American* develops. To a large degree, the novel's aim is to foreground the interpretive failures which accumulate as a result of living in a culture which sees capital gain as the *modus vivendi*. In Simmel's argument, people like Newman represent a way of being for whom "economic life, the web of their teleological series, has no definite content ... except making money" (433). James's comments in this sphere are startlingly direct: "Christopher Newman's sole aim in life," the narrator "nakedly" admits, "had been to make money":

what he had been placed in the world for was, to his own perception, simply to wrest a fortune, the bigger the better, from defiant authority. This idea completely filled his horizon and satisfied his imagination. Upon the use of money, upon what one might do with a life into which one had succeeded in injecting the golden stream, he had ... scantily reflected. (20)

As *The American* unfolds, and as Newman comes to learn what more there is to life than making money, readers must nevertheless hold in mind this early condemnation of the goals advanced by America's mercantile aspirations. It is no small irony that what is missing in Newman's conception of himself is what it is all for, nor should we miss the irony that the novel begins with Newman having left America to learn about life, as though having means in no way equals reaching ends. Interestingly, it is only at the novel's end, when Newman, like Strether, winds up getting nothing material out of the affair that he, like Strether, feels enriched.

This unswerving pursuit of "the golden stream" might serve as a model for the acquisitive theory of experience in James's fiction and is the apparent attitude Newman displays in his approach to Europe: "He believed that Europe was made for him, and not he for Europe," and that the world, "to his senses, was a great bazaar, where one might stroll about and purchase handsome things" (62). In contrast to the cumulative version of experience, *The American* also contains the seeds of James's idea that being experienced involves the Gadamerian notion of a vigilant and undogmatic "openness" (*Truth and Method*, 319).[1] This latter view of experience is the kind of understanding Newman, or, say, Lambert Strether, through inevitable disappointments and insights, eventually comes to acquire with the close of his European journey.

In James's hermeneutics the process of coming to be experienced in the full sense of the term[2] means both being disabused of one's heretofore putative understanding of *what is*, and confronting and accepting the irrefutability of what James, in his Preface to *The American*, calls "the things we cannot possibly *not* know, sooner or later" (1063). For Christopher Newman this lesson comes as he is carried by James through a series of experiences that bring him up against what even his wealth cannot do away with: the absolute absence of common ground between himself and the Bellegardes. Newman's shock is not so much that Urbain de Bellegarde, or that Madame de Bellegarde cannot see their way to permitting his marriage to Claire, but that Claire de Cintré too has internalized a culture so radically different from his that one might speak of an incommensurability between them. The painful recognition of this alterity changes Newman's understanding of everything and leads his early, naively bold announcement about Europe being made for him to make a mocking return at the close of the novel. The line with the most resonant truth at the novel's close, more resonant than Newman recognizes when he makes the assertion at the outset of his adventure, is his claim to Tom Tristram that "I seemed to feel a new man inside my old skin, and I longed for a new world" (23). For it is upon his initial, brief return to America that the change "inside" Newman becomes most apparent to himself and the reader. In explaining Newman's internal alteration James tells us that once back in America Newman "took no interest in chatting about his affairs and manifested no desire to look over his accounts," indeed, they "appeared unreal to him" (360–61). So extreme is Newman's change that he even questions his own identity: "he began to fear that there was something the matter with his head; that his brain, perhaps, had been softened" (361). It is here, where Newman confronts what he used to be and finds his past awkward and strange, that the full extent of James's concerns with experience and understanding begin to become apparent.

II

In *The American*, James gives us a character – "all-objective," in his words – so constituted that his openness is debilitating like a form of alienation (Preface, *Princess Casamassima*, 1095–96). For although objectivity is a goal in James's hermeneutics, the negative side of "all-objective" in Newman's case is his complete lack of internal disposition. He is what one could call an unformed subject. Because he suffers from a lack of subjectivity he is dependent upon external guides such as a Bädeker to tell him when he has had an experience. And since Newman, as we have seen, views being experienced through a mercantile lens and understands the goal as having accumulated a cache of impressions, as if experience itself were a mode of capitalization, external guides, such as a Bädeker, assume a value analogous to that of a stock certificate in one's portfolio. The more one has accumulated then, the more (experiential) wealth one has obviously amassed. Newman even has a laugh at himself over his objectified or commodified understanding of experience. In a letter to Mrs. Tristram in which he describes his European tour as a "placid, fathomless sense of diversion" (62), Newman confesses:

"You want to know everything that has happened to me in these three months. The best way to tell you, I think, would be to send you my half-dozen Guide-books, with my pencil-marks in the margin. Wherever you find a scratch, or a cross, or a 'Beautiful!' or a 'So true!' or a 'Too thin!' you may know that I have had a sensation of some sort or other." (73)

Here Newman is almost a parody of the disengaged observer. He has no sense of a distinction between experiencing "scenes" and experiencing "situations." How to travel from one to the other is basically what his story is about. James's irony in Newman's letter to Mrs. Tristram is not so much that Newman fails really to experience Europe as that he comes to understand the continent through a banal, impersonal text and accepts only those experiences which match his neutral textual "authority." Newman repeatedly allows some form of mediation to interfere with his critical perception which prevents him from attaining a perceptive understanding of his surroundings. To the extent he does so, Newman's lesson consists in learning to respond practically to situations as a participant and not simply an outsider who takes things over.

Of course James complicates matters by endowing Newman with an "all-objective" disposition. For James, being "all-objective" has positive and negative sides to it. The positive side seems to be what James the writer has in mind when in the Preface he describes Newman as a narrative tool. By using a protagonist purported to be "all-objective" or without prejudice, James constructed a character who (unlike his later characters) would not interfere with his narration. To the extent this is successful, Newman anticipates, if somewhat crudely, James's later developments in narrative form, principally the refinement of the center of consciousness as a way of dramatizing the process of understanding as it unfolds. James emphasizes the benefits Newman's unencumbered objectivity would afford both reader and writer when analyzing the novel's formal features years later in his Preface. For James, the perspectival privilege attendant upon Newman's role is clear:

the interest of everything is all that it is *his* vision, *his* conception, *his* interpretation: at the window of his wide, quite sufficiently wide, consciousness we are seated, from that admirable position we "assist." He therefore supremely matters; all the rest matters only as he feels it, treats it, meets it. (1067–68)

But being almost completely without prejudices makes Newman, paradoxically, a negative version of James's hermeneutics. Not being subjective, Newman's subjectivity does not get in the way of his understanding, but neither does it provide any space for understanding to occur. So Newman has no chance to question his own ability to take "the measure of reality" ("Art of Fiction," 51).

Newman's lack of subjectivity is a major source of comedy in the novel, as when Valentin de Bellegarde agrees to assist Newman in his marital quest but is somewhat bewildered at Newman's accepting his aid as a matter of course: "You will never understand [how I] have helped you, you will never be grateful, not as I deserve you should be" (115). Newman's exchange with Valentin, more specifically Valentin's immediate questions as to the degree to which Newman's genealogy permits his seeking to marry Claire de Cintré, adumbrates the more rigorous and, ultimately, destabilizing encounter Newman has with Madame de Bellegarde and her son Urbain. To Valentin's assertion that Newman is "not noble," Newman responds "The devil I'm not ... I say I am noble. I don't exactly know what you mean by it, but it's a fine word and a fine idea: I put in a claim to it" (110–11). Of course, Newman's staking a claim to the idea of nobility evokes, once again, the degree to which he is the product of a commercial society in which the operative term "*Combien?*" can make all things accessible, as Simmel puts it, "to the buyer who offers most for it, quite regardless of who or what he is" (*Philosophy of Money*, 436).[3] Thus, in James's characterization, Newman's being "all-objective" is a condition which facilitates the wide development of his acquisitive open-endedness – exactly the disposition which has allowed him to amass his enormous wealth from such varied sources just as it accurately represents the relentless consumerism of American culture. Again, Simmel's *Philosophy of Money* provides us with valuable insight into the way in which James uses Newman's epistemological dynamics as a representative example of a money culture's underlying bankruptcies. "Money," Simmel explains, as though speaking of this instant in *The American*, "represents the moment of objectivity in exchange activities, as it were, in pure isolation and independent embodiment." In other words, what James shows to some extent is that a money culture allows for and even promotes a subjective divestment, so as to promote the ease and immediacy of gain and to provide an adjustable measurement with which gain and loss can be calculated free from "biased relationship to any subjective economic element" (436). Newman's lack of subjectivity merely serves to enlarge the field of things he can undertake and acquire, something James takes care to note early in the novel when he describes Newman's history as "an intensely Western story" and has Newman remark how Europe fits in with his search for a wife: "I rather like the idea of taking in Europe, too. It enlarges the field of selection" (37).

Still, James does not simply leave it at that. It is not quite right to say that Newman is not subjective. Though without prejudices he is not without instincts – for example, his "natural impulse to disfigure with a direct, unreasoning blow the comely face of temptation," an attribute Noémie Nioche finds unintelligible (72). Newman's absence of prejudice is another way of describing his willingness, or at least availability, to encounter new experiences, a moral position – an ethical posture – that James thinks European culture has excluded from its norms and habits of conduct. Indeed, the Bellegardes are obviously experienced concerning the control of their world and therefore can simply be impervious to whatever is strange or unexpected. Really, nothing can either faze or reach them. Newman perhaps inspires openness, or perhaps the desire for openness in Madame de Cintré, but she cannot hold herself against the pressure of tradition. Consequently, when her mother and brother, Urbain, finally decide that they "really cannot reconcile [them]selves to a commercial person" like Newman, they remind Claire of the tradition of matriarchal authority: in "France," Mrs. Tristram explains, "you must never say Nay to your mother, whatever she requires of you" (252, 77).[4]

James's indictment of tradition as a rejection of what has not been repeated is dramatized in Claire's renunciation of Newman and ultimately of life itself. She responds to the pressure of tradition first with abject surrender and then by resigning her will altogether to the discipline of the Carmelite order. When Newman demands to know what has forced Claire's change of heart, Madame de Bellegarde responds by informing Newman that they "have used authority" (249). The collision here between Newman's understanding, Claire's unquestioning obedience, and Madame de Bellegarde's authority underscores the decay and sterility James associates with that aspect of European culture which views itself as complete. Characters such as the Bellegardes, argues John Carlos Rowe, "for whom the forms of society are already given and for whom adherence to such unreflective proprieties is considered a virtue and a duty," produce an atmosphere of "social stagnation." Be it "literary or historical," Rowe goes on to point out, "repetition is generally a sign in James of a culture that is secretly in ruins, that cannot find the imagination and passion to regenerate itself" (*Theoretical Dimensions*, 69). Thus, while James suggests Europe is at the end of its history, unable to do anything but reduplicate itself, Newman is suggested to belong to a history still waiting to happen. For this reason Rowe's idea of James's suspicion of repetition, though quite right, seems also to under-estimate what James understood as the strength of such cultures, especially their power to sustain themselves in the face of attempts at change. Therefore, however naive or innocent Newman appears, and however powerful the Bellegarde's Paris, Newman's willingness to taste something new is James's way of attesting to both the health of America as it is embodied in Newman's adventurousness, and the inherent danger of all attempts to regulate and manage experience. It is here that one should pause and note that James was not averse to commerce, documenting in many instances the democratic free-doms associated with commercial culture. He was well aware that a good measure of that "American" freedom people like Emerson valorized was a by-product of American mercantile aspirations. Like Simmel, James understood that a "money economy" plays an important role in "individual liberty" precisely because while it promotes a "mutual dependence" in order to carry out the business of getting and spending, it also, one could almost say, imposes on its citizens "a maximum of liberty" (*Philosophy of Money*, 295). Of course, those who find themselves swept up in the economic current suffer the negative consequences of a culture whose "maximum of liberty" is also understood to mean a minimum of care. This too James understood, as his *The American Scene* makes poignant. Nevertheless, to the extent that Newman is a manifestation of the maximum of liberty afforded the self-made man, he embodies James's declarations about the "exercise of freedom" as a requisite for the "good health of an art" ("Art of Fiction," 49). According to James, the ways in which a novel can be "interesting," which he sees as its primary "responsibility," can "only suffer from being marked out or fenced in by prescription" (49). In other words, control equals closure in James's hermeneutics, and closure poses a threat to the originary vitality of life and art.[5]

The dangers associated with the ossification of tradition as embodied in people such as the Bellegardes becomes manifest in Valentin de Bellegarde who is held captive by a "superannuated image of *honour*" (98). In a confessional moment Valentin admits to being a failure precisely because he belongs to a history which is complete, like a work of art. Because he was a Bellegarde, he explains the world was largely "ticketed 'Hands off!'." In his words, "I couldn't go into business, I couldn't make money, because I was a Bellegarde. I couldn't go into politics, because I was a Bellegarde – the Bellegardes don't recognize the Bonapartes ... The only thing I could do was to go and fight for the Pope" (95–6). However, this last honor is rendered empty when we learn that for Valentin fighting for the Pope was nothing more than a *pro forma* procedure. Honor, for these Europeans, James shows, has become nothing more than a dead tradition masquerading as a reality. Valentin's duel with a Brewer's son over a courtesan allows Newman to bring home James's point about the danger of allowing a blind allegiance to tradition to govern one's life. When Valentin admits that he will fight the duel not because he cares about Noémie, but because honor demands that "a man can't back down before a woman," Newman barks back "confound your sense of honour!" (242). James's indictment of this empty notion of honor is worth quoting at length since Valentin's defense of the idea underscores how hollow the notion of "honor" has become, and to what extent Europe has evolved, for James, into a culture whose people have lost the power of productive action. Indeed, Valentin's duel represents the recovery of action in the worst possible way, as Newman's charge suggests:

"Your duel itself is a scene ... that is all it is! It is a wretched theatrical affair. Why don't you take a band of music with you outright? It is d—d barbarous and it is d—d corrupt, both."

Valentin's response is predictable in its unquestioning allegiance to a romance version of the past.

"Oh, I cannot begin, at this time of day, to defend the theory of duelling ... It is our custom, and I think it is a good thing. Quite apart from the goodness of the cause in which a duel may be fought, it has a kind of picturesque charm which in this age of vile prose seems to me greatly to recommend it. It is a remnant of a higher-tempered time; one ought to cling to it. Depend upon it, a duel is never amiss."

Newman's reply to Valentin's theorizing cuts to the quick:

"I don't know what you mean by higher-tempered time ... Because your great-grandfather was an ass, is that any reason why you should be?" (244)

Newman's inability to understand, let alone sympathize with Valentin's captivity is directly related to his "all-objective" disposition. For Newman, understanding, at least at this point in the novel, involves a simple correspondence between word and deed, between what people say they mean and what they do. As James explains, Newman maintained a "life-long submissiveness to the sentiment that words were acts and acts were steps in life" (332). Nevertheless, what James points out through Newman's initial inability to become attuned to the Parisian social text is how little understanding has to do with any sense of objective truth, whatever that might prove to be.

Understanding, in James's hermeneutics, presupposes belonging, that is, it presupposes a background of concepts and beliefs, a familiar world into which alien events can be integrated and therefore understood. But in Newman, James gives us a classic American outsider who, not being subjective, is just to that extent impervious to the process of Europeanization that would constitute, let us say, the American's customary process of coming to understand an alien European culture. On the other hand, in the Bellegardes, James gives us a classic European family (and classic is accentuated in their being able to trace their genealogy back "eight hundred years" and the family home back to "1627") that, unlike Newman, is, if anything, *all-subjective* (115, 82). For the Bellegardes everything seems rooted in a fully determined self-interpretation where revision is impossible. The smallest revision, the revision of the past, would require a complete reconstruction of the whole. What James reveals in the conflict between Newman and Valentin, and between Newman and the Bellegardes, could be described as the tension between rival modes of interpretation James – the American in Europe – encountered in his travels and extended contact with (especially) Parisian culture. We recall that upon finally deciding to leave Paris in December 1876, James explained the move in his Journal by declaring that in Paris "I should be an eternal outsider."[6] James makes this point more elaborately in an essay he wrote for *The Nation* in 1878, shortly after completing *The American*. Writing in response to an issue which had been raised as to the position of

Americans abroad, such as himself, or Newman for instance, James said

Americans in Europe are outsiders: that is the great point, and the point thrown into relief by all zealous efforts to controvert it. As a people we are out of European society; the fact seems to us incontestable, be it regrettable or not. We are not only out of the European circle politically or geographically; we are out of it socially, and for excellent reasons. We are the only great people of the civilized world that is a pure democracy, and we are the only great people that is exclusively commercial. ("Americans Abroad," 208–9)

For James, his discovery was of the essential conflict between atomistic and holistic interpretations. In *The American*, he gives body to this conflict through Newman's struggle to understand the Parisian social text. For example, when arguing with Valentin about the prospective duel, James shows us that Newman misinterprets Valentin by thinking of him as separable from the whole, as though Valentin were someone – like himself – who has meaning all by himself because meaning for him is not a subjective affair. But Valentin, James shows, is holistic; he can only exist, can only have meaning, within the system that makes him possible. Newman mistakenly believes he can extract Valentin and Claire from their world, bring Valentin to America and put him "in the way of doing some business" (230). But both Valentin and Claire know that there is no existence for them except within the totality that gives them life. And, as we have seen "honour," within that totality, has a particularly heightened and self-affirming importance. Everything Valentin does is filtered through his subjective understanding of "honour." He goes so far as to die for it.

The inevitable collision between Newman's belief that understanding means accepting things at their face value and the Bellegardes' more thickened, personalized, and metaphorized construction comes when they reinterpret their position on Newman and put an end to his marriage plans. In the initial compact Newman is careful to exact from the Marquis and Madame de Bellegarde a promise, *on their honor*, that they would neither "interfere" with his suit nor use "persuasion" to influence Claire (248–49). However, when faced with the need to change their position, the Bellegardes use "authority," and, as Claire explains, command that she give Newman up. For the Bellegardes a world of difference exists between persuade and command, and it is just that world Newman cannot grasp, because for him the world looks and acts differently. And that is just it, as Newman notes:

"So you make a distinction ... You make a distinction between persuading and commanding? It is very neat. But the distinction is in favour of commanding. That rather spoils it." (250)

One last point about how the positive side of Newman's "all-objective" character shows itself to be a more democratic ethical posture than the Bellegardes' all-subjective stance needs to be made, since it highlights not only the more admirable qualities of Newman's character, but also accentuates a principal aspect of James's hermeneutics: namely the link between understanding and action. *The American* is chock-full of scenes borrowed from literary tradition.[7] Newman informs us that not only is a street scene "characteristically Parisian," but that Valentin de Bellegarde matches his picture of a Frenchman of literary tradition (91). Valentin's duel is, as Newman notes, "a scene" from the romance tradition, something James underscores by having Newman find "an old copy of *Les Liaisons Dangereuses*" by the dying man's bedside (264). Claire de Cintré's first marriage is described by Valentin as "a chapter for a novel" (107). And, of course, the Bellegarde home reminds Newman of something from a gothic novel (78). Newman's involvement in Claire's fate reads to him as "too strange and too mocking to be real; it was like a page torn out of a romance, with no context in his own experience" (326). Furthermore, in the midst of Mrs. Bread's story of Madame de Bellegarde's criminality, James breaks into the narrative to tell the reader that "the most artistic of romancers could not have been more effective. Newman made a movement as if he were turning over the page of a novel" (309). The comic irony in this persistent appeal to literary tradition as a contextualizing device is that Newman, who confesses almost in the novel's opening scene that "he had never read a novel," suddenly finds himself thrust into one where he is offered the opportunity to play various roles, principally the romantic hero and the avenger. The role Newman finally assumes, James reveals, has everything to do with how he learns to read himself in relation to the textual scenes that play themselves out before him. And it is in Newman's response to the interpretive challenge these various literary scenes present that the positive side of being "all-objective" is shown by James to be conducive to productive action.

III

Paul Ricoeur raises an interesting point about "the referential dimension of the work of fiction" which provides a valuable insight into James's presentation of Newman's struggle to understand, particularly as James employs literary scenes as constituent elements to highlight Newman's confusion (*Hermeneutics*, 141). Ricoeur suggests that "to interpret is to explicate the type of being-in-the-world unfolded *in front of* the text" so that what the reading or literary situation induces in the participant is a recognition of the text, or textual scene, as "*a proposed world* which I could inhabit and wherein I could project one of my ownmost possibilities" (142). In other words, works of art such as a novel or a poem open up "new possibilities of being-in-the-world" within a reader's quotidian reality (142). How one responds to the challenge of interpretation proposed by the literary scene is a measure, then, of one's ability to respond both to life and textual representations of lived reality. James sets the stage for just this type of interpretive dynamic in *The American* through Newman's tendency to translate living situations into textual scenes. Newman's consistent textualizing of social situations serves to enhance James's point about literature's ability to bring us a vision of reality from diverse and new perspectives. To be sure, James believed the novel's principal power lay in its ability to offer another and alternate world of experience into which the act of reading ineluctably projects the reader. While the novel's "*effect*" is "to entertain," its "main object," James claimed, "is to represent life." For James the novel "produces a certain illusion" which "makes it appear to us for the time that we have lived another life – that we have had a miraculous enlargement of experience" ("Alphonse Daudet," *Literary Criticism*, II, 242). Newman's larger experience in *The American* bears this out, a realization he eventually comes to when he "attempt[s] to read the moral of his strange misadventure" (358).

Indeed, James has Newman end his European experience as though Newman himself were finishing the last pages of a novel and finding that the "most unpleasant thing that had ever happened to him had reached its formal conclusion, as it were; he could close the book and put it away" (364). James's theoretical point is double. First, the degree of Newman's openness to the intersubjective transference experienced by the reading act is in direct proportion to his level of objectivity. Being "all-objective," Newman stands before every textual scene and experiences "new possibilities of being-in-the-world." In his own way Newman anticipates James's claim in "The Art of Fiction" that "the province of art is all life, all feeling, all observation, all vision" (59). Conversely, the degree of, say, Valentin's ability to meet the requirements of the literary scene, insofar as the textual breaches the boundary between the real and the not real, is in inverse proportion to the level of his subjectivity. It is perhaps because Newman has so little invested in a subjective sense of self that he is better able than Valentin to respond to situations which require productive action. But though this is the correct way to interpret Newman's response to Madame Dandelard, or to Valentin, it is not quite right to say that Newman's own subjective sense of self, or even his sense of what constitutes a self, does not get in the way of his ability to understand. This becomes apparent in his encounter with Claire de Cintré. Nevertheless, how well Newman meets the requirements of the situations he encounters, that is, how able he is to appropriate the consciousness necessary for understanding to occur, depends on the degree to which he is capable of resigning his ego, which enables his escape from the epistemological coerciveness of governing power structures and allows for his opening himself to the possibilities of the "*proposed world*" before him (Ricoeur, *Hermeneutics*, 142).

James offers a good example of the interpretive dynamic Ricoeur outlines when he has Valentin and Newman visit Madame Dandelard, a victim of marital abuse whose life is falling to pieces. For Valentin, ever the distanced observer of the aesthetic, Madame Dandelard represents a curious theatrical scene, someone he proposes "they should go and see" because she "was very pretty, very childlike, and she made extraordinary remarks" (102–3). Valentin's infantilism merely accentuates his aestheticized reduction of Mrs. Dandelard to a two dimensional literary text, something he can observe in a detached manner.[8] That Madame Dandelard's plight does not reach Valentin exemplifies his incapacity to get beyond the bounds of his carefully constructed ego, an imprisonment, James suggests, of an over-determined subjectivity that has been shaped by tradition, or, in more materialist terms, those institutional power structures which imprison subjectivity within determining constraints. James underscores Valentin's attitude when he reveals Bellegarde's perverse pleasure in looking over the unfortunate woman as though she were a text: "She had a blue spot somewhere," as a result of her husband's physical abuse, "which she showed to several persons, including Bellegarde" (103). For Valentin, James tells us, "the source of his interest in her was ... a curiosity as to what would become of her" (103). The upshot of this scene is that Valentin is not just disinclined to respond, but incapable of responding to the claim Madame Dandelard's scene makes on him. More to the point, James suggests through this encounter that Valentin is dead, that his interest can only be in detached observation, and that he goes to see women such as Madame Dandelard just to see an atmosphere of decay.[9]

It is interesting to note here that even at this stage of his career, in the late 1870s, James's concern with the more negative capabilities of aestheticism find their way into his work. Both *The American* (1877) and the earlier novel *Roderick Hudson* (1875) engage in a sustained attack against what James came to see as the immoral underside of aestheticism, at least insofar as the aesthete cultivated a hyper-sensual response to life. Valentin's pose here is one of unmistakable sensual detachment and matches the voyeuristic pleasures associated with the cavalier misappropriation of Walter Pater's conception of the self as an aesthetic being whose principal responsibility was to be engaged always in "habitual observation," to "burn always" and "maintain this ecstacy" before everything ("Wordsworth," 97; "Conclusion," 189). Since the young James found himself sharing close affinities with Walter Pater, in particular with Pater's cultivation of perception as a mode of being, to find the deeper artistic force James understood as growing out of studied observation reduced to disengaged voyeuristic titillation posed a threat not only to James's reputation as an artist, or to the public understanding of art, but to art itself. Valentin's inability to carry over his aesthetic detachment into meaningful action was James's way of revealing the moral corruption in this aspect of aestheticism and the implicit thanatotic drive associated with a hyper-refined aesthetic detachment. Valentin's fate in the novel bears this out as do his admitted motives in watching Madame Dandelard unravel.

"She is poor, she is pretty, and she is silly, ... it seems to me she can only go one way. It is a pity, but it cannot be helped. I will give her six months. She has nothing to fear from me, but I am watching the process. I am curious to see just how things will go. Yes, I know what you are going to say: this horrible Paris hardens one's heart. But it quickens one's wits, and it ends by teaching one a refinement of observation. To see this little woman's drama play itself out, now, is, for me, an intellectual pleasure." (103)

Now while Valentin's attitude is indicative of the threat to culture and society this form of aestheticist detachment posed, such attenuated refinement also posed a threat to the artist who could end up being refined to paralytic inertia. We see this in *Roderick Hudson* when Rowland Mallet finds Roderick Hudson "in his sitting room" which has been redecorated so as to resemble a burial chamber.

Here and there, over [the floor], certain strongly-odorous flowers had been scattered. Roderick was lying on his divan in a white dressing-gown, staring at the frescoed ceiling. The room was deliciously cool and filled with the moist sweet fragrance of the circumjacent roses and violets ... Roderick lay motionless except that he slightly turned his head towards his friend. He was smelling a large white rose, which he continued to present to his nose. In the darkness of the room he looked exceedingly pale, but his beautiful eyes quite shed a light. He let them rest for some time on Rowland, lying there like a Buddhist in an intellectual swoon, a deep dreamer whose perception should be slowly ebbing back to temporal matters. (1:393–94)

The point James makes here with Valentin and Roderick Hudson, and with Newman's notably different response to Madame Dandelard, underscores two important themes which run throughout his work. On the one hand, while James recognized within himself certain affinities with the aestheticist movement, he also recognized specific ways in which its more popular manifestations made it increasingly difficult for him to practice his own craft. Valentin and Roderick are to this extent *ficelles* which James employs in the larger text of his art in an effort to distinguish himself from this negative underside of aestheticism. Also, while *The American* attacks the blind consumerism of American culture, pointing up how little America knows in the way of being-in-the-world, James does make sustained efforts to show that as a growing and live culture America can learn and that its deep moral impulses do have productive consequences beyond the Puritan and Calvinist zeal which he depicts in *The Ambassadors*, "Daisy Miller," *The Europeans*, and a host of other works.

Newman's response to Madame Dandelard's disturbing situation bears this out. Unlike Valentin, or, one would imagine, Roderick Hudson, Newman is able to respond to Madame Dandelard more directly, without mediation of the aesthetic. When presented with "this little woman's drama" Newman, unlike Valentin, feels its application to reality and feels a need to act rather than observe. He

suggests Valentin "[t]alk to her; give her some good advice," something Newman has already done in offering to help Noémie Nioche
and her decrepit father, and something he will do in trying to offer
Valentin a chance to extricate himself from the text within which he
is caught. Newman's reaction to the scene Madame Dandelard
presents parallels the interpretive moment in Ricoeur's formulation.
"The moment of 'understanding'," Ricoeur explains, "corresponds
dialectically to being in a situation: it is the projection of our
ownmost possibilities at the very heart of the situations in which we
find ourselves" (*Hermeneutics*, 142). Madame Dandelard, then,
becomes a site on which James presents two modes of observation,
the passive and the active. Newman's is active because he is not
confined by the refinements of Valentin's aesthetic detachment. To
be sure, Newman's lack of subjectivity prevents him from joining
Valentin in the " 'intellectual pleasure' " of Madame Dandelard's
"prospective adventures." Indeed, it is precisely Valentin's all-
subjective nature that allows him to view Madame Dandelard as an
opportunity to refine his powers of observation. Accordingly, it is the
lack of a manipulative internal subjectivity that allows Newman the
freedom to meet the claim Madame Dandelard's scene makes and to
come to understand it practically in the way of action.[10] Where
Valentin recognizes in the scene its potential for "teaching one a
refinement of observation," Newman sees only the need to inter-
vene. He does not want to interpret it, he wants to change it, and in
so desiring dramatizes what Leon Edel has rightly called "the
American character in all its forthrightness and innocence as well as
in its predatory aspects" (*Conquest*, 249). In depicting the distinction
between Valentin's and Newman's mode of reaction, James underscores Newman's practical hermeneutics. What we see is how good
Newman is at hermeneutical praxis on the one hand, and how shaky
at understanding what is alien. His characteristic response to the
alien (Madame Dandelard in this case) is to want to change it into
what is recognizable and consistent with his own empirical outlook.

IV

In the opening sentence of chapter twenty-six James uses the word
"uninitiated" to describe Newman's "observation of the great
spectacle of English life" (357). James's choice of this word to
describe Newman's interpretive stance is curious in that it brings up

the negative side of what being "all-objective" might be. Since initiation is a social process, a way of becoming acquainted with a society's mores, the uninitiated observer, like Newman in London and Paris, would be at an interpretive disadvantage in an alien culture. Furthermore, being initiated means becoming, in a manner, subjective, at least insofar as one has an interpretive framework against which the alien and unknown can be compared so as to be made comprehensible. But if Newman is, as James claims, "all-objective," then he is to that extent an unformed or ill-formed subject and would as such be impervious to any knowledge offered beyond the face value of his experiences. Where the positive side of being "all-objective" instills in Newman a willingness to expose himself to what is strange without feeling the need to bring it under conceptual control, the downside is that he needs to be told what he is looking at and then can see only the two-dimensional surface of the thing. His only recourse for understanding then comes either through the mediation offered by his ubiquitous guidebooks, or through his own, narrowly developed impression of self. The danger of either interpretive method is readily apparent: on the one hand Newman can look to his Bädeker and impose its flattened, textually generated meaning, or he can choose the even more limited route and find in his impressions a mirror image of the viewing self. Newman does both.

James highlights the first of Newman's interpretive methods in the early stages of the novel by endowing Newman's "little red-guidebook" with almost talismanic status. The Bädeker assumes such a high degree of importance early on because James uses it as a narrative tool through which he dramatizes the hazards associated with a hermeneutics that looks to find understanding as a completion rather than an ongoing event. For James, retreating to the impressions of a guidebook is tantamount to a denial of life and evokes what he saw as the greatest threat to both understanding and art. The Bädeker offers Newman fixity and control, which translates in James's hermeneutics to closure or the refusal of hermeneutics. It is not surprising then, that during the course of the novel James shows how Newman's Bädeker-informed mind finds itself continually out of tune with the Parisian social text in which Newman moves.[11] In so doing, *The American* anticipates James's most intensive investigations into the nature of understanding represented through those centers of consciousness that strive to be individuals "on whom nothing is lost!" ("Art of Fiction," 53).[12] The manner of Newman's interpretive failures become a text played out in more and more minute and revelatory detail in James's more mature works: minute in that the concentration shifts from cultural clashes to interpretive conflicts between self and other and, eventually, in, say, *The Ambassadors* and *The Golden Bowl*, between self and self; revelatory because James is ultimately a writer whose works become a *vade-mecum* on understanding and becoming in tune with the self and the social reality in which the self is defined and understood. For James, achieving this level of understanding is the role art plays in human affairs. "Literature," he says "is an objective, a projected result; it is life that is the unconscious, the agitated, the struggling, floundering cause" ("The Lesson of Balzac," 118).

James begins his investigation of Newman's struggle to understand by inviting the reader into the novel through the doors of the Louvre where we meet Newman "reclining at his ease ... staring at Murillo's beautiful moon-born Madonna" (1). In our introduction to Newman, the narrator informs us that the American "had looked out all the pictures to which an asterisk was affixed in those formidable pages of fine print in his Bädeker" (1). By opening a work of fiction with a protagonist in a museum looking at a work of art James simultaneously calls attention to *The American*'s textuality and Newman's occupying the site analogous to the one occupied by the reader. In effect, this is the position James has Newman occupy throughout his Parisian experience, as though Newman were always in the space in front of the text. And in so positioning Newman, James succeeds in linking his hermeneutic struggle with the reader's own: both are involved in an interpretive task – Newman trying to take in Murillo's painting (and, as the novel progresses, Paris and "Europe"), the reader, as the novel progresses, trying to take in Newman and to gauge his ability to accomplish his task.[13] James's point is worth some attention. Since a connection is established between Newman and the reader, *The American* immediately succeeds in drawing readers into its textual frame and involving them in a complex intersubjective dialectic which continually juxtaposes the reader's understanding of events against Newman's, and, ultimately, James's vision of the whole from the Preface's distance.[14] Paradoxically, this is exactly why Newman's being "all-objective" allows James to achieve the full measure of his topic in *The American*. Newman's underdeveloped subjectivity allows him to blunder through the Parisian social text unfazed because unknowing that what he believes is occurring is exactly not the case. Since Newman takes all things at their face value – a condition of his over-determined objectivity and native mercantile instincts – James is able to foreground the ambiguities involved in all interpretation, particularly when one concentrates, as does Newman, on the spoken word. Thus the novel's elaborately developed layers of discrepant awareness – Newman's, the Bellegardes', Mrs. Tristram's, the reader's, and James's – constantly provoke the reader's attempts to unravel the ambiguous social text as represented in Newman's conception of what is happening, as embodied in the Bellegardes' more duplicitous mastery of language's inherent ambiguity, and as a representative characteristic of James's actively challenging aesthetics. One could say this is the condition of James's fiction. The interpretive dynamic locates itself in his texts' social language, in the "ambiguity of human motivation and psychology," as Rowe explains. "Learning not only how to recognize this fundamental ambiguity, but also how such ambiguity provokes necessary and inevitable efforts at determinate meaning and the institution of legal, political, economic, and familial authorities, is the hermeneutic imperative of James's fiction; such an imperative is directed at the reader, thematized by way of the characters, and finally returned to check the author's own will to mastery of his literary materials" (*Theoretical Dimensions*, 65).

The American's opening scene similarly calls attention to the implicit competition between the version of understanding James believes embodied in the narrative of Newman's European experience and the version Newman culls from his Bädeker. Newman's reliance on the guidebook in these opening scenes reminds one of Edward Said's remarks about "*textual* attitude[s]." According to Said, it is "a common human failing to prefer the schematic authority of a text to the disorientations of direct encounters with the human." Said goes on to explain that "[t]ravel books or guidebooks" abet the "human tendency to fall back on a text when the uncertainties of travel in strange parts seem to threaten one's equanimity" (*Orientalism*, 93). Just so with Newman who, as we have seen, tends to treat his encounters with the Parisian world, particularly the world represented by the Bellegardes, as a romance. What James shows when the world and Newman's textualized interpretations reach an impasse, as they do when the Bellegardes call off his engagement, is how unprepared Newman is to meet the requirements of the situation, how much he is the uninitiated observer. That the reader anticipates the Bellegardes' cancellation, and that it comes as a complete surprise to Newman (his first impulse is to laugh and accuse the Bellegardes of "fooling"), is further indication of the degree to which Newman's understanding has been thwarted by reliance on the textual authority of either a guidebook or a traditional literary stereotype (247).[15]

That the very nature of understanding is James's focus in *The American*, and that the novel is not the failed comic romance his initial readers and numerous subsequent critics claim is evident in the novel's super-structural design. One can view *The American* as a series of concentric circles, each operating as part of a larger vortex which ineluctably draws Newman and the reader deeper into the interpretive quandary Newman faces. Each circle presents a more grave and subtle interpretive trap, and the reader watches as Newman moves blindly from failing to perceive the obvious to being simply mastered by the nearly impenetrable precisely because Newman cannot read and cannot see in the way these social situations demand. At the organizational level of narrative, James plunges his protagonist into increasing degrees of impercipience until Newman finally is able to overcome all by experiencing what we would have to call a hermeneutic epiphany. But though this final releasement which accompanies Newman's moment of insight disabuses Newman with regard to his Parisian experience, James also suggests the experience of sudden insight forces Newman, in a sense, to begin his life again. And this new beginning ironically starts with Newman's obvious inability to read the world around him, made evident in the novel's opening encounter between the American and the Parisian adventuress Noémie Nioche. While lounging in the "Salon Carré" Newman's attention is captured by a "copyist" more intent on presenting herself than her copy of a Madonna to Newman as an *objet d'art* for purchase.

As the little copyist proceeded with her work, she sent every now and then a responsive glance toward her admirer. The cultivation of the fine arts appeared to necessitate, to her mind, a great deal of by-play, a great standing off with folded arms and head drooping from side to side, stroking of a dimpled chin with a dimpled hand, sighing and frowning and patting of the foot, fumbling in disordered tresses for wandering hair pins. These performances were accompanied by a restless glance, which lingered longer than elsewhere upon the gentleman we have described. (4)

After careful study of the painter and her product, Newman approaches and utters his first word in the story and the only French word he knows: "*Combien?*" The comic irony implicit in Newman's inquiry is his misunderstanding of just what is for sale. Mademoiselle Nioche, as she herself admits to Newman on another occasion, does not "know how to paint" (58), and Newman has already admitted he is an incompetent judge. Not until much later, when Noémie Nioche directly announces "[e]verything I have is for sale," does Newman fully understand this courtesan's discourse. And then, for all his commercial and democratic zeal, Newman is unable to recognize Noémie as anything more than a "prostitute" and unable to see the connection between Noémie's marketing of herself and Newman's collusion with the market forces Madame de Bellegarde manages in the "sale" of Claire (245). To this extent he reveals himself to be a bit of an American genteel prude who allows, as Edel remarks, "a strong and vulgar sense of materialistic self-satisfaction" to govern his idea of appropriate behavior (*Conquest*, 249).

But Newman's "*Combien?*" echoes, as we have seen, throughout *The American* in several crucial ways. It introduces us to Newman's reifying habit of mind, his belief that he can purchase the finished product – be it painting, artifact, the French language, or Madame de Cintré – simply by opening his ample wallet.[16] It adumbrates the commodifying tendency which leads Newman from misunderstanding to misunderstanding to his eventual total isolation at the novel's conclusion. And it links Noémie Nioche's willingness to sell herself with Newman's desire to purchase a wife, blurring the distinction between the supposedly immoral and supposedly moral Parisian worlds.[17] For James, Newman's "*Combien?*" is the descriptive term he uses to present the kind of subject a commercial culture produces. Newman conflates and commodifies everything so as to render things accessible and, ultimately, consumable. Since he thinks of himself above all else as a rich man and of life as "an open game ... he had played for high stakes" and won, Newman's natural tendency is to see Europe as a similar version of American commercialism (20). Certainly he approaches Europe as he does the American market, a point James makes succinctly when he has

Newman admit: "I have come to see Europe, to get the best out of it I can. I want to see all the great things" (21). And yet James's question here is difficult to fix. He seems to be asking the reader to decide whether Newman's entrepreneurial attribute is peculiar to Newman, or whether it makes him a representative American entrepreneur. The answer comes from Newman when he counters Mrs. Tristram's accusation that he has "no feeling" by suggesting life in a money culture such as America precludes the development of feeling: "The fact is I have never had time to feel things. I have had to *do* them, to make myself felt" (31). James's condemnation of a purely commercial culture seems clear here,[18] especially insofar as it produces individuals who, like Newman, or his more sinister manifestation, Adam Verver, exist solely as consumers rather than producers of culture.[19]

It is perhaps Noémie Nioche who makes the most insightful comment about this aspect of Newman's disposition when she responds to Newman's commission of "six or eight copies in the Louvre" with a mixture of sarcasm and incredulity (47):

"It must be charming to be able to order pictures at such a rate. Venetian portraits, as large as life! You go at it *en prince*. And you are going to travel about Europe that way?" (56)

In making her pejorative comment about Newman, about his idea of ordering art by the yard, Noémie gives voice to two issues James found most frustrating about Americans abroad: 1) appropriation; 2) copying. For James appropriation and copying are always signs of uncreative activity, of the consumer rather than the artist. James felt great frustration with Americans who traveled merely to collect or copy because what they ultimately were able to accomplish was a counterfeit version of culture. One of *The American*'s most powerful messages is that no amount of appropriative ability can deliver the real thing. For James, individuals such as Newman resembles, who come to a culture with rapacious designs, acquire works of art by seizure rather than as a result of some internal connection with it. So while they may possess the object, there is no aesthetic union between owner and owned, and without such a union, James believed one's consciousness would remain closed off to the "importunate *muchness*" of culture (*Henry James Letters*, I, 416).

V

I have suggested earlier that it is not quite right to say that Newman's subjective sense of self does not get in the way of his ability to understand. Nowhere is this more evident than in his relationship with Claire de Cintré. Newman's unqualified misreading of Claire becomes a drama through which James personifies the multiple dangers associated with any claim to objectivity and the more insidious ramifications of a subjectivity produced in a purely commercial culture. Claire de Cintré becomes the site on which James demonstrates how Newman's supposedly "all-objective" character winds up looking very much like the Bellegardes' pure subjectivity: only the cultural imperatives differ. In other words, what James accomplishes in dramatizing Newman's (mis)understanding of Claire is how much Newman's sense of himself overrides his experience of reality. Thus the distinction between "all-objective" and "all-subjective" disappears, which is an aspect of the novel that has led Leon Edel to argue that "in her own way the Marquise de Bellegarde is simply a European Christopher Newman; she sits upon her aristocratic sanctity with the same tough possessiveness and assurance as that with which Newman sits on his pile of dollars" (*Conquest*, 252). For Newman, this recognition brings about one of those truly negative experiences that first initiates a disabusement, as the world heretofore understood collapses under the weight of new insight, and then introduces an enlarged capacity to understand as one's horizon expands to incorporate (without reducing) what had been unfathomable.

James sets the scene for Newman's hermeneutic failure by having Newman reveal how much of his subjective package he imposes on his idea of what a wife might look like. Ever the commercial man, Newman constructs a mental cameo of himself and bride which he believes will match his image of himself as a successful man: "I want to marry very well," he announces; "I want to take my pick. My wife must be a magnificent woman" (34).

"I want a great woman. I stick to that. That is the one thing I *can* treat myself to, and if it is to be had I mean to have it. What else have I toiled and struggled for all these years? I have succeeded, and now what am I to do with my success? To make it perfect, as I see it, there must be a beautiful woman perched on the pile, like a statue on a monument ... I want to possess, in a word, the best article in the market." (35)

Though the Bädeker seems close here, what is perhaps more revealing in Newman's constructed image is how much his own subjective sense of self shows through the description. We recall, after all, that at the time Newman describes this future bride the woman is a phantom product of his imagination. What this secondary image shows is how much Newman conceives of himself as a rich man, and how for him being wealthy means playing a certain role. The picture of this "woman" serves to fill out the image proper. Thus the female ideal here is reduced to a marketable commodity, "the best article in the market." In carrying out this reification, Newman once again reveals the negative underside of a money-culture's reduction of all things to commodity status. As Simmel shows, one of the defining characteristics of a pure exchange economy is how money "ties being and owning together," since "ownership" provides an "opportunity for the Ego to find its expression in" objects (*Philosophy of Money*, 321). For Newman, possessing a wife, possessing Claire, as he comes to understand, becomes a form of validation in which Newman is validated and Claire is reduced to the means side of the means-ends exchange system with which Newman is most familiar and about which James is profoundly disturbed. It is interesting to note that Newman's reduction of the female to a material item is paralleled by every other male character in the text from Old Nioche's willing participation in and financial benefit from Noémie's sale of herself, to Lord Deepmere's pleasure in purchasing Noémie, to Tom Tristram's conception of his wife as a bank,[20] to Valentin's voyeuristic pleasures, not to mention his description of Claire as a statue come to life, a description that recalls Newman's perverse desire for a monument to perch atop his pile (105). James's point is interesting in light of the commercial ingredient of *The American* since in the novel every male character is powerless, in a sense emasculated, and caught up in circumstances which exceed his capacity for understanding. It is not without some degree of irony, then, that James tells us Newman "always came back to the feeling that when he should complete himself by taking a wife, that was the way he should like his wife to interpret him to the world" (117). Insofar as these themes converge in Newman and his relationship with Claire, James can be seen as suggesting the inherent limitations of purely commercial and, as a matter of course, masculine experience. What James seems to be getting at in this aspect of *The American* is the deficiencies of a money culture, deficiencies which restrict one's ability to think of others in terms other than cash value and exchange. In exposing Newman's limitations James shows his character to be "[c]onventionally masculine in his assumptions of the position of owner toward woman as commodity," as Peggy McCormack has argued. "Newman's blatant economic images of what he values in a wife," McCormack continues, "read like textbook examples of the essential presuppositions governing an economy based upon the exchange of women" (*Rule of Money*, 11). In each of the above cases, as well as Newman's commanding paintings by the yard or the Bellegardes' determination to sell Claire for the money in it, what James shows to be lacking is a third dimension. The first two, material good and money, enact the basic sequence which governs a cash-value exchange, but the deeper significance of what intrinsic value the article holds, of how the article can make one more complete, is always missing. Newman thinks of his prospective wife as an article long before he conceives of her as an individual woman, just as the Bellegardes always think of Newman as an American, which translates in their vocabulary into "a rich man." Only after Newman learns to look past Claire as "the best article in the market" does he begin to understand what she is herself and what she can mean to him. But this too takes some time.

How Newman goes about impressing himself upon Claire is worth examining since it reveals how much he is the product of his culture and also dramatizes the extent to which Parisian culture comes across as a text in which Newman finds himself suddenly forced to participate and in which he finds himself being rewritten. James points up the distinction between Newman's conception of the world as open arena and the Parisian social text as sealed tight against any foreign exegesis by first immuring Claire in layers of the Bellegarde house and then presenting Newman in the role of an observing theater-goer, but as much unable as unwilling to participate in the movements within. Indeed, the world (including Newman as part of that world) undergoes an alteration for Newman when he meets Claire in the sense that his power to impose understanding becomes less and less able to meet the requirements of the situation. When he first goes to see Madame de Cintré, Newman is pulled from the public and open world his objectivity can master into a private and cloistered world that exceeds his experience. James tells us Newman is forced to apply "for admittance at the stoutly guarded Hôtel

Bellegarde." Once he gains admission, Newman "crossed the court, entered the farther door, and was conducted through a vestibule, vast, dim, and cold, up a broad stone staircase with an ancient iron balustrade, to an apartment on the second floor" (80). Strangely, once he reaches the interior of this world his ability to react to textual scenes by projecting into them one of his "ownmost possibilities," as Ricoeur describes it, abandons him (*Hermeneutics*, 142). Instead of trying to experience the Bellegarde world as though he were involved in a situation that requires a practical response, Newman stands passively by, as an uninvolved spectator. In his visits to the Faubourg St. Germain drawing room Newman

sat by without speaking, looking at the entrances and exits, the greetings and chatterings, of Madame de Cintré's visitors. He felt as if he were at a play, and as if his own speaking would be an interruption; sometimes he wished he had a book to follow the dialogue; he half expected to see a woman in a white cap and pink ribbons come and offer him one for one or two francs. (101)

In this scene James reveals the complexity of his character. Where we have seen the man of praxis who seeks to change the world rather than simply read it, we now are presented with another side of Newman, that of passive voyeur. That Newman remains fixed in the role of nonparticipating observer, that he abandons the most basic reading strategy, the willing suspension of disbelief, and that he refuses to open up to the experience of the world unfolding before him highlights one of Newman's fundamental interpretive shortcomings. Rather than learn from his experiences, Newman instead reifies and then decontextualizes them as though experience too were something to be catalogued in a mental Bädeker.[21] And rather than allowing for experienced adjustment, his interpretive horizon confines and sets him apart as voyeur or interloper, causing him to remain known to the Parisian crowd as "the American," a title of isolation whose purpose is to differentiate him from everyone else.

James accentuates the danger of the outsider's susceptibility to culture-bound motivations through Newman's understanding of himself as different from the Parisians he is forced to deal with, especially as that difference is registered in his dealings with Claire de Cintré and her family. For Newman difference means, at least in his case, superiority.[22] For despite his claims to objectivity – he "observed a great many things narrowly, and never reverted to himself" – all of Newman's observations have an implicit element of judgment about them, as evidenced, for example, in his reaction to Paris: "the complex Paris world about him seemed a very simple affair; it was an immense, amazing spectacle, but it neither inflamed his imagination nor irritated his curiosity" (28). His opinions about Babcock, about Valentin and the other Bellegardes, about Paris and Europe, though couched in *laissez-faire* ideology,[23] tend to accentuate what Newman feels is the vastness of his good nature. Newman's very language belies his objectivity. He is the man, after all, who has "come to Europe to get the best out of it that [he] can" (21). One could say the very graciousness of Newman's magnanimity is the best example of his sense of supremacy, since for Newman the power to do is intimately connected with financial success and financial success with quality of character, but Newman himself is unaware of this position.[24] His idea in purchasing a wife is a good example of how Newman believes money talks, and that when it does speak, it only understands *Combien?* For Newman, this attitude prevails in every facet of his life. For instance, when Urbain de Bellegarde's wife remarks to him that, like her, he will "come into [the] family by marriage," Newman brusquely responds "Oh no, I don't! ... I only want to take Madame de Cintré out of it" (159). Also, James tells us Newman "liked doing things which involved his paying for people; the vulgar truth is that he enjoyed 'treating' them ... it was a private satisfaction to him" (226). It is no surprise that James undercuts his protagonist's magnanimity by exposing his action's underlying commercial rapacity time and again, going so far as to reveal that these acts of grandeur and their mercantile underpinnings are the most nearly natural state an individual like Newman possesses. This is what America produces, and Newman's testimony to Mrs. Tristram that he has "never had time to feel things," only "to *do* them, to make myself felt" eventually comes down, in James's sense, to something like this (31). Newman's capital ostentations are explained by Simmel's assessment of the psychological dynamics which develop between an individual and his or her money. The "possession of money," Simmel tells us, extends the self in a "very distinctive" way (*Philosophy of Money*, 326). Money is what allows the individual, such as Newman, "to set the stamp of his personality upon" objects and events, and that extending "monetary power" over things and people is a means by which the subject exerts control without any risk of intersubjective involvement. Newman's "private satisfaction" comes about *because* he is able to avoid any "qualitative relationship" with those who make up his party and *because* those for whom he is paying follow the basic principles of obedience to money which characterizes not only his native culture, but as well his understanding of himself as a self-made man. How closely James captures this component of American mercantile culture in Newman's behavior is perhaps made more evident when we find that Newman's actions fit almost perfectly the psychological profile Simmel depicts as endemic of the individuals in a society where money is the measure of all worth. For such individuals the "completeness with which money and objects as money-values follow the impulses of the person" becomes almost pathological and becomes the means with which he can materially and symbolically extend "his domination" (327). Viewed through this lens, Newman's "private satisfaction[s]," his desire "to possess the best article in the market," betray a peculiar will to power James identified as particularly American. In this sense Leon Edel is quite right when he suggests that Christopher Newman "wants to play god – to the whole world" (*Conquest*, 248).

The magnitude of Newman's interpretive error is most apparent in the way he courts Claire de Cintré. Newman commits the error all objectivists fall prey to. Rather than let Claire reveal herself, Newman commits what Tzvetan Todorov has described in a different connection as the "postulate imperative" (*Conquest of America*, 154). Newman's postulate involves the mistaken projection of *his* values as *the* values, of *his* understanding as *the* understanding, of his conception of who Claire is and what she wants as synonymous with her own idea of these aspects of her character. James tells us Newman "made no violent love to her – no sentimental speeches ... He explained to her, in talking of the United States, the working of various local institutions and mercantile customs" (167–68). Readers would be incorrect here, however, to see James as depicting Newman in a purely mechanical following of an imperative. Though he does follow an imperative, as I suggest, Newman's motives are more complicated. As the outsider, and, more importantly, as an individual who does not maintain a vigilant and "undogmatic openness to experience," Newman is shown to have no alternative to his own values or schema (Gadamer, *Truth and Method*, 319). In having Newman woo Claire with the operation of American "mercantile customs," James demonstrates the failings of an immature, or under-

developed, or poorly responsive discrimination as much as he does
the shortcomings in refinement he saw as symptomatic of an
American culture whose sole focus was always extended outward,
toward the material. But for Newman there is no other way to
interpret than *as* the American. And even though he is responsive to
Claire, he is unable to think of success as consisting in more than
taking her away from it all, an intention that simultaneously recalls
his entrepreneurial zeal, his status as outsider, as buccaneer, and his
hermeneutical praxis.

What becomes clear in the initial stages of their relationship is
that Newman is attracted to what he brings to Claire, to what he
imposes upon her rather than any of the qualities of her character
she tries to reveal. But as though testing the reader's subtlety of
perception, James takes care to ensure that the reader recognizes
also how Newman's descriptions of Claire suggest a consciousness in
some state of revision or development. The novel's language here is
notable for its openness and freedom. Claire's face has "a range of
expression as delightfully vast as the wind-streaked, cloud-flecked
distance on a Western prairie." And when Newman waxes poetic,
his choice of images betrays how much Claire is the site upon which
he not only projects his desires, but through which Newman is
forced to confront the consequences of his experience of her. "She
was a woman for the light, not for the shade; and her natural line
was not picturesque reserve and mysterious melancholy, but frank,
joyous, brilliant action, with just so much meditation as was
necessary, and not a grain more" (168). The internal dynamics of the
narrative in this scene dramatize the active quality of Jamesian
aesthetics. As we have observed, Newman often approaches situations as though he were a man occupying the space in front of the
text, but that he also has a tendency to react to scenes by wanting to
appropriate and change them. With Newman's courting of Claire,
James brings both sides of his American together and displays the
fundamentally destructuring and recreative quality of Jamesian
aesthetics. It is almost as though Newman has the ability to
disengage his consciousness and adopt the position of an observer
watching this marital foreplay. Interestingly, this is exactly the space
occupied by the reader. But what James succeeds in accomplishing
within this scene's narrative structure is to bifurcate Newman's
consciousness so as to allow Newman to observe not so much Claire
as himself in the act of wooing Claire, but from her perspective. By

adopting this position, Newman allows the text – the wooing couple – to educate him about himself. He then brings his practical side to bear on his own subjectivity and changes from being a man "who was also perfectly without words," to one whose language suggests a high responsiveness to the aesthetic qualities of Claire de Cintré. The subtle reader will notice that when Newman finds in Claire's face "a range of expression as delightfully vast as the wind-streaked, cloud-flecked distance on a Western prairie," his language is no longer economic, but has an aesthetic character. What Newman seems to be recognizing in Claire is the imagery of openness. Thus the narrative dynamics of this scene represent a significant moment in Jamesian hermeneutics because James intends his audience to go through the same scrutiny and revision of consciousness Newman experiences. And by having readers adopt the same perspective as his protagonist, James forces them into an active engagement with the process of interpreting the text and, by extension, their own consciousness. How this attempt to create a fundamentally active aesthetics influenced James's writing becomes apparent with his progressive refinements upon the center of consciousness technique and the eventual internalization of narrative in texts like *The Ambassadors*.

The discrimination Newman displays in this courtship scene, though comparable, fails to achieve truly Jamesian status. For James the cultivation of such a discrimination was not, as critics have suggested, a self-ratifying elitism, but instead, as Ross Posnock has argued, "an instrument of individual and cultural replenishment that propagates the 'more' – what James calls the 'margin'" and brings about an enhanced ability to see and feel, and do (*Trial of Curiosity*, 180). But such a level of discrimination required the renunciation of a socially fixed subjectivity and the cultivation of one which was receptive to individual changes and developments. Newman, we have seen, is unable to do either; and though he is momentarily able to get out of himself, he is unable to maintain this perspective and quickly slips back into his "American" identity. What James reveals as the ultimate danger in Newman's brand of objectivity is that it does not know how to make room for anything or anyone that is different. When Valentin asks Newman whether or not he is "afraid it may be a mistake for an American man of business to marry a French countess," Newman responds smartly with "[f]or the countess, possibly; but not for the man of business"

(207). Or when Claire warns Newman that he may be asking too much, that she is "weak," that even if for him "everything seems so simple" things really "are not so," Newman (dis)misses the point and suggests there is "only one thing to think about" (184). And that is just the point for Newman, the world is a simple place because he believes it to be so. Claire de Cintré, the real woman who depends on her world for her existence, never has a chance. The dark side of Newman's projection suggests itself if you view his description of Claire from her perspective:

"If you only knew ... how exactly you are what I coveted! And I am beginning to understand why I coveted it; and having it makes all the difference that I expected. Never was a man so pleased with his good fortune. You have been holding your head for a week past just as I wanted my wife to hold hers. You say the things I want her to say. You walk about the room just as I want her to walk. You have just the taste in dress that I want her to have. In short, you come up to the mark; and, I can tell you, my mark was high." (210)

Interestingly, Newman's projection upon Claire of an identity external to her own mirrors in a perverse way Madame de Bellegarde's similar institution of Claire's identity and foregrounds again the connection between Newman and the Parisian matriarch. Claire herself is always left out of the picture, always being forced to define herself by negation.[25]

James accentuates the limitations of Newman's reflexivity when Claire de Cintré, contrary to saying just the things Newman wants her to say, does the unexpected by announcing "something very grave has happened ... I cannot marry you" (247). When Newman gets beyond the idea that Claire is "fooling," he finds that the reality of her words causes him for the first time to experience the limits of his understanding. Though he correctly accuses Urbain and Madame de Bellegarde of using force, Newman's incapacity to understand why Claire acquiesces to their "authority" is a further indication, James suggests, of his inability to see things as different from the way he has assumed they are (249). And though Newman is also correct in suggesting Claire's refusal of "him and his future and his fortune and his fidelity" so as to "entomb herself in a cell" as a Carmelite nun is "a reduction to the absurd" that stretches even the bounds of the reader's experience, he incorrectly tries to exonerate Claire from complicity in the debacle, an indication, once more, of his reluctance to question his interpretive skills (285).[26] Thus, by

having Claire turn nun and move in such an extreme and unexpected direction James points up the sheer gulf between Newman's
conception of her and who she conceives herself to be. In the
context of the novel's presentation of how Newman's experience of
reality is overwritten by his conception of himself as a self-made,
commercial success "impervious," as Edel suggests, "to all save his
own anchored dollars and the sense they give him that he can do as
he pleases," the shock of Claire's refusal becomes a particularly
effective way to demonstrate how far afield Newman has been in
trying to read the Parisian social text (*Conquest*, 252). Furthermore, in
extending the dramatization of Newman's moment of bewilderment
and his having for the first time come up against the limits of his
understanding, James foregrounds the limits of fixity, whether it be a
fixity of self, or a general cultural fixity such as *The American*'s Paris or
The Ambassadors' Woollett. Claire's refusal brings about a moment of
radical self-understanding for Newman, in the sense that everything
Newman thought was the case comes crashing down. What the
novel so forcefully shows is that Newman has been undergoing a
self-exposure, and here his divestiture becomes part of what he
experiences.

VI

In James's fiction the moment of bewilderment such as Newman
experiences is almost immediately followed by efforts of attunement
in which the characters attempt to (are forced to) reconstruct their
understanding of reality in such a way as to incorporate the new
insight into an expanded and qualitatively different understanding of
how things are. One could say that James texts repeatedly reveal
characters who, because of some moment of radical self-understanding, are forced to rebuild their world after experiencing the destruc-
tion of it. Furthermore, James suggests this constant revision to be
analogous to life, and his representation of it in his texts is what
imbues Jamesian aesthetics with its active and vital quality. For
James's characters, as for his readers who live outside of (or, more
likely, within their own) texts, James shows this rebuilding to be a
central part of understanding and to be a slow and painful process
that, for Newman at least, may only be beginning at the end of the
novel. In *The American*, this epiphany plays itself out as Newman sits
before the corpulent duchess, Madame d'Outreville, awaiting "the

opportunity to tell his story" that "the Bellegardes were traitors and that the old lady, into the bargain, was a murderess" (344, 345).

As I have mentioned,[27] the scene between Newman and "the comical duchess" reveals an hermeneutic change in Newman's capacity to understand. James shows Newman able to respond to a social situation by measuring the present event against a developing body of lived experiences and then converting the event's subtext into useful knowledge which contributes to his enlarged understanding of himself, other people, and the world. This scene is perhaps the finest in the novel as it demonstrates James's mastery of his material while disclosing, between the lines of the duchess's amiable dialogue, the novel's most profound critique of European culture. After all, if it is correct to assume James used Newman as a representative example of an individual produced by a commercial society, or, to state this another way, that only a purely commercial society could produce an "all-objective" subject such as Newman, the novel also suggests that Europe is a society which produces an "all-subjective" subject. Valentin and Claire de Cintré answer to this title as perhaps even more completely do Urbain and Madame de Bellegarde. While the authoritarian elder Bellegardes' actions provide little Newman cannot imagine, both Valentin and Claire act for reasons Newman cannot determine. Claire in particular acts in ways entirely internal to herself, leading me to conclude she has internalized a culture so radically different from Newman's that, as I have suggested, one might speak of an incommensurability between them.

James seems to be developing the idea that Newman lacks practical wisdom – Gadamer's *phronēsis* – which is something that only age and experience can produce, including age and experience of the world in which one grows up.[28] *Phronēsis* is not needing a guidebook or book of rules to get you through tight situations. Rather, James suggests that America, like its representative Christopher Newman, lacks *phronēsis*. James's thoughts on this aspect of his country are implied when he has Mrs. Tristram refer to Newman as "the great Western Barbarian, stepping forth in his innocence and might" (32). More to the point, Newman's America is a culture of *techne*, as demonstrated by Newman's having made fortunes in the manufacture of wash tubs, copper, leather, and railroads. James's most sustained examination of commercialism's limitations comes in *The American Scene*, but his statements there offer a good vantage onto his feelings about why Newman is the way he is. Upon his arrival in

New York in 1904 James found an America given over to the vulgarity of commercialism. Manhattan, in his mind, was "crowned not only with no history, but with no credible possibility of time for history, and consecrated by no uses save the commercial at any cost." And while in Boston James came to conclude that Americans will put up with unlimited frustrations and boorishness because their only concern is to make money: "To make so much money that you won't, that you don't 'mind,' don't mind anything – that is absolutely, I think, the main American formula" (*American Scene*, 77, 237).[29] But Europe too lacks *phronēsis* in James's opinion. It is a culture of over-refined *aisthēsis*,[30] where people have lost the power of productive action because they refer everything back to themselves. Even more so than Newman, the Bellegardes are guilty of committing a postulate imperative. That *the* values are synonymous with *their* values is in their mind an *a priori* truth, an actuality James captures when he describes the Marquise as "a striking image of dignity which ... may reside in the habit of unquestioned authority and the absoluteness of a social theory favourable to yourself" (162). It is on the basis of this attitude that the Bellegardes have cultivated a mode of perception which virtually dispenses with material reality since it refers everything back to themselves and sanctifies their own self-serving certitudes.

Where Aristotle means *aisthēsis* to suggest a mode of understanding in which interpretation is refined so as to provide the interpreting subject with an ability to judge any particular situation without needing recourse to a culture-bound orthodoxy, James suggests the Bellegardes have appropriated understanding by collapsing the distinction between the universal and the particular and made themselves arbiters of both. *Aisthēsis* means being able to see the application to reality of the particular as apart from its relation to the universal. As Martha Nussbaum explains, perception in this sense of the term is meant to develop an ability to "respond to nuance and fine shading, adapting its judgement to the matter at hand in a way that principles set up in advance have a hard time doing." The aim of both *phronēsis* and *aisthēsis* is to bring about good judgment and a "superior responsiveness or flexibility." But flexible is exactly what the Bellegardes are not. They live and judge as though there were only one truth, a mode of behavior which James suggests places them outside the categories of living and dead, vital and inert. That "it is not possible for a simple universal formulation intended to cover many particulars to achieve a high degree of correctness" does not faze the Bellegardes because they recognize no reality except that which conforms to their conception of self (*Fragility*, 301). This ability to have power over and manipulate interpretation is a crucial and often misunderstood feature of James's novels as it reverses the usual understanding of Jamesian passivity. Traditional critical opinion has held that the Jamesian observer purposely takes a purely passive stance toward the world because he or she is incapable of acting. These observers, we are told, are more content to be seated on the side watching life as opposed to participating in its process. But this distinction relies, as I have suggested, on a mistaken understanding of Jamesian discrimination as an escapist elitism. Rather, James cultivated discrimination so as to be more engaged with life, so as to enhance one's experience of reality, so as to make available to himself and his audience a mode of understanding which brought the full measure of reality into one's consciousness. In this way, throughout his fiction James was able to document the growth of consciousness and develop an aesthetics which converted the novel from a passive form into "an act of life," as he says of his *Notes of a Son and Brother* (*Henry James Letters*, IV, 706).

When we examine the Bellegardes from this perspective, what we see is a people who, though they say they "have been used to set the example," actually establish their power over others not through an active engagement with life, but by sealing themselves off from the world. Within the corpus of James's fiction, the Bellegardes take their place alongside individuals such as Gilbert Osmond who falsely empowers himself over others by claiming to be "convention itself" (*Portrait of a Lady*, 4:21), Mona Brigstock, *The Spoils of Poynton*'s "massive maiden" who establishes her "supremacy" by presenting an "image of successful immobility" (10:199), and Mrs. Newsome and Sarah Pocock who similarly derive their power over others by establishing themselves as a self-ratifying authority. Maria Gostrey perhaps explains it best when she remarks to Strether that "[t]here's nothing so magnificent – for making others feel you – as to have no imagination" (*Ambassadors*, 22:223).[31] James's point is not that worldly power emanates from a general passivity with respect to the world, but that such power is a result of rendering the world passive. James addressed this inversion throughout his fiction and made it part of his hermeneutics because he saw it as imposing dangerous constraints on the individual's consciousness and on the collective consciousness of humanity. Individuals such as the Bellegardes are threatening because they can become like a culture, and their conception of *aisthēsis* does not spring from worldly experience, but from making themselves "the world," and admitting as legitimate only experiences which fall within that artificially circumscribed border. What James tries to show is that such an over-refined conception of *aisthēsis* poses a dangerous threat to art and life, constraining the former within tightly defined generic restrictions and the latter within a potentially destructive personalized ethnocentrism. It is perhaps because the Bellegardes have developed a hyper-aesthetic version of *aisthēsis* that James sees them as representative of a culture which is at the end of its history, incapable of productive action, able only to express itself anew through sterile reduplication. And, finally, in completing its revolution of the traditional opposition between passivity and activity, observation and participation, imagination and a lack of imagination, James's fiction ultimately suggests that the lack of imagination which leads to a type of worldly power eventually brings one to a lethal astringency such as we find in *Washington Square*'s Dr. Sloper.

How much Europe has given over *phronēsis* and turned toward a hyper-aesthetic version of *aisthēsis* is evident in every European in *The American*. The Bellegardes' final inability to "reconcile [them]-selves to a commercial person" is perhaps the most obvious example of their exclusionary self-ratifying authority passing judgment on the particular (252). Newman is reduced to a type and cast out, not only by the family he was trying to enter, but by the entire Parisian crowd, an action which simultaneously corroborates the Bellegardes' status as arbiters of tradition and universalizes James's critique of European culture in *The American* as destructively reflexive. "Our friends approve of us," the Marquise explains to Newman, "there is not a family among them that would have acted otherwise. And however that may be, we take our cue from no one. The Bellegardes have been used to set the example, not to wait for it" (252).

When Urbain and Madame de Bellegarde, or even Valentin and Claire for that matter, insist that they live according to principles rooted in tradition, they do so with the understanding that tradition and the Bellegardes are synonymous. It is for this reason "the Bellegardes don't recognise the Bonapartes," and see no need to take a role in what they consider is the aberration of contemporary affairs (95). The decaying Bellegarde fortune, the obscene marriage

between Claire and Monsieur de Cintré, the foolish duel between
Valentin and the Brewer's son, the plan to marry Claire to Lord
Deepmere, the murder of the old Marquis de Bellegarde, the blind
allegiance to tradition, Urbain de Bellegarde's book on the "history
of The Princess of France who never married," and even Claire's
refusal to fight for herself are all examples of a culture which can no
longer act so as to regenerate or reinvigorate itself (107). When one
looks closely at the Paris Newman encounters, its chief talent, James
demonstrates throughout the novel, lies in *preventing* things from
taking place, as when the corpulent duchess, with marvelous empty
mots, prevents Newman from carrying out his revenge.

In Newman's meeting with Madame D'Outreville, James allows
each of these cultural dynamics to present itself to the reader *and* to
Newman through the dialogue. Eager for vengeance, Newman
comes to the duchess to put before her the Bellegardes' sinister
history. But, as James explains, though "Newman had come to her
with a grievance,... he found himself in an atmosphere in which
apparently no cognisance was taken of grievances; an atmosphere
into which the chill of discomfort had never penetrated, and which
seemed exclusively made up of mild, sweet, stale intellectual
perfumes" (343). Rather than allow Newman to introduce the topic
she knows is on his mind, the "comical duchess" talks "to him about
flowers and books" before "getting launched" into remarks "about
the theatres," the "humidity of Paris," the "complexions of American ladies," and Newman's own "impressions of France" (342–43).
As James implies in and through the narrative of this scene, the
duchess's "brilliant monologue" is an example of "an affirmative
rather than an interrogative cast of mind." In this way the duchess is
"like many of her country women" (such as the Marquise de
Bellegarde) who "made *mots* and then put them herself into circula-
tion" (343). In James's fiction, to be of an affirmative cast of mind is
to be controlling, just as the duchess controls Newman's ability to
introduce his topic. But it is precisely by way of her "brilliant
monologue" that the duchess absolutely prevents Newman from
carrying out his intentions. It is as though the duchess's sole purpose
were to prevent things from taking place. And that is exactly James's
point. That the duchess asks Newman "no questions about their
common friends," the "circumstances under which he had been
presented to her," and behaves "as if the Bellegardes and their
wickedness were not of this world" arises from the same reticence as

the Bellegardes' defensive allegiance to tradition and to an aristocratic decorum whose superficiality astounds Newman (343). For
James these Europeans' behavior demonstrates a strategic and
seemingly comfortable avoidance of the present, and a denial of the
possibility of a future different from what has already come down to
them from the past. That this is a cultural compact meant to thwart
outsiders as well as social change is an insight Newman cannot
avoid: "They all hold together bravely, and whether anyone else can
trust them or not, they can certainly trust each other" (343–44).[32] To
the extent that this attitude manifests itself in the armory of James's
Europeans, Europe, since it admits nothing alien, can be seen as
representing the denial of hermeneutics. Newman observes as much
when he finds in the duchess "not a symptom of apprehension that
[he] would trench upon the ground she proposed to avoid" (343).

James renders Newman inactive before the duchess so as to
foreground the active unfolding of Newman's developing hermeneutic skills. Rather than retreat to a socially constructed conception
of the event, or to pass it off as unfathomable, Newman places
himself in a reading position "in front of the text" (Ricoeur,
Hermeneutics, 143). To some extent, it is in this very scene that the
entire novel coalesces around James's main point. In situating
Newman as a reader essentially open to the experience of life,
perceptive in a (truly Jamesian) way which allows an escape from the
interpretive prejudices that confound our ability to understand,
James gives *The American*'s readers an active demonstration of what is
possible when we learn to see without the interpretive filters that
normally govern our encounter with the world. Newman learns not
just about the duchess's and, through her, the Old World's motivations, but he learns too about who he is, and who he has almost
become. In other words, Newman discovers the private space in
which interpretation of a very large order can be accomplished. And
through the demonstration of Newman's discovery and the vast
enlargement of his interpretive horizon, James affords the reader a
similar opportunity. For both Newman and the reader, this interpretive event follows the pattern I have characterized as the
negativity of experience in Jamesian hermeneutics. For it seems that
what Gadamer and James mean by depicting experience in this way
is for readers to understand that experience which simply meets our
expectations, or experience which is shaped by the constrictive
forces which mediate our encounter with reality, really do no more

than ratify our expectations. To the extent that this is so, we find ourselves in a situation similar to the Old World Europeans James criticizes for having lost the power of productive action. But in breaking free of his prejudices, in accepting his responsibility to take an active role in coming to understand, Newman imparts an unforgettable lesson, a lesson James saw as the novel's principle power. For the reader, this lesson leaves an indelible mark, for we expect and perhaps even wish Newman to carry out his revenge. But we do not expect the unexpected because everything about Newman tells us otherwise. And we wonder why.

VII

It is no small irony, given his life-long advocacy for ever more refined powers of observation, that understanding always takes the form of action in James's hermeneutics.[33] That James reserves these moments of meaningful action for the conclusion of his protagonists' experiences underscores his idea that perspicuity and understanding are conditions we come to through becoming experienced. And this is exactly where Newman arrives at the close of *The American*. Laboring under the ignominy that "above all he was a good fellow wronged" by the Bellegardes' sabotage of his prospective wedding, Newman finds himself "disposed to sip the cup of contemplative revenge" (360, 317). Yet, when he confesses his vengeful plans the reader becomes aware of how much they have of *re*action rather than action in them. Reaction, of course, is a condition of will, not understanding in the larger sense of the term.

"I am very angry, I am very sore, and I am very bitter, but I don't know that I am wicked. I have been cruelly injured. They have hurt me and I want to hurt them." (301–2)

However, after Newman has time to reflect on his desire to exact revenge he comes to understand not just the senselessness of trying to injure his antagonists, but, more importantly, how much vengeance is not a part of his character.

Paradoxically, Newman's decision not to act according to the prodding of his will brings about the internal actions which result in his enlightened understanding of self and others. In Gadamer's language, Newman's final epiphany "involves an escape from something that had deceived us and held us captive" (*Truth and Method*,

321). Newman's captivity is two-fold: first his inability to recognize the radical alterity between himself and Claire de Cintré (or if not his refusal to see the difference between them, his belief that he can simply pay the difference to disappear); second, his penchant for reifying all things so as to be able first to quantify and then to purchase them outright as possessions, or, in the case of the Bellegardes' traditions, buy their silence or allegiance. Newman is disabused of this mercantile understanding of reality when he acts against his immediate *re*action and gains the self-knowledge and insight which constitutes an experienced person.

James's presentation of Newman's final moment of insight shows Newman to have achieved a level of understanding qualitatively different from any he has yet displayed. After staring at the impregnable convent walls behind which Claire has been locked up for life, Newman turns and walks away until he arrives at the "vast towers of Notre Dame."

Newman sat in his place, because while he was there he was out of the world ... He leaned his head for a long time on the chair in front of him; when he took it up he felt that he was himself again. Somewhere in his mind, a tight knot seemed to have loosened. (364)

When his thoughts return to the Bellegardes, Newman admits to having almost forgotten them, remembering them only as "people he had meant to do something to." This recollection evokes an annoyed groan and a relieved sensation that "the bottom, suddenly, had fallen out of his revenge" (364). That the idea of revenge evokes shame in Newman is indicative of how far beyond *re*action Newman has moved, how far, that is, he has moved past a reflexive will and allowed himself to be open, to "accept the unchangeable," or, to borrow from the Preface, to accept the presence of "the things we cannot possibly *not* know, sooner or later" (358, 1063).

The unraveling of the tight knot and the renunciation of revenge parallel the experience that sent Newman to Europe in the first place – his letting a business competitor get away with sixty thousand dollars. In this earlier episode, as in the latter, Newman's actions take place, as he explains, "quite independently of my will" (22). Ross Posnock sees this resignation of will as an example of James's willingness to "revise the bounded self of 'bourgeois circumspection'" so as to make "a permeable self" which could become the sum total of all that it has encountered (*Trial of Curiosity*, 168).

Posnock's "permeable self," insofar as "permeable" suggests a retention of lived experiences, is another way of describing the process by which James's characters come to be practically wise through the course of their respective experiences. Posnock makes an insightful point when he draws a connection between Newman, James, and Lambert Strether. Despite "their individual differences," he suggests, "Newman, Strether, and Henry James share a relaxation of will that permits them to open themselves up to others as well as to their own internal otherness" (*Trial of Curiosity*, 316n.2). But Newman offers a further and telling reason for his pleasure in giving over this financial battle. Instead of acting as he had planned, Newman engages in an act of hermeneutic revision when he finds himself experiencing what one could call an out-of-body experience. He tells Tom Tristram how he "sat watching" the deal slip away as though it were part of the action of "a play at the theatre" (23). This admission of voyeurism serves to substantiate James's claim about Newman's over-determined objectivity while it simultaneously offers an example of what Jamesian hermeneutics often comes down to, namely that the failure of understanding often becomes the medium of understanding. Newman attempts just such an explanation of this quintessential Jamesian paradox when he tells Tom Tristram, "I could feel it going on inside of me. You may depend upon it that there are things going on inside of us that we understand mighty little about" (23). Interestingly, though he understands "mighty little," Newman is able to take away enough to know that his understanding of himself and his world has changed. The important point here is in recognizing how the process of becoming experienced in James depends on how an openness to the possibility of experience allows in one a continual revision of understanding.

But as is the case in every James work, there are consequences associated with becoming experienced. For instance, in both *The American* and *The Ambassadors* becoming experienced is connected in different degrees to a marriage which does not occur. (Whereas in *The Portrait of a Lady*, Isabel becomes practically wise as a result of a marriage which should not have occurred.) James was criticized at the time of *The American*'s publication for not giving in to the desire for "cheerful endings." His excuse to W. D. Howells is as important to the understanding of *The Ambassadors* as it is to the understanding of experience's role in *The American*. James explains that marriage between Newman and Claire de Cintré "would have been impossible." Despite having, as Newman pleads, "the whole world to choose from," the world was essentially closed. "Mme de Cintré couldn't have lived in New York ... and Newman ... couldn't have lived in France" (*Henry James Letters*, II, 104–5). The purpose of the experience for Newman is, James goes on to explain, "its exemplification of one of those insuperable difficulties which present themselves in people's lives from which the only issue is by forfeiture – by losing something" (105). Newman, as we have seen, gains in the loss of his naivety, in the understanding, that is, of difference. James's comment also seems a particularly keen anticipation of Strether's experience and his inability to accept Maria Gostrey's offer of marriage. For Strether too experience has a negative quality about it. Strether gains an understanding of himself that is dependent upon his being disconnected from Paris, from Woollett, and from Maria Gostrey. Thus, as James points out in *The Ambassadors*'s "Project," "marrying Miss Gostrey would be almost of the old order" ("Project," 390). The irony of texts like *The American* and *The Ambassadors* is that the hard-won experience always comes too late, and always prevents any attempt at traditional closure. But then for James experience is just *that* way; it thrives on an open-ended multiplicity that challenges any sense of rootedness or closure.

Perhaps the most profound irony of *The American*, and what makes it most similar to *The Ambassadors*, is where James leaves Newman at the end of his experience.[34] In his own way, Newman, like Strether, emerges on the other side of it ("Project," 390). As *The American* closes James allows us a glimpse of Newman recalculating himself, trying to "read the moral of his strange misadventure." This late, transformed Newman, "his commercial imagination ... dead," adopts a new-found "reflective mood," and comes to accept the presence of "the unchangeable" (358, 359, 358). In reaching this point Newman achieves a type of practical wisdom.[35] But that understanding, James suggests, also leads to a worldly detachment. Newman, we recall, ends the novel unable to find his old comfort in either New York or San Francisco. He chooses finally, he believes, to "fix himself in Paris forever," only to find that Paris too can no longer offer sanctuary (362). Newman's final destination remains indeterminate. He has revised his compact to stay forever to mean, as he has it, "that I was going to stay away forever" (365). The novel ends, then, with Newman suspended between worlds, neither an "American" to the Parisians, or a fellow-exile to Mrs. Tristram and her circle of American expatriates. This lack of finality in *The American* is replayed time and again in James's works. The point being, I suggest, that James understood experience as something that leads to an open-endedness, as something that takes away from us the world we had before and leaves us disconnected. Experience, in other words, leads one to understand the inherent uncertainty of life, the impossibility of controlling it, the foolhardiness of predictions (*Truth and Method*, 320). Such an understanding, James implies, is what allows one to achieve an ethical condition of openness indispensable for a good life. Such an understanding prepares one for the alien and frees one from the constraints of having to imprison what is strange within a self-serving certitude. Such an understanding prevents one from ever again being caught by surprise. This, too, we shall see, is what Isabel Archer and Lambert Strether come to understand through their experiences.

CHAPTER 3

Bondage and boundaries: Isabel Archer's failed experience

> She was a person of great good faith, and if there was a great
> deal of folly in her wisdom those who judge her severely may
> have the satisfaction of finding that, later, she became consis-
> tently wise only at the cost of an amount of folly which will
> constitute almost a direct appeal to charity.
>
> Henry James, *The Portrait of a Lady*

> Then we,
> As we beheld her striding there alone
> Knew that there never was a world for her
> Except the one she sang and, singing made.
>
> Wallace Stevens, "The Idea of Order at Key West"

I

About a quarter of the way through *The Portrait of a Lady* Isabel
Archer and Ralph Touchett carry out a seemingly innocent conversation which underscores James's conception of art's civic and
heuristic value. I am referring to the conversation in which we find
Ralph Touchett, sick and dying, confessing to Isabel his inability to
participate actively in life and his desire, therefore, to observe Isabel
live hers: "What's the use of being ill and disabled and restricted to
mere spectatorship at the game of life if I really cannot see the show
when I have paid so much for my ticket?" (3:209–10). Touchett's
plea awakens in our memory the Jamesian artist isolated, peering
down on the human scene from behind a window in the house of
fiction. But it also awakens another image of spectatorship, an image
recalled by James in his autobiographical *A Small Boy and Others*
explaining how he lacked "the intrinsic faculties" to "go in for
everything and everyone" and therefore used "the sense and image
of it all" to cultivate an artistic life (*Autobiography*, 164).[1] In this

conversation Ralph assumes Isabel is one of the world, one who could "go in for everything" and suggests she "drink the cup of experience," to which Isabel hotly responds "No, I do not wish to touch the cup of experience. It is a poisoned drink! I only want to see for myself" (3:213). And when Ralph suggests "that the world interests" Isabel and that she will "want to throw [her]self into it," Isabel responds flatly, "I never said that" (3:214). Her response is surprising. Readers are left wondering what she means. Why does Ralph ascribe to her values typically associated with James's artist figures when she seems so far from the measure? And what does the intertwining of spectatorship, experience, and participation have to do with collective wisdom? What, we wonder, is this a portrait of?

The answer suggested in James's authorial intrusion I have quoted as an epigraph to this chapter has to do with practical wisdom and lived experience, of how the latter leads to the former. In Isabel Archer's case practical wisdom is intimately associated with a process of disillusionment, which strikes me as an accurate way of reading Gilbert Osmond's role in her life. Furthermore, Isabel's disastrous marriage, her seeming incapacity to recognize Osmond for what he is, can be seen as a vehicle through which James expresses his concerns about the difficult challenge of freedom and independence for the kind of originary aesthetics he saw as particularly Jamesian. To this extent, Isabel's being the victim of Osmond's predatory designs (I have left her involvement in the affair unclear because, as I will show, Isabel is not quite so unwitting as many critics would have her) carries with it two important considerations. 1) The obvious gender questions. Isabel's being an independent woman of means comes with the suggestion that she is in the market for a husband. (James's references to Jane Austen in *The Portrait of a Lady* are purposeful.) More importantly, James genders aesthetics through Isabel and thus articulates, through the sense of predation surrounding Isabel, the rapacious threats art faces in an aggressively commercial culture. 2) In addition to the questions of gender and predation, Isabel Archer also dramatizes important issues of sensibility James found misunderstood or underappreciated in the public at large. Being a figurative rendering of a Jamesian sensibility, Isabel reveals, in her seeming impercipience, James's concerns with both the requirements of aesthetic freedom and the price one pays either for a neglect of the aesthetic or, more importantly, for an aesthetic which attempts an artificial circumscription of one's perceptual horizon. So in an important way gender and art play an interanimating role in *The Portrait of a Lady*, but James's emphasis is upon the challenge of aesthetic action and the threat posed by those who are not up to the task. Unfortunately Isabel shows, eventually, her deficiencies in this struggle when she restricts her world by granting Osmond jurisdiction over her worldly encounters, a move which leads Isabel from being a kinetic (Jamesian) sensibility to being a static (Osmondian) one. Read this way, *The Portrait of a Lady* becomes James's indictment of the purely passive spectator's understanding of the world, a cautionary tale about how the mind, however gifted perceptually, is prey to the hazards of a spectatorial understanding when it remains untempered by lived experience. Practical wisdom, *phronēsis*, in cases like this, we learn, comes only after a measure of suffering because, echoing the Greeks, James suggests it is only through suffering that we arrive at a position from which the truth begins to come into focus.

II

In the above conversation Ralph Touchett represents the role of the detached spectator-artist who approximates the perceptual productivity characteristic of the Jamesian sensibility: there to observe, to document "the joys of contemplation," but forbidden the "riot of expression" (3:53, 54). James's counter view in *The Portrait of a Lady* is embodied, as we shall see, in the sterility of Gilbert Osmond. The connection between Ralph and James is best established in the juxtaposition of James's original intentions for the text, for Isabel, against an explication of Ralph's involvement in the text of Isabel's life. In his Preface James explains that the "single small cornerstone" of *The Portrait of a Lady* is "the conception of a certain young woman affronting her destiny" which is, to him, "artistically speaking, the circumstance of interest" (1076–77). This would require the following structural architecture:

"Place the centre of the subject in the young woman's own consciousness ... and you get as interesting and as beautiful a difficulty as you could wish. Stick to *that* – for the centre; put the heaviest weight into *that* scale, which will be so largely the scale of her relation to herself." (1079)

The novelist's next question is " 'what will she *do*?' " (1081). Like the ideal Jamesian novelist, Isabel attempts to convert the sense of her adventures " 'into the stuff of drama or, ... *story*' " which James, the observing artist, uses to create his *Portrait* (1083).

James's prefatory comments clearly indicate the rewards attention to this character will pay. To some extent James speaks of the creative process as one of autogenesis. He endows Isabel with certain attributes and opportunities and then sits back and lets the text compose itself. This too is in effect what Ralph Touchett does. The Preface and text show how, for both James and Ralph, Isabel is a person who "hovered before him, soliciting him, as the active or passive figure, interesting him and appealing to him just as they were and by what they were" (1072). The particularity of James's attachment to Isabel Archer is further underscored by several possessive statements he makes in the Preface and echoes once Isabel announces her intention to follow a path different from the one he has plotted. James characterizes himself as "a wary dealer in precious odds and ends," and Isabel as a "rare little 'piece' " he has kept locked away "in a cup-board door." He even implies Isabel has, as Diana Collecott has suggested, "a consciousness of her own – that the 'creature' has the power to be independent of her creator," an acquisition which ultimately casts Ralph in a Pygmalion-like light once Isabel behaves in a fashion contrary to his expectations ("Framing *The Portrait*," 46).

Furthermore, like *The Golden Bowl*'s Bloomsbury shop dealer who realizes his golden bowl will only really be appreciated by a select few, James speaks of "the feminine nature I had for so considerable a time all curiously at my disposal" and admits to his initial fear of sharing his "young woman" with others:

I quite remind myself thus of the dealer resigned not to 'realise,' resigned to keeping the precious object locked up indefinitely rather than commit it, at no matter what price, to vulgar hands. (1076)[2]

The question of subjective possession here – James's, Ralph's, Isabel's – is striking. In her reading of *The Portrait of the Lady*, Collecott questions James's motivations with regard to his construction and possession of Isabel Archer. Collecott argues that the book's title draws attention to the "act of representation" and "implies that an actual person is being represented." To be sure, the portrait rendered follows James's own prescriptions for proper portraiture in his *Partial Portraits* (1888). Citing this text, Collecott shows how James "entices the reader to consider Isabel as potentially real" and that the portrait rendered is James's attempt to "'catch a talent in the act'," where "the act" is the observation of Isabel's encounter with the world by the male observers James, Ralph, and Osmond (*Partial Portraits*, qtd. in "Framing *The Portrait*," 47). Collecott sees these power relations as central to *The Portrait of a Lady*, claiming that "independence is an indulgence granted to Isabel" by male characters and "not least by the author himself." As Collecott has it, Isabel's "personality is contained within the frame of observing male consciousness"(51). And so it is, within the confines of the text. But to impute to James a "gentleman's club" titillation in describing Isabel via "sexual double entendres" endows Isabel with a consciousness as though she *were* real and as though James somehow violates her by giving her life within the text (46–47).[3]

But to return for a moment to Collecott's suggestion that James's aim is to lead readers to "consider Isabel as potentially real." In a specific and important way this is exactly the case, but not in the way Collecott imputes. Rather than playing a perverse game of sexual manipulation and intrigue with his female character, James is linking her potential as a created representation of a real-life being with categories of aesthetics. What is real about Isabel is how she represents figuratively the power of artistic creation, and how the depiction of her under constant scrutiny and, in some instances, predatory aggression is indicative of the manipulative suspicion and determining constraints aesthetic categories constantly find themselves under. Think, for instance, of Osmond's complaint that Isabel's main problem is that she has "too many ideas," that she thinks too much. Her plenitude represents the originary capacity of art (3:412). What happens to her in the course of her experience throughout *The Portrait of a Lady* is, in James's view, an accurate depiction of the daily threat art faces from an unresponsive, or inflexible, or unreceptive audience, from an audience which simply refuses to think about aesthetics in a way different than that which has been handed down to it from the past. By making the connection between Isabel and art, between the feminine and aesthetics, James effectively accentuates the lack of freedom art enjoys in a principally commercial, male society. So in a way Isabel is real, as art, and she is "contained within the frame of observing male consciousness," and, as James suggests, more's the pity.

Here again Ralph Touchett's role as a projection of the author is important. For as the shadow of James roaming through the novel observing Isabel, vicariously living through her encounters, and authoring her being with his endowment, Ralph Touchett allows James to play out his own authorial fantasy with his "female fry" and make a positive statement about his understanding of the voyeuristic component of the artistic mind on the one hand, and the dangerous terrain artists must daily negotiate as a matter of course on the other (Preface, 1077). For while Isabel can be read as art under threat, Ralph can be seen as the artist prevented from enjoying the full measure of his passion. Taken together, the figurative representations of Isabel and Ralph are a powerful testimonial for the need to recognize freedom as a primary requisite for originary artistic production. That they cannot *be* underscores the force of bondage in a society where the material supersedes the asethetic and the personal.

James admits the principal motive behind a work of art, in his mind, is "the highly personal plea – the joy of living over, as a chapter of one's experience, the particular intellectual adventure":

Here lurks an immense homage to the general privilege of the artist, to that constructive, that creative passion ... the exercise of which finds so many an occasion for appearing to him the highest of human fortunes, the rarest boon of the gods. He values it, all sublimely and perhaps a little fatuously, for itself – as the great extension, great beyond all others, of experience and consciousness. (Preface, *The American*, 1060–61)

James continues, accepting the "toil and trouble" of artistic production as insignificant given the rewards. Paraphrasing Robert Louis Stevenson, he explains "that the partaker of the 'life of art'" who

repines at the absence of rewards, as they are called, of the pursuit might surely be better occupied. Much rather he should endlessly wonder at his not having to pay half his substance for his luxurious immersion. He enjoys it, so to speak, without a tax; the effort of the labour involved, the torment of expression, of which we have heard in our time so much, being after all but the last refinement of his privilege. It may leave him weary and worn; but how, after his fashion, he will have lived! (Preface, *The American*, 1061)

In explaining the artist's reward James brings us round full circle to his prefatory confessions of Isabel's being as "interesting" and "beautiful a difficulty" as he "could wish" (1079). And the joy the creative experience brings, "so to speak," explains much of Ralph Touchett's role in having a hand in Isabel's "fate"; for though Isabel leaves Ralph "weary and worn" she enables him, "after his fashion," to live.[4] Ralph ultimately admits this motivation to Isabel (and the audience) explicitly when near death. In a confessional moment between him and Isabel, Ralph acknowledges "[i]t was for you that I wanted – that I wanted to live. But I'm of no use to you" (4:307).[5]

Ralph Touchett's artistic characteristics are what lead Tony Tanner to label him a "recurring Jamesian artist figure – the subtly debarred spectator who enjoys everything in imagination and nothing in action" ("Fearful Self," 78). Tanner's explanation seems to parallel James's own description of himself as one fated to experience only "the sense and image" of life because his mind was "naturally even though perversely, even though inordinately, arranged as a stage for the procession and exhibition of appearances" (_Autobiography_, 164, 105). In _The Portrait of a Lady_, Ralph carries on this discussion, initiating it early by exclaiming to Lord Warburton "I'm not in the least bored; I find life only too interesting," a statement which, given Ralph's infirmities, can be more readily interpreted when compared to James's assessment of the life of observation in _A Small Boy and Others_: one could "be as occupied, quite as occupied . . . on only a fifth of the actual immersion" (164). However, though similar, Ralph is not Henry James, and it would be incorrect to extend the analogy between the two any further than according the character a shadowy similarity. For while Tanner is correct to classify Ralph as a "debarred spectator," James, as his autobiography shows, cultivated perception as a form of power which enabled him, through art, to take an active role in the world. It is important to recall in these discussions which attempt to classify James as a genteel aesthete James's own understanding of his role as artist as a commitment to the "high and helpful, and, as it were, civic use of the imagination" (Preface, "Lesson of the Master," 1230). For both Ralph and James, it is the action of art which makes interest. One could make the following analogy: what Ralph is to Isabel within the text, James was to the world through his art. Both sought to develop a form of perception and discrimination which would enlarge the impression of reality by enhancing the mind's capacity to perceive, experience, and understand the world.

Yet more of the Ralph Touchett–Isabel Archer relationship needs examining; what is at stake for Ralph amounts to his struggle between life and death itself. Without Isabel, Ralph's waning years would be dark and empty. Her advent provides him with opportunity to gather "some direct impression of life" (Preface, 1074). In the narrative's words: "It was very probably this sweet-tasting property of the observed thing in itself that was mainly concerned in Ralph's quickly-stirred interest in the advent of a young lady who was evidently not insipid. If he was consideringly disposed, something told him, here was occupation enough for a succession of days" (3:54). By seeing Isabel as "occupation enough" Ralph echoes James's prescriptions for true artistic experience. He takes an outward phenomenon, an impression, and transfigures it into a work of art. Such creative activity represented for James the pinnacle of human endeavor. Ralph's motives about art thus follow James's in general and allow James to employ Ralph as a textual embodiment expressive of the wide-reaching limits of art. Speaking more generally about James's conception of art, Stephen Donadio argues a point which fits Ralph as well. For James, says Donadio, "art will ultimately reveal itself to be a form of power not only over his own experience but over the perception of other people with respect to their own experiences as well" (*Nietzsche, Henry James*, 47).

But Ralph does not simply reify Isabel as does Gilbert Osmond; rather, as Tony Tanner points out, Ralph "appreciates her living qualities artistically," something Osmond is unable or refuses to do ("Fearful Self," 79). When Ralph shows Isabel his collection of art he finds his eyes drawn away from the framed portraits and captured by his cousin: "She was better worth looking at than most works of art" (3:61). Later he confesses to Isabel's being "entertainment of a high order":

"A character like that,... a real little passionate force to see at play is the finest thing in nature. It is finer than the finest work of art – than a Greek bas-relief, than a great Titian, than a Gothic cathedral. It is very pleasant to be so well treated where one has least looked for it. I had never been more blue, more bored, than for a week before she came; I had never expected less that anything pleasant would happen. Suddenly I receive a Titian, by the post, to hang on my wall – a Greek bas-relief to stick over my chimney-piece. The key of a beautiful edifice is thrust into my hand and I am told to walk in and admire." (3:86)

Here again Ralph's language is reminiscent of James's own comments in the Preface to *The Portrait of a Lady*; for both, Isabel is a "rare little 'piece'" whose observation brings untold reward and pleasure to the "imagination that detains it, preserves, protects,

enjoys it, conscious of its presence in the dusky, crowded, hetero-
genous back-shop of the mind" (1076).

Readers at this point may find the trope of Isabel as figurative
representative of art wearing a little thin, given the description of her
as a "rare little 'piece'," a "real little passionate force" that falls into
the male observer's collection in order to relieve his boredom. To be
sure, James has deployed in his characterization of Isabel all the
linguistic force of infantilism and repression which characterizes the
stereotypical depiction of woman as, to borrow James's own term,
"female fry." And while this is the wrong place to carry out an
examination of James's complicated attitude toward gender, it is
worth noting that James was more than well aware of the difficult
position women were made to labor through in their private and
public lives. His sister Alice never allowed him to be unaware, and
his devotion to her in the latter years of her life shows he never
forgot. To this extent James exposes in *The Portrait of a Lady* what
Priscilla Walton has argued is the "reductio ad absurdum of nine-
teenth-century Realist/humanist ideology" (*Disruption of the Feminine*,
68). As Walton shows, humanist ideology purports to advocate a
subject's freedom of determination while the reality for female
subjects is that their identity is carefully constructed by a ruling
patriarchy. Women are invited to "participate" in the discourse of
freedom while simultaneously being "subject to a specifically feminine discourse of irrationality, submission, and passivity" (52).
Furthermore, the ideological structures which imprisoned women
within a particular subject position were also at work constructing
acceptable and unacceptable modes of subjectivity for men. The
accepted role of masculine identity as wage earner or business man
left little room for sensibilities more at home in aesthetic production.
To some extent the man of art was no man at all. These ideological
dynamics, and the murky terrain which characterizes James's own
sexuality, even for himself, make glib accusations impossible. And,
throughout the course of the novel, much as James may hold Isabel
at fault for preemptively foreclosing her artistic and intellectual
development, he does hold her plight continuously before the reader's eye and leaves us with no way but to acknowledge that much of
what Isabel suffers is because she is a woman and as a woman not
free to be herself, whatever that might have been. This, I take it, is
what he means by charging his audience not to "judge her severely"
and to recognize the "direct appeal to charity" her case makes

(3:145). I would go so far as to say James recognized in Isabel's struggle for independence the very struggle he felt characterized his own life, that her capitulation to forces which eventually beat her down was an indication of how much harder he had to fight for his own independence and recognition, within his family and his world, as an individual and an artist.

III

I began this chapter by touching on a conversation in which Ralph confesses to Isabel his role as spectator "at the game of life" (3:210). The conversation is crucial because Ralph announces to Isabel her role in his new-found occupation: "I content myself with watching you – with the deepest interest" (3:211). And with full authorial power Ralph explains:

"Ah, there will be plenty of spectators! We shall hang on the rest of your career. I shall not see all of it, but I shall probably see the most interesting years. Of course if you were to marry our friend [Warburton] you'd still have a career – a very decent, in fact a very brilliant one. But relatively speaking it would be a little prosaic. It would be definitely marked out in advance; it would be wanting in the unexpected. You know I'm extremely fond of the unexpected, and now that you've kept the game in your hands I depend on your giving us some grand example of it." (3:212)

What this conversation reveals is the nature of Ralph's spectatorship: he is both the isolated spectator and the author figure subtly manipulating the field "by the need of the individual vision and by the pressure of the individual will" (Preface, *Portrait of a Lady*, 1075). The choice of language Ralph uses to explain Isabel's situation is illuminating for the connections it has with discourse and novelistic production. Ralph is speaking of modes of discourse, of the require-ments of a Jamesian novel. As the shadow of James, Ralph explains that were Isabel to marry Lord Warburton there would be no story to tell, the career "would be a little prosaic," more in line with an Anthony Trollope novel than a woman "affronting her destiny."[6] But Ralph is composing a Jamesian text, one in which a good deal of the unexpected will complicate the plot as well as his own precon-ceived understanding of its completed version. The characters' actions will also be charged with the unexpected, a testament in James's mind, to his characters' ability to develop beyond the author's initial conceptions, or, as the narrative has it, "Isabel's originality was that she gave one the impression of having intentions of her own" (3:87). Thus, what James indicates in this exchange between Ralph and Isabel is the degree of Ralph Touchett's involvement in Isabel's story. In Ralph's words, "I should like to put a little wind in her sails ... I should like to see her going before the breeze!" (3:260, 262). When Daniel Touchett finds something perverse in his son's voyeuristic desires, stating directly "You speak as if it were for your mere amusement," Ralph openly admits: "So it is, a good deal" (3:262). In effect, what Ralph does is recognize his role as spectator and take an active hand in producing the most rewarding spectacle a connoisseur like himself could want. By means of a large endowment Ralph purchases an aesthetic interest which will engage his interest (the "amusement" ends sharply) for the rest of his life.[7]

The connection between Ralph and James, between Ralph's monetary gift and James's offer of a very particular and personalized (for artist and audience) art to the world, needs some elaboration. What is perhaps most interesting is that the gift of each, that within the boundaries of the text and that within the circumference of life, so to speak, brings the recipient into contact with a series of experiential limits. First, for Isabel, Ralph's gift introduces the responsibilities of freedom; as she says, "A large fortune means freedom, and I'm afraid of that" (3:315, 320).[8] That introduction quickly brings Isabel up against the limits of her capacity to understand her experience of her own subjectivity and that of those others with whom she comes into contact. Ralph's gift, in short, brings on the crisis that typically confronts James's "centers of consciousness": it forces her to encounter the limits of her understanding. How she reacts to this confrontation forms the principal interest of the novel. The reader of James's texts is brought by the reading experience up against a similar limit. James's narrative, as we shall see, forces the reader to question his or her own capacity to understand in a way quite similar to Isabel's, and to ask how much one's own sense of self and one's own subjectivity takes for granted external and internal shaping forces. How the reader is made aware of and led to confront these forces through his or her interpretive engagement with the text is perhaps the most subtle and powerful challenge of James's art.

James orchestrates this dialectic of limit and freedom by continually introducing the element of surprise. The surprise of *The Portrait of a Lady* is that given all her advantages, intellectual and financial, Isabel's destiny proves so needlessly tragic. And that is also Ralph's tragedy. The point becomes explicit in a conversation between them in Ralph's death chamber. Isabel, aware that Ralph is the author of her fortune, rhetorically asks if "all I have is yours?" to which Ralph responds "Ah, don't speak of that – that was not happy ... I believe I ruined you" (4:414). Ralph's surprise at Isabel's willingness, through marriage to Osmond, to have herself "put into a cage" has served as an example of Jamesian bewilderment, an example of how one's interpretive horizon is exceeded by some unexpected and unassimilable brute fact (4:65).[9] Ralph has been bewildered by the discovery of something in Isabel's character that cannot be done away with. As James explains, "Ralph was shocked and humiliated; his calculations had been false and the person in the world in whom he was most interested was lost" (4:61).

The oft-discussed exchange which follows Ralph's bafflement can simultaneously be read as Ralph's and the reader's attempt to salvage their investment (Isabel) and to reconstruct their interpretive frame of reference. The argument between Isabel and Ralph elicits several of Ralph's most candid admissions as to his intended construction of Isabel for his own viewing pleasure and James's most direct indications of Ralph's role as shadow of the author. As Ralph confesses: "I had treated myself to a charming vision of your future ... I had amused myself with planning out a high destiny for you. There was to be nothing of this sort in it. You were not to come down so easily or so soon" (4:69). From all early indications of her character and temperament, indeed, from her own statements ("I'm not a candidate for adoption ... I'm very fond of my liberty" [3:23–24]), Isabel has presented herself to Ralph and her audience as one on whom nothing was to be lost. And so James describes her as one with "a comprehensiveness of observation" and a remarkably active imagination (3:21, 66). Like her audience, Ralph reads Isabel from these clues, and, like her audience, Ralph finds himself baffled by this sudden anomaly in her character: "You must have changed immensely. A year ago you valued your liberty beyond everything. You wanted only to see life." Isabel's infamous response stuns everyone: "I have seen it ... It does not look to me now, I admit, such an inviting expanse" (4:65). Ironically, James has here thrown up for reconsideration his prefatory question "what will she *do*?" and admitted Ralph Touchett's own authorial limitations, and also that Isabel, if her life is to be engaging, must have some degree of autonomy for her story to be in any way an approximation of life (Preface, 1081).

Throughout the text the portrait of Isabel Archer has been one presented not directly, as a result of Isabel's own comments, intellect and imagination; rather, our admiration and expectations come through mediators such as the narrator, Madame Merle, and Ralph. In fact, Isabel says and does little on her own to justify the reader's great expectations. Ralph's praise is the way we come to understand Isabel. In this way James uses Ralph as a narrative device to transfer information to his audience. To be sure, having someone of Ralph's acumen be stunned by Isabel's turn-around afforded James the perfect vehicle by which to present the magnitude of Isabel's change. The degree of Ralph's bafflement is the measure of Isabel's fall; had he not been so baffled the extraordinary qualities attributed to Isabel would become suspect. In Ralph's words, Isabel's fall "hurts me ... hurts me as if I had fallen myself" (4:70). A great part of Ralph's pain at Isabel's decision to wed Osmond is his recognition of his own complicity in Isabel's decision to have herself "put into a cage," a willingness Isabel makes all too explicit in the following tragically ironic statement:

> "I've fortunately money enough [to marry Osmond]; I have never felt so thankful for it as today. There have been moments when I should like to go and kneel down by your father's grave: he did perhaps a better thing than he knew when he put it into my power to marry a poor man." (4:73)

Ralph's displeasure in Isabel's actions thus gives voice within the text to the reader's own frustrations with her behavior, and his lament over his complicity in Isabel's choice of partner is meant to parallel, again within the text, the reader's own sense of having incorrectly composed and projected a rather different configuration of Isabel Archer. James's point is double: first, in acting quite differently from what the reader anticipates, Isabel shows the reader the limitations of an understanding based on assumption and projection; and second, by having Isabel act contrary to everyone's expectations, including her own, James reveals the extent to which the self is fluid, and always in process. Isabel, unfortunately, as *The Portrait of a Lady* goes on to show, rejects the notion of a fluid self and attempts to seal herself off from the requirements such a notion of self demands, only realizing her mistake when it is too late, at least within the context of the novel, to make a change.

The ironic allusion to Ralph's involvement with Isabel's "fate" takes us back to our opening discussion of spectatorship where the disabled Ralph explains to Isabel: "What's the use of being ill and disabled and restricted to mere spectatorship at the game of life if I really cannot see the show when I have paid so much for my ticket?" (3:209–10). Isabel's decision to marry Osmond largely ends the show for Ralph: Isabel has nothing of interest left to present, or what she does trot across the stage is not a show he wishes to watch. In Ralph's mind Isabel has indeed "affronted" her destiny, affronted in the sense of openly abused and slighted rather than faced head-on, something James himself is hinting at in his Preface when he says that the novel centers on "the conception of a certain young woman affronting her destiny" (1076). Left with nothing to see, with "the person in the world in whom he was most interested ... lost," Ralph's role necessarily diminishes; but it is not over, despite his illness. The exigencies of the text require a measure of Osmond and the danger to art he represents. To facilitate this comparison James allows Ralph to linger, chorus-like, on the margin. James explains the need for his peripheral presence by claiming what "kept Ralph alive was simply the fact that he had not yet seen enough of the person in the world in whom he was most interested: he was not yet satisfied. There was more to come; he couldn't make up his mind to lose that. He wanted to see what she would make of her husband – or what her husband would make of her" (4:146–47). Isabel's marriage takes her destiny out of Ralph's hands, and since Ralph seems aware of the inevitable outcome of her story, to have him hang on as an agent would subvert James's intention regarding the openness of the novel's form. What remains is for the reader to follow the unfolding of Isabel's destiny and arrive at the level of understanding Ralph has reached.

In a way, James's presentation of Ralph as author-surrogate and his elaborate and convoluted Preface to the novel form a peculiar dynamic of manipulation and estrangement. By so cluttering the text's horizon with competing and complementary explanations of who Isabel Archer is or who she could be, James effectively succeeds in presenting the reader with the same question he attaches to Isabel: how does she affront her destiny? For the reader the affront is the experience of *The Portrait of a Lady*. Burdened with expectations of Isabel (even her name – Archer – recalls a specific type of heroine), the reader enters the interpretive project already the victim of interpretive manipulation. In this sense the reader experiences an estrangement from self akin to Isabel's own. James expends so much energy setting up this dynamic in order to allow the reader simultaneously to experience what Isabel experiences and, through that experience, come to understand more fully the degree to which interpretation is always already mediated. James felt that only when the reader was brought to this latter awareness could understanding take place. By being manipulated and then estranged the reader is made aware and, when made aware, made free of all foreconceptions or, as Gadamer says, "the tyranny of hidden prejudices" that color our interpretive horizon (*Truth and Method*, 239).

IV

Our first impression of Isabel Archer is manipulated to elicit a degree of fascination. Before she enters the scene on the Gardencourt lawn at the opening of *The Portrait of a Lady*, James has his characters begin constructing her identity for us, going so far as to let us know she matches Lord Warburton's conception of "an interesting woman" (3:12). James presents her as an independent spirit, one who brings to life "a comprehensiveness of observation," "an immense curiosity," one who is captivated by impressions and is "constantly staring and wondering"(3:21, 45). In depicting Isabel as one "on whom nothing is lost" James grants her all the requisite requirements for artistic understanding ("Art of Fiction," 53). But despite all her above gifts, Isabel also reveals a number of important flaws. For one, "[h]er imagination was by habit ridiculously active; when the door was not open it jumped out of the window" (3:42). And, more significantly, she suffers from a lack of discernment: "at important moments, when she would have been thankful to make use of her judgement alone, she paid the penalty of having given undue encouragement to the faculty of seeing without judging," as though she has some faculty in place which necessarily leads her to premature judgment based on an overactive imagination (3:42). Like *The American*'s Christopher Newman, Isabel Archer's lack of discernment seems to be the product of a failure of practical wisdom. She believes the world corresponds to the image she has created: "she had a fixed determination to regard the world as a place of brightness, of free expansion, of irresistible action" and has determined her "life should always be in harmony with the most pleasing impression she should produce" (3:68–69).

Yet throughout *The Portrait of a Lady* Isabel consistently misreads the impression in part because her "fixed determination" produces an impression she has willed; what is at stake in the misreading is Isabel's understanding of herself, of her desires, and of the experiences she has through the course of her encounter with the world.[10] In creating such a dialectic between subjective and intersubjective understanding James is able to draw readers into the text and force them to be wary of any rapid judgment. In this fashion, the reader shares, to a degree, Isabel's hermeneutic project. Knowledge and understanding for both are dependent upon being able to distinguish between the "real" and the "apparent." James makes this task explicit once Isabel comes to Rome and encounters Gilbert Osmond. Confronted with a juxtaposition of the real (Roman treasures) and the spurious (Osmondian affectations of the real thing) Isabel is given the opportunity to develop discernment. What James reveals through the interpretive quandary Isabel falls into is that discernment is dependent upon some degree of prior knowledge and a similar degree of openness to what is. Isabel's problem, we come to realize, is that not only has she nothing to fall back on – her active imagination has leapt from experience to experience without pausing to assess and assimilate the encounter – but that even her ability to be open to the demands of her Roman encounter is circumscribed by her resistance to accepting the full measure of what that experience has to offer. And, as the novel shows, there is literally a world of difference between the two.

Earlier I discussed a conversation between Ralph and Isabel wherein Ralph is attempting to gauge Isabel's attitude toward engagement with the world. We recall how Ralph almost covertly explains to Isabel her desire to "throw herself into" the flow of life and "drain the cup of experience," a suggestion which elicits Isabel's peculiar recoil that the "cup of experience" is a "poisoned drink" (3:214, 213). What Isabel stresses in her discussion with Ralph is her desire to remain on the periphery, her desire "to look about me" and "see for myself" (3:213). What needs a moment of consideration is not Isabel's desire to experience the world on her own: as a young woman with her desire for experience the prospect of taking in Europe would be powerful. What is peculiar, however, is Isabel's calling the "cup of experience" a "poisoned drink." What, we must ask here, is she basing her knowledge on? What understanding has she reached which has led her to see experience as so bitter? Nothing in the text up to this conversation affords the reader the confidence necessary to accept Isabel's statement as an informed one. What we do know, however, is that her "thoughts were a tangle of vague outlines which had never been corrected by the judgement of people speaking with authority" (3:67). Given her limited exposure to the world (we are led to believe Isabel has spent most of her youth in self-isolation, reading books chosen for their covers in her grand-mother's Albany study) and the experience she comes to have through the course of the novel, Isabel's statement is both naive and prescient. Isabel does come to understand experience as a poisoned drink, but she is also complicit in blending the cup. As James notes, the story is primarily one of Isabel's "relation to herself" (Preface, *Portrait of a Lady*, 1079).

In his penetrating study of freedom and necessity in the novel, Paul Armstrong points out that initially Isabel is "the perfect embodiment of freedom in the eagerness with which she opens herself to the possibilities Mrs. Touchett has almost magically made available" by taking her to the Continent (*Phenomenology*, 104). James characterizes Isabel's zeal for knowledge and experience by having her describe to her aunt the fascination she has with places "in which things have happened," places which have "been full of life" (3:34). Europe, through Isabel's memory (3:44), and her active reading (3:31, 45), is a place "full of experience," and Florence is something she would "promise almost anything to see" (3:35). Even Isabel's family is convinced "[s]he's just the person to go abroad" in order for her to "develop" (3:40). But there is an ambiguity in Mrs. Ludlow's hope that Europe will provide Isabel with the experience she needs to develop. James presents a picture of Isabel in her sister's eyes which suggests the latter's concern over her sister's lack of the practical wisdom required to make one's way through the world. As a child Isabel "protested against" the "laws" of the primary school and abandoned formal education altogether. As a young woman Isabel moves through the world blind to the claims day-to-day living makes. James makes the point subtly by interjecting comments such as "Isabel new nothing about bills," or having her admit "I don't know anything about money," a truth brought into sharp focus when Mrs. Touchett explains to Ralph that Isabel "has a small income and she supposes herself to be traveling at her own expense" (3:28, 34;

3:57). Isabel's financial naivety influences Ralph's desire to endow her with means:

"She has nothing but the crumbs of that feast [her father's small bequest] to live on, and she does not really know how meagre they are – she has yet to learn it ... it would be really painful to me to think of her coming to the consciousness of a lot of wants she should be unable to satisfy." (3:263)

James's use of Isabel's pecuniary simplicity as a leitmotif establishes an important point about Isabel's blindness or inability to consider what it takes, quite literally, to live in the world. Through Isabel's innocence about the role capital plays in every life, especially the life she wishes to experience, James qualifies Isabel's own understanding of her freedom, suggesting, as Armstrong has pointed out, that she believes "possibility need suffer no limit" (*Phenomenology*, 104–5).

Herein lies the danger inherent in Isabel's unchecked and "ridiculously active" imagination: since she imagines the world corresponds exactly to her own experience of it (in this case experience financed by the Touchetts) she is able to pass through whatever worldly obstacles would check her exuberance and understanding. Thus, as Armstrong explains, Isabel's "imagination can be dangerous because it covers up limits by leaping beyond them without notice. It obscures the resistance of reality because the absolute freedom of fantasy knows no 'feeling or effort' or 'coefficient of adversity'" (*Phenomenology*, 105). By making contact only with those details of the landscape that match her own mental map, Isabel mistakes interpretation for free impression and demonstrates the partial manifestations of artistic sensibility which seem, in her case, to be thwarting her ability to take a full measure of reality.[11] Since she cannot recognize her impressions as "produced" and since she produces nothing with them, Isabel remains an artist manqué and leaves her self open to the suffering which results when her impressions are violated or overwritten by Gilbert Osmond who clearly understands how impressions are produced and received. That Isabel believes how she feels the world is how the world is marks her as somewhat a romantic, as Daniel Mark Fogel has suggested ("Framing James's Portrait," 1). We see this in the naivete of her desire to "find herself some day in a difficult position, so that she should have the pleasure of being as heroic as the occasion demanded" (3:69).

This attitude manifests itself in peculiar ways, such as her admission to Lord Warburton that if she were to consent to his offer of marriage "I should try to escape my [fate]." When pushed she elaborates her response to be "I cannot escape unhappiness ... In marrying you I shall be trying to" (3:186). In a frighteningly real way her marriage to Osmond allows her to put to the test her youthful idealism and raises questions about the exact nature of her attraction as well as casts a good deal of suspicion on her testimonials toward openness. But close reading of the novel shows these imprisoning characteristics as determining aspects of Isabel's personality long before she meets Osmond; think, for instance, of her childhood reading environment. It is clear from James's description of her appetite for texts that we are to see her as exceptional, but it is just as clear that her decision to read while locked away in a musty, dark upper room is something more than escapism (3:30). Isabel's seeming comfort behind closed doors manifests itself in her hyper-conscious concerns over her appearance. James presents just this image of Isabel in his early descriptions of her character. Along with having a "great desire for knowledge" and "an immense curiosity about life" Isabel is uncharacteristically (in the sense that she makes loud claims to the contrary) concerned with the impression she makes (3:45). James tells us of "her desire to look very well and be if possible even better" (3:69). She is careful to produce a predetermined "effect" upon people and afraid of appearing "narrow minded" (3:74, 83). Isabel's conscious concern with these impressions is what makes them relevant, for as normal apprehensions about being in the world they are of no consequence. This element of her portrait becomes more clear in an exchange with her aunt wherein Isabel explains her desire "to know the things one shouldn't do." When Mrs. Touchett asks if Isabel's concern is with obeying custom, Isabel explains that she desires only "to choose" whether or not following convention is convenient (3:93). But Isabel's assertion of independence is rather ambiguous, for true independence of spirit would be unconcerned with convention. For wanting to know convention in order to "choose" when to follow it is quite different from acting openly in spite of or without regard for convention. The person Isabel wants to present in the conversation with her aunt is one who would respond freely to any situation. Isabel does not. James makes this ironically clear in the conversation about outward appearance Isabel has with Madame Merle. When Serena Merle explains to Isabel that the self is "an envelope of circumstances ... a cluster of appurtenances" whose beginning and end form a continuum of which "the clothes" one should "choose to wear" are but an expression, Isabel responds in her naively independent posture:

"I know that nothing expresses me. Nothing that belongs to me is any measure of me; everything's on the contrary a limit, a barrier, and a perfectly arbitrary one. Certainly the clothes which, as you say, I choose to wear, don't express me; and heaven forbid they should! ... they're imposed upon me by society." (3:388)

Madame Merle's abrupt "Should you prefer to go without them?" effectively measures the simplicity of Isabel's understanding of social independence and brings to mind the snags associated with an understanding of the world not rooted in the landscape of fact.[12]

James details Isabel's character at such length early in *The Portrait of a Lady* for a number of reasons. One, the detail provokes from readers expectations of grandeur from Isabel. We need to see some indication that she matches Ralph's comparison of her with "a Titian, ... a Greek bas-relief" and a "Gothic cathedral" (3:86). And we need to be convinced of her own zeal to take in life's grandeur and make herself into the best possible person as a result of her lived-experience. We need to think as well of Isabel as she thinks of herself (3:67). Anything short of being sold on Isabel's potential would undermine the shock we are to feel when she resigns control of herself to "a sterile dilettante" (4:71). Theoretically, James elaborates the conditional and willed quality of Isabel's understanding so as to underscore the implications of consciousness in any construal of reality, and that interpretive failure results precisely because her consciousness manufactures a reality quite different from that in which the others in her world move. Therefore, in presenting Isabel as an example of how one's consciousness can deceptively map the landscape of fancy onto that of fact, James opens *The Portrait of a Lady* up as a study of how consciousness is always at work composing our understanding of the world and how that understanding is dependent upon the individual perceiver's capacity for openness and discernment.[13] By dramatizing Isabel's collision with the world at large, James uses Isabel as a vehicle through whom he can investigate the price of experience and what is at stake when you are not perceptually and epistemologically disposed to welcome experience on its own terms.

V

Not surprisingly, James develops this line of analysis in *The Portrait of a Lady* through a series of journeys, the well-wrought Jamesian technique of understanding through travel. As with *The American*'s Christopher Newman, James, perhaps more fully than any other writer, understood the power of travel as a narrative tool through which the author could systematically expose the traveler's prejudices and interpretive methodology. Also, and perhaps more importantly for James's understanding of art's role, the formal structure of travel narrative, especially when interpolated within a not specifically travel novel, functions as a method which demands response. In other words, to some extent the traveler's journey, Isabel's in the novel, becomes ours. Her response to what she encounters evokes the reader's response, which often is somewhat different, if not contrary. And if in this difference of opinion we become aware of Isabel's peculiarity of response, so too do we become aware of our own idiosyncracies. For James, awareness of the latter, of course, was the first step toward emancipation from the public and private forces which have constituted our understanding. And for James, this reflexive process was how art became active and responsible.

Once she finds herself in Europe with the world all before her Isabel makes three journeys of increasing significance. The first, a trip to London with Ralph and Henrietta Stackpole, shows Isabel following the path Ralph and the audience have come to expect. She approaches London willing to let the experience of the city imprint itself upon her. In the encounter she compares the landscape of London with that which she has anticipated and, more importantly, allows the city to penetrate and modify her expectations.

Isabel was full of premises, conclusions, emotions; if she had come in search of local colour she found it everywhere. She asked more questions than [Ralph] could answer, and launched brave theories, as to historic cause and social effect, that he was equally unable to refute. (3:198)

James underscores Isabel's openness by employing Henrietta as a foil, or *ficelle* who demonstrates all the wrong ways of encountering something new.[14] In London Henrietta tears a page out of Christopher Newman's book and believes taking in the city means marking off sights mentioned in "her guidebook" (3:199). Unlike Isabel, Henrietta wants textual verification that a sight has been consumed.

Later, in Rome, Henrietta, following the lead of Mark Twain's innocents abroad, finds herself "obliged in candour to declare that Michelangelo's dome suffered by comparison with that of the Capitol at Washington" (3:425). In both cases Henrietta's philistinism points up Isabel's sensitivity and openness to the encounter. Unlike Henrietta, Isabel is willing to be impressed by London, by Rome, impressed in the sense that she welcomes the epistemological alteration of the experience. Isabel wishes Europe to leave a mark. James allows her to express the point more directly in her refusal of Caspar Goodwood's proposal, "I don't need the aid of a clever man to teach me how to live. I can find it out for myself" (3:223). And she stakes her independence against Goodwood's desire to rein her in as his:

"I try to judge things for myself; to judge wrong, I think, is more honourable than to not judge at all. I don't wish to be a mere sheep in the flock; I wish to choose my fate and know something of human affairs beyond what other people think it compatible with propriety to tell me." (3:228–29)

Thus, Isabel's London encounter ends with Ralph and her audience convinced of her as a free and open intelligence ready to experience the world. To this extent audience and character remain united by the interpretive project. And by maintaining this unison between the reader's and his character's experience, James is able to solidify the bond between reader and text and draw more apparent attention to the actual process of interpretation when these united paths begin to diverge.

Isabel carries this receptivity to the London scene with her to the Mediterranean. She finds that "Italy, as yet imperfectly seen and felt, stretched before her as a land of promise, a land in which a love of the beautiful might be comforted by endless knowledge" (3:320). With Isabel's movement into Italy, James makes a value judgment about the role of art in life (4:32). James was convinced that contemplation of art could lead one to a depth of understanding. For James the experience of art put one in touch with the "beautiful" which in turn opened one to the "endless knowledge" embodied in aesthetic work. James believed that in contemplating art the viewer's mind was made aware of and could thereby educate itself as to the possibilities inherent in the mind's contemplation of the art work, and, by extension, one's experience of life. "The effect, if not the prime office, of criticism," explains James in "The New Novel," is to make "the mind as aware of itself as possible, since that awareness quickens the mental demand, which thus in turn wanders further and further for pasture" (*Literary Criticism*, 1, 124). Translated into the language of *The Portrait of a Lady*, James's injunctions in "The New Novel" suggest that for Isabel, Italy serves as an opportunity for "reaching out" so her "interest can grow more various." Both Ralph and James believe critical observation such as is made available to Isabel in Italy "is the very education of our imaginative life" and instructs one in "the general question of how to refine" understanding (124). This was what James meant when he described his goals as an artist as "the high, helpful civic use of the imagination" (Preface, "The Lesson of the Master," 1230).

The connection between James's advice in "The New Novel" and Isabel's situation as a traveler in London and Italy is made explicit through James's discussion of the "act of consideration" further on in his essay. In language strikingly similar to his description of Isabel's response to London, James explains that the "effect of consideration, we need scarce remark, is to light for us in a work of art the hundred questions of how and why and whither, and the effect of these questions, once lighted, is enormously to thicken and complicate, even if toward final clarifications, what we have called the amused state produced in us by the work" ("The New Novel," 146). Paul Armstrong makes James's concerns with the value of art, particularly the novel as a mirror image of humanity, explicit in his discussion of the novelist's understanding of the impression: "The epistemological and existential function of art here relies heavily on the imagination. Epistemology and imagination meet in the activity of projecting life into art and reflecting on art's meaning for life. They meet when we try to understand 'the image in the mirror' held up to us by the novel" (*Phenomenology*, 68). Within *The Portrait of a Lady* this dialectic between epistemology and imagination is realized in the image Italy offers Isabel. In the reflection of Italy, Isabel discovers a wealth of thought-provoking potentialities which lead her "constantly [to] pictur[e] to herself by the light of her hopes, her fears, her fancies, her ambitions, her predilections," her "career" thus far (3:321). She finds herself "lost in a maze of visions" and convinced that to "live in such a place [Florence] was . . . to hold to her ear all day a shell of the sea of the past," a "vague eternal rumour" which "kept her imagination awake" (3:355). For both James and Isabel, the Florentine vista offers a contemplation of what it was, is, and could be to be alive. The seashell echoes of the lived-experience embodied in the impression of all that is Florence. James's aim is to allow the reader to experience the potentialities associated with the mode of perception he called discrimination and realize the attendant enlargement of experience discrimination brings about. One need only be open to the impression to be presented with the possibilities of "endless knowledge." Should Isabel stand in proper relation to the mirror of Florence, as her sensibility warrants, she could become the portrait Ralph Touchett imagines possible. Ralph's advice to Isabel seems a paraphrase of James's own comments in "The New Novel": "Don't try so much to form your character – it is like trying to pull open a tight, tender young rose. Live as you like best, and your character will take care of itself ... Put back your watch. Diet your fever. Spread your wings; rise above the ground. It is never wrong to do that" (3:319).[15] Isabel, holding "a shell of the sea of the past," is at a rare moment of conflux in *The Portrait of a Lady* where James, Ralph, and Isabel appear in imagination all compact: the life of art and the art of life are intimately intertwined and can present a wisdom to those whose perceptual process allows them to transfigure the impression into a product of artistic imagination – so James of the novel, so Ralph of Isabel, so Isabel of life.

Isabel fulfills Ralph's injunctions during her initial "pilgrimage to Rome" where she matches the reader's and Ralph's expectations of her character:

It is enough to say that her impression was such as might have been expected of a person of her freshness and her eagerness. She had always been fond of history, and here was history in the stones of the street and the atoms of the sunshine. She had an imagination that kindled at the mention of great deeds, and wherever she turned some great deed had been awarded. (3:413)

James continues to develop this completion of Isabel's character by presenting her as the ideal open tourist or impression-collecting individual determined to get all she can out of travel:

Her consciousness was so mixed that she scarcely knew where the different parts of it would lead her, and she went about in a repressed ecstasy of contemplation, seeing often in the things she looked at a great deal more than was there. (3:413–14)

Though Isabel appears to take in Rome as expected (in Ralph's words "Isabel would become a Rome lover; that was a foregone conclusion"), James's language foregrounds another, more crucial development in her character – the lack of discernment or hermeneutic ground on which to judge (3:408). It is not by accident James chooses to describe Isabel's encounter with Rome as the end of a "pilgrimage," a comparison which adds a religious connotation to Isabel's adventure.[16]

The sense of pilgrim and pilgrimage here assumes a relevance in the immediate context of *The Portrait of a Lady* and the larger context of Jamesian aesthetics. Since Rome is the place Ralph sees as the center of art and beauty, it necessarily becomes a testing ground where Isabel can prove herself as one who is able not only to take the true measure of things, but as one whose understanding and wisdom set her above the common weal. Furthermore, James uses Isabel's Roman encounter as a vehicle through which he can present his larger concerns with aesthetics as a means to an enlarged ability to understand the world. By lending Isabel's Roman experience a religious connotation James conflates the spiritual and the aesthetic and, in doing so, allows the latter to absorb the higher insight normally attributed to the former. This is not to say that James's art should be recognized as particularly spiritual or religious; on the contrary, his aesthetics remains purely secular, but secular with a penetrating and transfigurative power. And it is the ability to learn this discriminating perception James presents Isabel in Rome. For while Rome is described as a place of beauty and "endless knowledge," it remains worldly, a secularized objective in all senses and is therefore the place where one does not see things as they are, but must learn to distinguish between the genuine and the counterfeit. Thus, it is rather telling that Isabel's inability to understand herself and her world becomes most evident in Rome. James underscores her failure to *see* by having her fall for Osmond in Rome – the place Osmond (the text's most flagrant example of a counterfeit) is said to have created himself. And from Rome on Isabel's world begins to grow more and more narrow as what was once all before her now becomes increasingly inaccessible. What Isabel comes to experience in Rome is the consequences of relying too heavily on a "faculty of seeing without judging," or seeing "in the things she looked at a great deal more than was there" (3:42, 413–14).

James thus uses Rome as a turning point in Isabel's life and as an inflection point in the narrative. It is in Rome that Isabel comes up against the limits of her experience. James shows Isabel caught between the demands of freedom and the security of an enclosed interpretive system. Up to her Roman pilgrimage Isabel is following, primarily, a sensibility directed by Ralph Touchett which, like the Jamesian artist, privileges observation as a subtle form of participation. Once "through" Rome, however, Isabel finds herself exchanging the world offered by Ralph for the one she believes has been offered by Gilbert Osmond. James prepares us for this shift in Isabel's focus by sending her on one last journey, to the Eastern Mediterranean with Madame Merle. The Isabel who makes this trip is different in kind from that who went to London, Florence, and came to Rome. Madame Merle notes that her companion is "restless," and "that even among the most classic sites, the scenes most calculated to suggest repose and reflection, a certain incoherence prevailed in her." Rather than opening herself to the possibilities of Greece and Turkey, Isabel closes herself off, traveling "rapidly and recklessly . . . like a thirsty person draining cup after cup" (4:38).

That James recalls the metaphor of experience as draining a cup, the poisoned drink Isabel refused much earlier but is freely tossing off now, suggests the qualitative change that has come over her. The former Isabel wanted to see and judge for herself, the latter Isabel finds herself frustrated by the level of self-reliance necessary for the type of independence she earlier advocated. And since this shift in character has occurred off-stage, so to speak (James allows us only to hear of Isabel's trip through the mediation of Madame Merle's observations, forcing the reader to undertake the same character revaluation underway in Isabel's mind), the reader has to go back and re-read Isabel's encounter with Rome and find the causes of Isabel's change. For after Rome, Isabel turns from accepting Ralph's injunctions to be open and free with the world and looks toward those who are more willing to tell her what she ought to do given her circumstances. I have suggested this movement is one from kinesis to stasis, from understanding to opinion. Not surprisingly, the figuration of Isabel as art becomes particularly relevant in this movement. Historically speaking, Isabel's decision to marry, her decision to look to Osmond for guidance would match quite well *The Portrait of a Lady*'s contemporaneous audiences' expectations. For many the question "what will she do?" is answered appropriately with marriage, something Caspar Goodwood gives voice to within the text when he explains part of his desire to marry as a determination to make Isabel "independent": "an unmarried woman – a girl of your age – isn't independent. There are all sorts of things she cannot do. She's hampered at every step" (3:228). James plays upon this expectation in two ways. No one can read the novel and see in Isabel's marriage a happy situation. Those whose expectations are initially met are subsequently forced to reappraise their initial opinion, and perhaps, even their opinion of what traditional expectations amount to. Such a provocation toward sympathy and tolerance is what James is after. As figuration of art, Isabel brings to focus a similar need to rescue aesthetics from projected and preconceived expectations. For art to achieve its full potential as a living and educative medium it must be free to choose its own path just as an individual, especially a woman, given the traditional lack of freedom, must be free to be herself. In a culture which inscribed a fixed identity for women, Isabel was never given that chance. Try as she did, her understanding was shaped by the understood opinion that she would marry to complete herself. Her tragic fate is the measure of that freedom's lack.

James's theoretical aim here is important. By taking Isabel off stage he creates the authorial distance necessary for the reader's own reappraisal of Isabel. What the reader discovers in this re-examination is the degree to which he or she has, like Ralph Touchett, been authorially involved in constructing expectations of Isabel based upon a number of assumptions, which include assumptions based on gender and on what other characters say as opposed to an understanding of the particular circumstances of her situation. By involving the reader thus James follows his own instructions laid down approximately fifteen years earlier in his essay on "The Novels of George Eliot" (1866). James's explanation is worth quoting at length:

In every novel the work is divided between the writer and the reader; but the writer makes the reader very much as he makes his characters. When he makes them ill, that is, makes them indifferent, he does no work; the writer does all. When he makes him well, that is, makes him interested, then the reader does quite half the labour. In making such a deduction as I have just indicated, the reader would be doing but his share of the task; the grand point is to get him to make it. (*Literary Criticism*, 1, 922)[17]

Caught between rival and incompatible demands: of being female and what that requires, of the "sense of freedom, of the absolute boldness and wantonness of liberty" Ralph's world holds, Isabel turns to travel as a distraction. One of the problems Ralph's offer of expansiveness presents is that it relies on a degree of imaginative freedom the "world" would never, realistically speaking, grant a young woman, particularly in the circles Isabel moves in. As Priscilla Walton has noted, as a woman Isabel is free "only to submit to socially determined notions of subjectivity" (*Disruption of the Feminine*, 53). Anyone who has read James's "Daisy Miller" or *Washington Square* would see in these stories of repression and forced conformity how aware James is of the restrictions placed upon women and why James continually feminized art in order to show art under threat. In *The Portrait of a Lady* this threat is measured in Isabel's changing attitude toward the experience of travel. The moment she looks on travel as a form of tourism through which one collects impressions like so many snapshots, Isabel admits her failure. Travel becomes an escape rather than an experience which could truly enlarge her horizon. Both Paul Armstrong and John Carlos Rowe see Isabel's trip to the Eastern Mediterranean as an avoidance and substitute. Armstrong argues that in one of "its less felicitous forms, travel can provide a way of changing our position frequently enough to give the illusion that we have avoided situating ourselves," a means of self-deception to which Osmond has forced Isabel (*Phenomenology*, 110). In addition to using travel as a method of avoiding the question of Osmond's professed love for her and her own unclear desires for him, Isabel manipulates her understanding of the entire experience so as to convince herself that mere observation of the world holds nothing more of value for her. The trip, then, becomes a way for Isabel to convince herself she has largely completed her character and accomplished the education a life of wandering can yield. Thus completed she frees herself for a life of refinement under Osmond. Isabel reveals this thought process upon her return from the east when she finds herself "[g]rave" and "weighted" from "the experience" of having spent a year "seeing the world":

She had ranged, she would have said, through space and surveyed much of mankind, and was therefore now, *in her own eyes*, a very different person from the frivolous young woman from Albany who had begun to take the measure of Europe on the lawn at Gardencourt a couple of years before. She *flattered herself* that she had harvested wisdom and learned a great deal more of life than this light-minded creature had even suspected. (Emphasis added, 4:32)

James deflates Isabel's claims to wisdom and understanding by including the qualifier "in her own eyes" and remarking her tendency toward self-flattery. Isabel has "ranged ... through space," taking in a rather unexamined, distanced survey she has yet to assimilate. In believing she has completed her education Isabel errs on the side of naivety. Rowe explains that "Isabel's tour has been little more than an interlude in which the 'scenic' offers itself as a substitute for wisdom, which for James is never to be achieved short of one's full involvement in the social and historical network" (*Theoretical Dimensions*, 196). Isabel's scenic consumerism takes her out of the realm of artistic sensibility where she was able to educate her understanding of things beneath the surface, and subjects her to the "confusion" of the "splendid waste" where she finds herself baffled by "a certain incoherence." In Rowe's argument, Isabel's method of consuming experience prevents her from accomplishing what the travel could have given: "a conscious investigation of one's social, familial, and historical relations" (197). What the whole Roman and Eastern Mediterranean experience indicates, then, is Isabel's move from self-reliance to reliance on Osmond, the man whom she believes can whisper in her ear the same voices as "a shell of the sea of the past" and draw a filtering (or exclusionary) circle around her world. No longer content just to observe, Isabel makes a studied and conscious effort to ground herself through attachment to Osmond, a man largely the product of her imagination (3:355, 383, 399).

James dramatizes the retraction of Isabel's consciousness in the excuses she gives for closing herself off to the world. Her change in attitude toward experience and the way one comes to understand self and world follows the paradigm of a gestalt shift[18] in that she has repeated on a number of occasions her abhorrence of marriage for more reasons than that it will interfere with her experience of Europe: "I too don't wish to marry till I have seen Europe" (3:213); "I really don't want to marry, or to talk about it at all now. I shall probably never do it – no, never" (3:222); "I don't need the aid of a clever man to teach me how to live" (3:223); "If you should hear a rumour that I'm on the point of [marrying] ... remember what I have told you about my love of liberty and venture to doubt it" (3:229). Isabel had equated marriage with a confinement. And even if we accept her conviction that she has taken Europe for all it is worth and is now free to consider marriage, nothing in her character has indicated any inclination to being so bonded to another, let

alone to having her perceptual horizon so restricted. The prospect of
marrying Osmond startles even her: "No one can be more surprised
than myself at my present intention" (4:50). In fact, Osmond's
declaration of love evokes images of imprisonment and violation
similar to those evoked by Warburton's and Goodwood's proposals
and, *ironically*, to the image of her grandmother's "mysterious apartment" with its door "that had been condemned" and was "secured
by bolts which a particularly slender little girl found it impossible to
slide" (3:30). When James tells us that with Osmond's courtship
Isabel believed she could hear "the slipping of a fine bolt – backward
and forward," we are meant to recall that Isabel "was guided in the
selection" of her reading material "chiefly by the frontispiece" (4:18,
3:29–30).

James foregrounds the change in Isabel's understanding and calls
her reasoning into question shortly after Ralph fails to get through
to her with his reminder of her passion for liberty. Isabel responds to
this reminder with "I have seen it [life], ... it does not look to me
now, I admit, such an inviting expanse ... One must choose a corner
and cultivate that" (4:65). In his exposé of Isabel's mind James notes
the radical shift in her goals and foregrounds the lack of discernment
and self-understanding which has exhibited itself throughout as a
debilitating feature of her character.

The desire for unlimited expansion had been succeeded in her soul by the
sense that life was vacant without some private duty that might gather
one's energies to a point. She had told Ralph she had "seen life" in a year
or two and that she was already tired, not of the act of living, but of that of
observing. What had become of all her ardours, her aspirations, her
theories, her high estimate of her independence and her incipient
conviction that she should never marry? (4:82)

Here the mystery of Isabel's motivations seems to rest more clearly
on the claim made by the need to follow the requirements of one's
imagination. That Isabel should tire of a life of observation reveals
more about her failure to open herself to that which she has
observed and to allow her encounters to impress themselves upon
her than it does about the deficiencies of observation in itself. In fact,
James is suggesting Isabel has mis-observed the entire European
adventure, approaching all she has seen and done as one outside the
frame looking in, as a passive spectator. Isabel has recorded but not
processed most of what she has seen, that is, she has observed things
but her consciousness has not transfigured them into understanding.

And that she desires to rein her energies in "to a point" and focus on "the act of living" seems to attest more to her pending marriage as an escape than as a conscious choice.

In both instances James shows how Isabel manipulates her own understood openness to events by fabricating an impression of the outside world to match the landscape of her imagined understanding – imagined in the sense that she has constructed it from fantastic ideals rather than worldly phenomena. To this extent Isabel's radical disappointment of the reader's expectations similarly reveals the reader's own sub-conscious textual assumptions and foregrounds the two-sided manipulation at work in any interpretive event – in this case the reader's and the author's. Ralph comments on how once Isabel chose to focus her energies on Osmond, she "invented a fine theory" about him in order to justify the marriage (4:75). And James explodes the whole motivation behind the marriage by presenting Isabel's own understanding of it as a *deus ex machina*: "It simplified the situation at a stroke, it came down from above like the light of the stars, and it needed no explanation" (4:82). Isabel's resignation here, her acceptance of "no explanation," is indicative of something perhaps greater than a gestalt shift, for James has now forced us to ask what Isabel has shifted from. One could argue Isabel never had a fixed gestalt in the first place, or that the gestalt was fixed for her when she was born female; it is this lack of ownership which allows her to find life vacant, to tire of unlimited expansion, to fool herself into believing she could see life in a year or two, to boast of goals never to be met, to feel a need to "gather one's energies to a point." For without a fixed center Isabel's consciousness has been too diffuse to work the transfiguration of her lived-experience into a viable understanding and practical wisdom.

It is here we should recall her "faculty of seeing without judging" and understand Isabel's inability to judge as rooted in her lack of a fixed center of self-understanding. Isabel has, in a sense, floated through her experiences, being neither open nor closed to them, but untouched. She has watched the world as though seated before a stage, watched a performance she has largely constructed, not from outward phenomena, but inward fancy. Ralph Touchett's authorial hand has led her through the scenes safely and securely. And it is the unexpected appearance ("down from above") of Osmond, a phenomenon over which Ralph has no control, an impression of his being "like no one she had ever seen ... a specimen apart," which forces Isabel to rely on her own judgment (4:375–76). Thus, in a very real way Isabel's encounter with the unexpected Osmond is a textual example of the perceptual process we live every day. James would say Osmond represents one of those things which have not yet come our way. Our ability to respond to these unexpected events is commensurate with our ability to understand at all. Isabel fails to respond to Osmond in a fundamental way when she allows herself to impose an internally generated image so as to escape from the requirements of interpretation. Within the context of Jamesian aesthetics this circumvention represents an artificial and threatening boundary for art and a denial of hermeneutics.

VI

Within the context of Jamesian aesthetics the question as to how Isabel sees Osmond becomes particularly important. In *The Portrait of a Lady*, Isabel's self-generated vision of Osmond attests to her mind's weakness when confronted by the pressures of interpretation. Isabel's infatuation with Osmond is, on her side at least, rather straightforward. Osmond represents to her all the high beauty and culture the lure of Europe held for her as an ideal. In her understanding, life with Osmond "seemed to assure her a future at a high level of consciousness of the beautiful" (4:82). But what James wants his readers to struggle with is how Isabel actually *sees* Osmond. For it is the complexity of Isabel's vision, how she falls into an inactive role and relies on projected assumption, that requires attention if one is to understand how she so completely misreads him. On her first meeting with Osmond Isabel does what is natural to her – she assumes the stance of spectator and watches the progression of life before her as though it were so much action on a stage.[19] As Osmond and Madame Merle meet, "Isabel took on this occasion little part in the talk; she scarcely even smiled when the others turned to her invitingly; she sat there as if she had been at the play and had paid even a large sum for her place." Isabel's disconnectedness from the scene allows her to consider Osmond and Madame Merle as "distinguished performers figuring for a charity" (3:355). Yet as an observer at a play Isabel approximates the reading subject and, like a reader, is presented with surface events and required to engage in constructing an understanding from what she has been watching. So was she to do with the experience of Europe. In

Ricoeur's language we can recognize Isabel's refusal to acknowledge
the responsibilities and potentialities associated with finding oneself
"in front of the text" and an almost frightened retreat before the
requirements of interpretation such a position affords (*Hermeneutics*,
143). In denying her role in the dialectical nature of interpretation
Isabel disables the opportunity of recognizing how much the "text is
the medium through which we understand ourselves." To this extent
she demonstrates the mode of detached observation critics have too
easily accused James of adopting. But James understood observation
in a far more potent manner. Like Ricoeur, James believed it was
"not a question of imposing upon the text our finite capacity of
understanding, but of exposing ourselves to the text and receiving
from it an enlarged self, which would be the proposed existence
corresponding in the most suitable way to the world proposed"
(142–43). Isabel's error of passivity with Osmond is a redramatiza-
tion of her similar passive stance toward Europe. And as with
Europe, Isabel focuses only on the aspects of Osmond which match
the portrait she wants to see. Thus the structure of Isabel's
perception determines the appearance of all that comes before it.
Within the context of Jamesian aesthetics such a displacement of
active discrimination rendered art lifeless and life either an artificial
process in which one referred everything back upon oneself, as
though the perceiving subject were a self-ratifying authority, or
rendered the whole idea of culture impossible since each subjectivity
would exist, for the most part, within its own established monad. In
either case, James understood the need to be wary of mistaking self-
generated perceptions for the real thing, so he created an aesthetics
whose narrative process ineluctably brought readers up against the
natural tendency to impose upon reality.

In *The Portrait of a Lady* we can see this tendency toward projecting
a self-generated reality in Isabel's portrait of Osmond.

She had carried away an image from her visit to his hill-top which her
subsequent knowledge of him did nothing to efface and which put on for
her a particular harmony with other supposed and divined things, histories
within histories: the image of a quiet, clever, sensitive, distinguished man,
strolling on a moss-grown terrace above the sweet Val-d'Arno and holding
by the hand a little girl whose bell-like clearness gave a new grace to
childhood. The picture had no flourishes, but she liked its lowness of tone
and the atmosphere of summer twilight that pervaded it. (3:399)

It seems clear James intends Isabel's portrait of Osmond to reveal both the artistic tendencies of her consciousness and its failure to produce a completely representative picture.[20] Furthermore the internal and external reflections in this portrait call up the other references to portraiture in this novel. That catalogue is rather extensive: Isabel creates a portrait of Osmond; Ralph creates a portrait of Isabel; Isabel creates a portrait of herself; Osmond creates a portrait of himself; and James creates a *Portrait* of all these projected portraits. Of course, this list mentions only those most obvious examples of portraiture in the novel with one notable absence. The proliferation of representations should also include the reader's own portrait-making practice. After all, what else is the reading act but a process by which one actively constructs pictures of what one believes to be transpiring within the text. So when within the novel James brings his characters up against the limitations of their portraits' ability to contain reality, he means his readers to encounter a similar experience when their expectations of the novel are either challenged or overthrown by the novel itself. This dynamic of portraiture then is an aspect of Jamesian aesthetics which is meant to point up the inevitable limitations of any attempt to fix or enclose reality, within or without fiction. Thus, in Jamesian hermeneutics, the need to recognize our tendency toward portraiture is an injunction aimed at the reader, dramatized by the characters' failures and, ultimately, imposed by James upon his own aesthetic system.

Furthermore James's concern with portraiture's ability to exert a destabilizing force upon reality is implicit in the phrase "histories within histories" that Isabel employs in her portrait of Osmond. By constructing a history for Osmond, Isabel believes she can ground him as historically verifiable, as belonging to history in a way she feels she does not. One could say Isabel's wanderings have kept her outside history, a part of everything and therefore a part of nothing. Grounded in history, Osmond has a place of belonging (he is inextricably linked to Rome and Florence), which is exactly what Isabel covets. Thus, Isabel comes to see Osmond as an opportunity to step into history and be part of a world she has only heretofore observed. But the implied question, of course, is into what "History" does Isabel step? Certainly not Osmond's, as the novel eventually shows. James, as we have seen, was convinced that "the real represents ... the things we cannot possibly *not* know, sooner or later, in one way or another" (Preface, *The American*, 1062–63). Isabel's active construction of a version of history based on desire and a "lowness of tone" is a challenge to "the real" and will eventually crumble either upon contact with that "real" James suggests lurks out there, or when it comes up against a history such as Osmond's, which in a more subversive and powerful way overwrites those histories it comes into contact with. The danger, James suggests through this depiction of willful histories, is not that Osmond or Isabel can overwrite "the real," but that the proliferation of self-determined and self-ratifying "histories" poses a threat to the whole notion of culture, of epistemology, of subjectivity, and of understanding. One of the focuses of Jamesian hermeneutics is to challenge so as to overthrow this threat, by exposing the novelistic or compositional quality of interpretation in general. Since we make sense of experiences by narrativizing them, we are always in danger of forgetting the degree to which we fill in the blank spaces of our experiences so as to make their narrativized recreation whole and to which we use the recreated version for the basis of our understanding of the immediate experience and its role in our future actions.

VII

The full measure of James's critique of our tendency to revert solely to our own subjectivity when confronted with difficult decisions or powerful desires is made apparent in the consequences of Isabel's attempt to appropriate Osmond and her sudden recognition of her mistake. If Ralph Touchett's plea of being "restricted to mere spectatorship at the game of life" conjures up images of James's prefatory description of the house of fiction and shapes our understanding of Ralph as shadow of James (3:210), Isabel's unexpected departure from Ralph's project suggests her inability to follow the artistic precepts Ralph outlined. That she chooses to follow Osmond, the man, who, despite superficial similarities, is least like Ralph, is indicative of a perceptual shift Isabel willingly accommodates. In marrying Osmond, Isabel subjects herself to the authorial stance of a sterile dilettante. For Osmond, as surely as Ralph, is a textual embodiment of authorial control.[21] But where Ralph welcomes and in fact demands the complete freedom of his charge to experience the world and develop her own understanding as she sees fit, Osmond demands stasis and closure, and aggressively manipulates Isabel's encounter with the world. This dichotomy is what leads

William H. Gass to see the difference between Ralph's and Osmond's style of author/artist as "self-effacing" on the one hand and "appropriative" on the other ("High Brutality," 188). This difference in understanding art's function, according to James, goes a long way to discovering the antipathy these men share for each other. Ralph seems to understand exactly who and what Osmond is and his disdain is shared by the reader. But Osmond seems to have no legitimate grounds for his aversion to Ralph, for accusing him of being a "jackanapes," other than resentment of Ralph's ability to recognize him as a counterfeit (3:349). In this way Osmond's hatred of Ralph is a product of the anger and humiliation he feels in being first discovered and then dismissed by Ralph.

But the friction between Osmond and Ralph offers even more in the context of James's larger artistic argument. If we understand Ralph as authoring Isabel – particularly with regard to the financial endowment, and accept Osmond as being appropriative, and if we come to see Isabel as Osmond's museum piece and the Palazzo Roccanera as the museum Isabel's money has allowed him to establish, then we can accept Osmond's resentment of Ralph as founding benefactor. Though neither Osmond nor Isabel know that Ralph is immediately responsible for the bequest, his being linked to it is cause enough for Osmond's antipathy. For in being familially connected to both Isabel and the endowment, Ralph's claim to celebrate their worth is more legitimate than Osmond's, especially considering Osmond's duplicity in acquiring both. Osmond can only be seen, then, as an imposter and counterfeit in comparison with Ralph. Isabel makes this point explicit when she recognizes that "it didn't make Gilbert look better to sit for half an hour with Ralph" (4:203).

And when we allow this elaborate comparison to extend beyond the text the obvious point is that James employs Ralph and Osmond to show up the danger to art the copyist and sterile dilettante presents. As a negative example of the artist, all Osmond produces is counterfeit and dead art – Isabel included. Jonathan Freedman makes the fraudulent and sterile aspects of this attitude explicit:

In Gilbert's form of vision, the self is understood to be a smug, observing entity, a private and self-satisfied "point of view," while all others are treated as objects of this contemplative vision, to be either appreciated or rejected but always transformed into signs of the supreme taste of the observer. Gilbert's aestheticizing vision, in other words, might also be said to be a reifying vision. Despite the nobility of his rhetoric, Osmond perceives all the others he encounters as detached, deadened objects of his purely passive perception, and seeks to make those who refuse to be so into such beautiful objects. (*Professions of Taste*, 153)

In Osmond's and Ralph's countervailing views of Isabel as a work of art James gives voice to two competing forms of art: the static and the dynamic. Not surprisingly, these two views of art correspond in Jamesian hermeneutics with what he saw as the two modes of understanding, the false being static, with the subject hermetically sealed within the confines of its own ego, the true being active, with the subject being hermeneutically open to the possibilities of experience and its attendant potential for subjective enhancement.

James foregrounds this collision between modes of interpretation with Osmond's initial and most lasting complaint against Isabel's intellectual plenitude: "She has only one fault ... Too many ideas" (3:412). But rather than celebrate it as potentiality, Osmond slowly snuffs out Isabel's mind and transmogrifies her from kinetic sensibility to static artifact. He looks upon Isabel as a "figure in his collection of choice objects" and counsels her to make her life "a work of art" (4:7, 15). The rub for James is the difference between Isabel as work of art in Ralph's sense, that is, kinetic and vital, always in process because open to the phenomena of the world, and Isabel as work of art in Osmond's sense, that is, as artifact, completed, sterile, static, and, effectually removed from the shaping influence of the world. Isabel chooses the latter through a super-subtle (mis)reading and (mis)understanding which exemplifies, to James, the danger putative and formulaic art presents to the individual subject and culture as a whole. In order to follow James's nuances here we need to examine the connections Isabel inadvertently draws between Osmond and the artist seated before a window in the Preface's house of fiction. The parallels between Osmond and the silent watcher are doubly relevant. First, they provoke understanding of the danger to art and life Osmond's sterility presents; and second, they expose Isabel's own complicity in Osmond's vision, her desire to remove herself from life and join Osmond at the window.

James represents the consequence of Isabel's misreading of Osmond by an elaborate parallel between Osmond's influence upon her and a journey in which Isabel "had taken all the first steps in the purest confidence and then suddenly found the infinite vista of a multiplied life to be a dark, narrow alley with a dead wall at the end" (4:189). The house of fiction is similarly described as offering an infinite vista from "mere holes in a dead wall" (Preface, *Portrait of a Lady*, 1075). Like the Preface's house with its "posted presence of the watcher," Osmond's mansion too has at its aperture "the consciousness of the artist" (1075): "Osmond's beautiful mind seemed to peep down from a small high window and mock at her" (4:196). But James's description of the house in the Preface is to explain the place wherein the phenomena, the impressions of the world, are transfigured into the vital beauty of art. The Preface's house has a vitality about it; Osmond's is "the house of darkness, the house of dumbness, the house of suffocation" (4:196). James's condemnation of Osmond's manner of artistic production and Osmond's sensibility is most forcefully apparent in this description of the dank and sterile abode which reflects his mind. Isabel strengthens the condemnation when she laments Osmond's "faculty for making everything wither that he touched" (4:188). And James's declaration "Tell me what the artist is, and I will tell you of what he has *been* conscious" effectively completes his portrait of Osmond and the threat his sensibility poses to both life and art (Preface, 1075). For by cultivating convention Osmond has sacrificed creativity, one of the most vital features of a life of the imagination. Paul Armstrong captures the dangers James indicates in Osmond's system nicely by noting "Neither [Osmond] nor Madame Merle show that serious engagement of artistic freedom with the limits of structure without which art's transcendent powers lapse and only banal conventions remain" (*Phenomenology*, 114).

James marks a crucial failure or lack of practical wisdom in the perceptual disjunction between what Isabel believes Osmond to be and who he really is. Isabel does mistake Osmond's courting of convention, misreading his tightly drawn perceptual horizon as an ambiguity which promises limitlessness. In trying to take Osmond's measure she celebrates his "*pose*" for intellectual certitude and his negativity as plenitude. In justifying herself to Ralph she explains Osmond's lure as being his freedom to be and do whatever he wants exactly because he is nothing and has no claims upon him: he has "no property, no title, no honours, no houses, no lands, nor position, nor reputation, nor brilliant belongings of any sort. It is the total absence of all these things that please me" (4:144, 74). Yet, as James suggests through the rhetoric of Isabel's argument, in celebrating

Osmond's lack she effectively decontextualizes Osmond in an (un)conscious effort to recontextualize him according to her desire. In other words, Isabel commits the error that social living often leads one into.

By presenting Osmond as superficially attractive, James simultaneously reveals the flaw in Isabel's capacity for judgment and suggests, more generally, the need to cultivate discrimination. For though Osmond does mislead Isabel to a certain extent, he cannot be accused of being duplicitous in any vulgar way. He does not lie in any generally understood sense of the term. He simply admits to embodying a standard, to being "convention itself" (4:21). What he never explains to Isabel is that he lives "exclusively for the world," for convention, after all, can have none but a communal/public mode of existence (4:144). But then this is exactly what attracts her to Osmond, the opportunity to become the standard-bearer of taste. Isabel's moment of folly is in accepting a counterfeit for the real thing, and wrongly seeing in Osmond's spurious version the grandeur she wants to embody and take possession of. As Armstrong similarly notes, "She makes culture the object of an extravagant dream of innocence that idealizes and idolizes it" (*Phenomenology*, 114).

It is here, in Isabel's desire to become a standard-bearer, that we find her complicity in the bargain she makes with Osmond and the (un)conscious understanding of and attraction to exactly what Osmond represents. Isabel sees in Osmond the opportunity to join him at his window, to judge the world as he does, to make herself an object of envy. But in Jamesian aesthetics, envy, or an attempt to produce envy is often associated with the collector, always a dubious title in James's work. For instance, in *The Portrait of a Lady*, it is envy which Ned Rosier – the little collector – feels for Madame Merle's collection, and envy which attracts Rosier initially to Isabel and Pansy, whom he sees as "really a consummate piece" (4:90). Isabel's admission of this motivation accompanies her criticisms of Osmond's narrowness, never recognizing her own desire for perceptual constriction. "Instead of leading to the high places of happiness, from which the world would seem to lie below one, so that one could look down with a sense of exaltation and advantage, and judge and choose and pity," her life with Osmond "led rather downward and earthward, into realms of restriction and depression where the sound of other lives, easier and freer, was heard as from above, and where it served to deepen the feeling of failure" (4:189). What James shows in this explanation is how much Isabel neglects to see her own appropriativeness, her own desire to remove herself from the world, to elevate herself and pass judgment, her own exaltation at having become a measure of convention. Life under Ralph's system put the burden on Isabel's imagination and her creative response to experience, a burden she readily throws off in favor of the opportunity to follow and emulate a finished product. In other words, she throws off the task of original in favor of the ease of the copyist's versions: "she felt a delicate glow of shame as she thought how easy [life] now promised to become for herself" (4:60).

By choosing stasis over kinesis, finished product over process, sterility over vitality, Isabel precipitates the end of her personal development and thus betrays one of the most vital requirements of a life of the imagination which, by necessity, is always in process. James was adamant that "[t]he *whole* of anything is never told" as he explained in defense of the novel end in his Notebook entries (*Notebooks*, 18). Isabel's desire to effectuate a delusive appearance of finality suggests her acceptance of herself as finished artifact rather than creative artist. It is in depicting Isabel as an artifact that James most suggestively reveals her failure to meet the requirements of a life of the imagination. The irony in *The Portrait of a Lady* is that despite her plea for freedom Isabel just fits too well into Osmond's museum. The skill with which she presents a "mask" to the world, and the finesse with which she manages her "Thursday evenings," undermine arguments like Ralph's (and much criticism) that lay the blame on Osmond's tyranny. Isabel's ability to emulate Osmond is uncanny, so much so that Ralph is moved to comment that he recognizes in her "the hand of the master" (4:141, 142). Like Osmond, Isabel has developed an ability to produce an impression of being enviable. Ralph notes "she appeared to be leading a life of the world," people speak of her as "having a 'charming position'":

it was supposed, among many people, to be a privilege even to know her. Her house was not open to everyone, and she had an evening in the week to which people were not invited as a matter of course. She lived with a certain magnificence, but you needed to be a member of her circle to perceive it; for there was nothing to gape at, nothing to criticize, nothing even to admire, in the daily proceedings of Mr and Mrs Osmond. (4:142)

James wants the reader to question whether Isabel's fitfulness and tendency toward "exaggerations," that "she had been curious, and now was indifferent," are indicative of a consciousness which has been extinguished by Osmond, or of the closure of Isabel's mind, which would be indicative of her complicity in drawing the experiential boundaries (4:143). That is, could Isabel's lack of rebelliousness toward being drawn into Osmond's dungeon be more indicative of her willingness to accompany Osmond than of Osmond's tyranny? When Ralph discovers that she "represented Gilbert Osmond," and Goodwood finds her impenetrable, "perfectly inscrutable," we have to wonder whether Isabel's ability to emulate and "pose" suggests a skill worthy of Osmond but not produced by him. These images Isabel produces on her own. To say Osmond is wholly responsible is to render Isabel so meek as to discount her entire experience. But to inculpate her is to find in James's *Portrait* a critique of a certain brand of what James saw passing as art and artist, and the dangers such art and artists present to life. This spurious version produces lifeless impressions, art manqué. As Freedman has argued, Isabel "shares a good many of the more problematic qualities of Osmond's aestheticism," and "it is these qualities that cause her to fall under his control" (*Professions of Taste*, 155). James makes the point by showing Isabel's world grow dark, by commenting in passing on the death of Isabel's and Osmond's child "six months after his birth" (4:96). The utter lack of commentary on what would otherwise be a central and agonizing event in most marriages, suggests how fully James wants us to see the aesthetic attitude Isabel has joined as sterile. That the product of this union should die is a matter of course.

VIII

James impresses upon his audience the consequences of perceptual constriction through Isabel's midnight vigil. In his Preface to the novel, James proudly explains how "the vigil of searching criticism ... is obviously the best thing in the book," representing a "landmark," not just for Isabel, but for himself.[22] For Isabel, the vigil, sparked by the "anomaly" of coming upon her husband "sitting while Madame Merle stood," allows her to reread her life and come to a more complete understanding of who and what she is, who and what Osmond is, and how she and Osmond came to be (4:164). While consciously recomposing her life to date Isabel reaches the height of her capacity to absorb and transfigure impressions as a Jamesian figure of the artist. By presenting Isabel "motionlessly *seeing*," James allows the form of the narrative, its internal process, to contain as much transfigured impression as there is in the novel as whole (Preface, 1084). Seated by a dying fire Isabel redramatizes before her mind the impressions her life with Osmond have produced and transfigures them into knowledge she uses to construct a more complete understanding of herself and her world. In so doing, Isabel translates the impressions of her lived experience and produces a text which approximates James's outlines for artistic production.

Furthermore, "motionlessly *seeing*" aligns Isabel with the artistic consciousness seated before the window studying the world. The discoveries Isabel makes as she watches the shades of her past move through her present frame of reference reveal not only what James explained elsewhere as the multifoldness of reality,[23] but the nature of understanding itself. "Experience is never limited" and reality "is immense," as James duly noted, so the demands of our understanding necessarily place us in the position of having to construct a picture of the world based on what we see and what we expect lies hidden but follows from that which is present ("Art of Fiction," 52). In this sense understanding is in a perpetual dialectic between a present situation which always remains partially hidden but requires action and a retrospection which often brings what was hidden into focus and allows one to complete the picture. The narrative structure of chapter forty-two thus imitates the process of Isabel's hermeneutic struggle, laying bare her struggle to understand on the one hand, and her dawning awareness of how much she is the author of her own present misfortunes on the other.[24] The chapter forty-two vigil can be seen then as representative of Isabel's continuing movement from her early idealism to a more historically verifiable "realism," as Elizabeth Deeds Ermarth uses the term. In Ermarth's system Isabel could be described as encountering the implications of "the realist technique," in that the vigil provides a manageable distance which allows "the subjective spectator or the subjective consciousness to see the multiple viewpoints and so to find the form of the whole in what looks from a closer vantage point like a discontinuous array of specific cases" (*Realism and Consensus*, 35). Certainly Isabel discovers upon reflection more than one "anomalous" situation in her past relations with Madame Merle, with Osmond, and in her own perceived understanding of herself, discovering in the process the power of reflection.

Wolfgang Iser's explanation of the discovery process as it is
involved in the act of reading helps explain James's achievement
with Isabel's vigil, especially since Isabel's vigil adopts the dynamic
of reader (Isabel) confronting text (Osmond and her marriage). Iser
sees reading as an "activity" which "can be characterized as a sort
of kaleidoscope of perspectives, preintentions, recollection" which
come together and form the "virtual dimension of the text," that is,
the union of "text and imagination" (*Implied Reader*, 279). In reading
through a text we commit incidents to memory and develop
anticipations of what each sentence to follow will hold. Thus the
reader endows the text with expectations based on assumptions
drawn from what has been revealed and what retained or hidden. As
the reader moves through the text the dynamics between the present
unfolding, the past memory, and future anticipation reveal both the
construction of the text and the implications of the reader's own
desires in the construction of understanding. Thus, as Iser notes,
"the reader, in establishing these interrelations between past, present
and future, actually causes the text to reveal its potential multiplicity
of connections. These connections are the product of the reader's
mind working on the raw material of the text, though they are not
the text itself" (278). Iser explains this process elsewhere as the
reader's "wandering viewpoint," a special relation between text and
reader characterized by "a moving viewpoint which travels along
inside that which it has to apprehend" (*Art of Reading*, 109). Since the
reader digests aspects of the text "not in isolation but embedded in a
particular context" when one of these "recalled context[s]" is called
forth, it "can be viewed from a point outside itself," enabling the
possibility of revealing aspects which had heretofore been hidden
"when the fact had settled in the memory" (116). Textual apprehension then involves a constant juxtaposing of past background against
present reassessment in light of the present situation of the wandering viewpoint, an "apperception" which throws light on the
present:[25]

This feature of the reading process is of great significance for the
compilation of the aesthetic object. As the reader's conscious mind is
activated by the textual stimulus and the remembered apperception returns
as a background, so the unit of meaning is linked to the new reading
moment in which the wandering viewpoint is now situated. But as the
perspective invoked already possessed a configurative meaning and does
not return in isolation, it must inevitably provide a differentiated spectrum

of observation for the new perspective which has recalled it and which thereby undergoes an increasing degree of individualization. (117)

In other words, Iser's explanation of the reading process can also explain how Isabel's remembered impressions of Osmond and herself constitute an apperception which impresses itself upon her present frame of reference and allows her to reconstitute her understanding in light of the retroactive enlightenment.[26]

In the course of her meditative vigil Isabel comes to recognize the manifestations of her own fancy in her construction of Osmond's virtual dimension. The current perception of her wandering view-point forces her to acknowledge the degree to which the Osmond she became enamored of and desirous to possess was a product of his surface text and her fanciful imagination that he was "the first gentleman in Europe." The thought of him being so, she admits, "was the reason she had married him" (4:197). Isabel's rereading of Osmond involves a perceptual shift because the apperception of her earlier understanding of Osmond's virtual dimension reveals itself to have been based on the deceptive and faulty assumptions of her understanding. Her narrative documents the deceptions of fancy which led her to imagine "a world of things that had no substance. She had had a more wondrous vision of him, fed through charmed senses and oh such a stirred fancy" (4:192). But the "new perspec-tive" which has recalled the past shows it to be the product of a misreading – "she had not read him right":

she had seen only half his nature then, as one saw the disk of the moon when it was partly masked by the shadow of the earth. She saw the full moon now – she saw the whole man. She kept still, as it were, so that he should have a free field, and yet in spite of all this she had mistaken a part for the whole. (4:191)

It is just this mistake which inculpates Isabel in the misreading. For it is not convincing enough to pass off her disappointment with an "I just didn't read him right!" That Isabel mistakes a part for the whole is true, but not expiatory. Isabel also constructs a whole from a part, creating in Osmond and their marriage a grandeur which would exclude the responsibilities endemic to the world Ralph has offered her.

James's determination to foreground the dangers of misinterpreta-tion or of selective and preconceived interpretation through his exposure of Isabel's hermeneutic struggle accentuates his belief in the need to cultivate perceptual awareness. The greater part of this cultivation means being aware of one's own interpretive categories and the subconscious influence those prejudices exert. The narrative structure of Isabel's vigil therefore is meant to compel readers to carry out their own inter- and extra-textual revaluation. In realizing the degree to which we have been incorrect in our projections of *The Portrait of a Lady*'s outcome, we are led, by extension, to an awareness of the dangers we expose ourselves to by our subconscious projections upon the world at large. In James's hermeneutics, the extended exegesis Isabel's vigil provokes is an example of the fundamental destructuring and recreative quality of Jamesian aesthetics and a plea for Jamesian art's active quality. More specifically yet, for James Isabel's vigil was a vehicle through which he could expose, via her own discovery, the deficiencies of her particular "aestheticizing vision," as Freedman has argued. In Isabel's movement "beyond this form of apprehension," beyond the "reifying aestheticism of an Osmond," James shows how his own brand of aestheticism was more "informed by the original sense of *aesthesis*, as a heightening or perfection of the act of perception" (*Professions of Taste*, 162–63). The shift in emphasis is crucial for an understanding of James's art. Critics have long focused on this aspect of Jamesian aesthetics and used it in order to classify James as a genteel asethete whose valorization of perception allowed him to adopt the perspective of the disengaged, superior observer whose fiction mirrored that stance. If we recall from our discussion of *The American*, the Aristotelian notion of *aesthēsis* as "a faculty of discrimination that is concerned with the apprehending of concrete particulars, rather than universals," and couple that with James's understanding not only of art's civic value, but of his conception of himself as an artist whose role was to cultivate in his audience a power of perception which would enhance their civic imagination, then the charges of detached connoisseurship seem in error (Nussbaum, *Fragility*, 300). Thus in contesting the reification of James as detached aesthete Freedman has shown how James's aesthetics, as captured in Isabel Archer's developing ability to use perception as a hermeneutic tool, "emphasizes" a deep "embeddedness in historical process[es]" and a committed "participation in the human community" (*Professions of Taste*, 165).

James brings his audience to this deeper conception of his aesthetics by allowing us to witness Isabel's reawakening, which includes allowing us to see with her exactly where she went wrong. Once again Iser can help us arrive at a more clear understanding of Isabel's effort at reconfiguration. For instance, Isabel finds in Osmond a reflection of her own inclinations just as, according to Iser, the "manner in which a reader experiences a text will reflect his own disposition" (*Implied Reader*, 281). Isabel thus endows Osmond with a reflection of her own desires which she then seeks to satisfy. In this way Isabel finds herself a victim of not understanding and ignoring the fact that one is always already situated in the present moment, an unavoidable condition of being in the world. But Isabel errs in believing she has a more critical, more discerning and reflective understanding of the situation. In the opening stages of her relationship with Osmond the implications of this situatedness and Isabel's lack of discernment mean that not only is Isabel unable to get a more distanced perspective of Osmond, what Gadamer calls "effective-historical reflection," but that during the initial moments of contact between the pair Isabel imbues Osmond with the desires of her own mind, making Osmond into something quite other than what he really is (*Truth and Method*, 269). From that point on Isabel becomes relatively blind to the Osmond Ralph and the reader see. The degree of Isabel's blindness and refusal to *see* Osmond is represented, as we have noted, in her travels to the Eastern Mediterranean. In Iser's words, by reflecting one's "own disposition," the "literary text acts as a kind of mirror" (*Implied Reader*, 281). And so on the one hand Isabel finds in Osmond the mirroring of her desire to experience a life altogether different from that which Ralph opened to her, and on the other, the reader discovers Isabel's complicity in the deception practiced by Osmond and her own, probably unconscious, desire to allow Osmond to reform her as an artifact reflective of his own mind (4:194–95).

That Osmond turns out such a tyrant whose "egotism lay hidden like a serpent in a bank of flowers" is certainly an unanticipated development, but Isabel deceives herself when she professes shock at Osmond's demand for social recognition (4:196). James's point here is that one can be an arbiter of taste, the measure of convention only by tacit community approval. Osmond, the narrative explains, "was a gentleman who studied style" (3:328). But in James's aesthetics there is a tremendous distinction between *studying* style and *creating* a style. That distinction, of course, is measured in the difference between a passive and active stance toward reality. James cultivated an active stance through an aesthetics which was fundamentally destructuring and recreative. This was *his style* and it required one to read his aesthetics as active and engaged. Unfortunately, it is perhaps only when James's aesthetics is juxtaposed against the more detached and passive aesthetics of the aesthetes Osmond represents, or the aesthetic paralysis he portrayed in *Roderick Hudson*, that the full power and subtlety of James's style is most evident.[27] Osmond, as a collector, a follower of style, cultivates a purely detached because completely disengaged aesthetics which wins approval from those who know no better, and from elevating himself as a self-ratifying authority. Indeed, the novel suggests Osmond's smallness proves even more rude: "this base, ignoble world ... was after all what one was to live for; one was to keep it for ever in one's eye, in order not to enlighten or convert or redeem it, but to extract from it some recognition of one's own superiority"; but Isabel also admits to relishing "a sense of exaltation and advantage" superiority affords (4:197, 189).[28] Her successful presentation of herself at the Thursday evening gatherings is an example. And though Isabel is right to note how Osmond actively extinguished the light of her perceptual horizon, how he "deliberately, almost malignantly ..., put the lights out one by one," what she neglects to note or accept is her desire that he do and in so doing finish what she started. James reveals the consequences of such a choice by foregrounding the difference between Isabel's desire for a degree of perceptual limitation and Osmond's perceptual tyranny. The world is the difference, for rather than allow a flexible circumference to Isabel's horizon, Osmond permits her the vision of a "dark, narrow alley with a dead wall at the end" (4:189–90).

The virtual dimension produced by Isabel's meditative vigil can be seen then as the realization of Isabel's potential as a Jamesian artist figure. For in redramatizing her impressions Isabel is able to transfigure them from a spurious and benighted version into an understanding which matches the landscape of fact. James's irony here is that the understanding Isabel arrives at, the work of art she produces, merely catches up to that which was present to her perception originally. In this sense the apperception allows her to catch up to the present. What the vigil fails to provide is a means for encountering the future, a predicament made manifest by Isabel's rather glaring inability to see exactly who Madame Merle is until she is told bluntly by the Countess Gemini and Madame Merle herself:

"*Ce me dépasse*, if you don't mind my saying so," the Countess exclaims, "the things, all round you, that you've appeared to succeed in not knowing" (4:365). As it is on Osmond, James's statement about what the artist's consciousness reveals is an apt commentary on Isabel, whose meditative vigil produces an accurate rendering of her perceptual imprisonment. Here we call forward once again Isabel's cry to Ralph that the cup of experience is a poisoned drink. In chapter forty-two Isabel learns how she has been involved in mixing the cup of her experience, the poison of which reduces her capacity for openness so that she can only continue to experience impressions which fall within the rubric of Osmond's perceptual limitations.

Within the context of the novel the consequences of tasting the mixture she and Osmond concoct are that it conditions Isabel's future. The novel's hotly disputed end thus seems to suggest Isabel's return is a result not of pride, nor of obligation to her marriage vow, nor of a desire to aid Pansy who is as ground in Osmond's mill as Isabel. Her final return is a return to the only world Isabel can know. Her experience has been such that the rest of the world is effectively closed to her, is a world she can only watch but in which she can never be, which matches, ironically, the common perversion of James's explanation of the artist as observer. This is the background against which we must come to understand the absolute disarray into which Goodwood's kiss throws Isabel. James implies this reading of the end by having Isabel feel her world suddenly "take the form of a mighty sea, where she floated in fathomless waters" (4:435). Goodwood's kiss comes from a world outside the perimeters of Isabel's perceptual horizon, and it causes her to feel "herself sink and sink," to "beat with her feet, in order to catch herself" and reach an understanding amidst "the confusion, the noise of the waters" (4:435–36). Isabel reacts to the collision between worlds by returning to Rome, where, having tasted of a certain type of experience she can find her feet on the ground and deal with what she knows. However limited she finds life with Osmond, her knowledge of that world affords her a measure of power. In choosing to return she demonstrates how Osmondian sensibility destroys true artistic sensibility and controls the world not by perception but by limitation.

Does she then really become consistently wise, as James notes upon the outset of her European adventure? Is a return to Osmond an example of Isabel's hard won wisdom? One wonders if James suggests wisdom comes at the expense of having one's illusions shattered and learning to live within that disenchanted world. If so, then, we can say that in *The Portrait of a Lady* Isabel frames herself by virtue of the experiences she has and those she chooses to have. She frames herself in a world of her own design.

But there is something more at stake in the novel's claim about Isabel's hard won practical wisdom. There is an essential irony in having what we could call Isabel's *phronēsis* come to her somewhat too late. At the conclusion of this stage of her portrait Isabel has committed herself to a world she constructed, but her knowledge of that world at the end of her textual experience leaves the reader with the sense that it is a world the present Isabel Archer can no longer inhabit. It is as though the completion of Isabel's experience leaves her estranged from her past and disconnected from her future. Thus, it is not with some small irony that James ends *The Portrait of a Lady* with Isabel said to be on a train going back to Rome. That we never see her arrive is James's way of bringing this chapter of her life to a close while yet retaining the text's essential open-endedness. Leaving Isabel caught between worlds – the London she has just quit and the Rome she left behind – James leaves her within the realm of potentiality, forces the reader to shoulder the burden of conclusion, and demonstrates once again, the active component of his aesthetics.

CHAPTER 4

Lambert Strether and the negativity of experience

And then the justice,
In fair round belly with good capon lined,
With eyes severe and beard of formal cut,
Full of wise saws and modern instances,
And so he plays his part.

William Shakespeare, *As You Like It*

I

The conclusion of James's outline for *The Ambassadors* raises a difficult question for readers of James's fiction. The outline calls for a final conversation between Maria Gostrey and Lambert Strether in which Strether is given "a clear vision of his opportunity" with Maria ("Project," 390). In the final text James remains faithful to this last attempt at connection between the pair. The interesting question comes in James's reason for Strether's refusal of Maria's offer of marriage. James explains how Strether "*can't* accept," how he "won't," or "doesn't," that it is "too late" for such an intimate partnership at this stage of his life. These are reasons we can understand given our insight into Strether at the conclusion of all that has happened. But James goes on to explain how Strether "has come so far through his total experience that he has come out on the other side – on the other side, even, of a union with Miss Gostrey" (390). The question here is what does it mean to pass so through an experience that you come out on the other side, that you emerge into a world completely altered? Into what world, that is, does Strether emerge? To reason through James's suggestion is to confront the whole notion of experience and understanding not only in *The Ambassadors*, but in all of James's projects up to this late novel.

The difficulty of making sense of *The Ambassadors*'s end, particularly Strether's refusal to ground himself in Maria Gostrey, is doubly compounded, first by the permutations of Strether's subjectivity throughout the course of his Parisian experience, and second by the ambiguity of the novel's closing comment – "Then there we are!" (22:327). Readers have long wondered where "we are" points to, for Strether and Maria Gostrey as much as for themselves. To ask this question, one James purposely plants at the novel's close, is to ask about the basic structure of understanding as it functions in James's hermeneutics. We recall that *The Ambassadors* closes with Maria Gostrey offering sanctuary to Strether and that he refuses it on the grounds that his "only logic," is "[n]ot, out of the whole affair, to have got anything for myself" (22:326). But Strether's idea of pulling his pockets out to show how he comes away from the affair empty handed is really an underhanded way of disguising how much he has secured for himself.[1] We could say that had Strether accomplished something with Chad and Madame de Vionnet, in the sense of having Chad remain faithful to their affair, Strether would have been compensated. By refusing to stay Strether does get nothing out of it all, but in getting "nothing" refutes Woollett's claims to the contrary. In taking this stance Strether is finally able to throw off the bonds of Woollett and achieve the freedom his Parisian experience evokes. To achieve this is to achieve something indeed from "nothing"; it is to achieve a height of dignity long since abandoned by the Woollett Strether.[2] To read the novel this way is to see it as an elegiac recovery of, to borrow Strether's own phrase, "the pale figure of his real youth" (21:83–84).

II

In a persuasive and insightful deconstructive reading of *The Ambassadors*, Julie Rivkin, employing what Derrida refers to as " 'the logic of supplementarity'," argues rather forcefully that what I refer to as the permutations of Strether's subjectivity are "supplementations," a manifestation of the "logic of delegation" which governs the entire novel's narrative structure; in Rivkin's words, a "principle" of "displacement . . . compensating for sacrifices by creating a chain of ambassadors" beginning with James, moving through the Preface, embodied in the text, and made manifest in the "plurality dictated by the text's own logic of delegation – not *The Ambassador* but, rather, *The Ambassadors*" ("Logic of Delegation," 819–20). The outcome of

Rivkin's analysis is to show that what Strether discovers "as he replaces one truth about experience with another is that there is no stopping point in this logic of revision" (828). But in focusing on supplementarity, Rivkin deconstructs all notions of self in the novel and leaves Strether without *any* ground on which to come to understand the personal and public impact of his Parisian experience insofar as it assists in the development of his conception of self as permeable.[3] And one wonders here whether an argument which focuses on a deconstruction of the self in *The Ambassadors* retraces the ground Strether has already deconstructed over the course of his Parisian experience. After all, is not the goal for James and Strether not to get rid of or to "supplement" the self, but to make that self porous? To this extent *The Ambassadors* can be read as a text which tries to relocate rather than get rid of the self, and this includes a relocation outside deconstruction.

Furthermore, Rivkin's reading of the novel not only intensifies the ambiguity of Strether's final "Then there we are!" because just as it leaves Strether stuck, looking for yet another possible supplementary authority, it also leaves the reader out of the interpretive equation, in that all too typical role of passive spectator only too willing to watch but not be engaged in (Strether's) interpretive adventure. And while Rivkin rightly accords the concept of revision a crucial place in James's aesthetics, particularly revision of self, her deconstructive "supplementarity" is based more on a principle of replacement than revision, on resignation and passive observation than active participation. To this extent Rivkin sees Strether as continually displacing himself, continually living vicariously through the experiences of others as opposed to coming to understand and revise himself through the collective body of his personal and observed experiences. The difference here between Rivkin's "supplementarity" and what I call Strether's "permutations" is crucial because it suggests, in Rivkin's argument, that all Strether can ever come to understand of himself comes through "an infinite chain, ineluctably multiplying the supplementary mediations" which stand between Strether and himself (Derrida, qtd. in "Logic of Delegation," 819). "Permutations," on the other hand, suggest Strether is consistently and actively revising and expanding *his* conception of self and is more in keeping with James's own remarks about understanding from his Preface to *The American* where he says "The real represents to my perception the things we cannot possibly *not* know, sooner or later, in

one way or another" (1062–63). If we substitute "self" for "real" in
James's formulation, a substitution James's fiction encourages, then
reading Strether's developing sense of self and his conception of
what has and is happening both in Paris and in Woollett as a series
of permutations allows us perhaps to get a more clear picture of how
the process of understanding functions in James's hermeneutics and
the extent to which it depends on an attitude which regards
experience as shaping rather than corroborative.

In order to get a clear picture of who Lambert Strether is James
makes it clear that the reader must first come to understand
Strether's initial author-figure – Mrs. Newsome. All initial expressions of power and the text's initial interpretive direction emanate
from Mrs. Newsome. In a curious inversion James casts the Woollett
matriarch in a masculine authorial position only to undermine both
her authority as matriarch and interpretive coordinator. As Julie
Rivkin has noted, Mrs. Newsome functions as a parodic version of
the omniscient author whose allegiances belong to a narrowly realist
tradition James believed limiting to fiction because it is the product
of a covert ideology which purports to present a real picture of life
while secretly confining that life within an artificially closed system
("Logic of Delegation," 824). As realist author Mrs. Newsome
follows a line of strict referentialism, cementing words and referents
together in order to impose understanding on what James understood to be an ever-evolving and fluid reality. James accentuates the
putative security of the Realist position embodied in Mrs. Newsome
by allowing her the function of overseer whose control of understanding is so great that she need not present herself as mediator.
Indeed Mrs. Newsome's absence is the most powerful presence
throughout the novel as each of the characters try in successive and
various ways to accommodate their experience of the world with
Mrs. Newsome's determined version.[4]

Mrs. Newsome is, of course, the author of Woollett's purely
referential approach to reality. We recall that Strether early on
admits to having once referred to Mrs. Newsome as "Queen
Elizabeth" (21:51), a comparison which not only establishes Mrs.
Newsome's position as the power in opposition to the events which
transpire in Europe, but also the interpretive medium through
whom everything must pass in order to be legitimized. One can see
Mrs. Newsome's attempt to control interpretation in her decision to
deploy an ambassador. An ambassador is chosen for similitude, how

well he or she matches the disposition of those in power.[5] By sending Strether to read Paris, Mrs. Newsome first assumes he will see things just as she would, but in so doing explicitly establishes herself as an opposing author figure in that her choice of an ambassador is an attempt to write the novel in her way. In Mrs. Newsome's novel Strether is to function as a matronym, the synecdochical manifestation of Woollett's voice heard in Paris. That he unexpectedly differs from his putative author is James's way of saying, first, that even authorship must give way to the requirements of individual vision, and second, that the constrictive rigor of American comfort in likemindedness embodied in Mrs. Newsome's political system cannot sustain its own weight when its representative travels beyond the umbra of her control. Thus, Lambert Strether becomes the site on which James's critique of narrow referentialism and its attendant epistemological limitations is played out. And what James shows in the conflict between Mrs. Newsome's and Strether's understanding is how completely Mrs. Newsome has perfected a management of reality and the attendant epistemological limitations that go along with such a narrow and exclusive referentialism.

It is interesting to note how often commentators identify Mrs. Newsome with philosophical positions, especially those positions which claim to possess a sure-fire method for understanding and behavior. Ross Posnock, for instance, has cited Mrs. Newsome's "implacable rationality" as an indication of her "Cartesian method" (*Trial of Curiosity*, 225). As a New Englander of her time Mrs. Newsome strikes one as an example of the Puritan internalization of the Law that both Henry Jameses – Sr. and Jr. – held with a good deal of impatience and skepticism. Henry James Jr.'s complaint with Puritan rigor such as Mrs. Newsome's was centered on his conception that individuals such as the Woollett doyenne draw their absolutes and certitudes from within and carry out their own self-serving positions through a self-ratifying spiritual authority. It is perhaps this aspect of Mrs. Newsome's persona that Strether hears as "the hum of vain things" in her letters to the ambassador (21:82). Both descriptions – Mrs. Newsome as the embodiment of a strict interpretive methodology or of Puritan zeal – are apt, for Mrs. Newsome leaves nothing to chance, refuses to accept the possibility that the individual has anything less than absolute control over her own moral agency.[6]

Indeed, without exception, each of Mrs. Newsome's acts – from wanting to bring Chad home, to choosing an ambassador who will act her agent in Paris, to redeploying an alternate in Sarah Pocock, to severing relations with Strether – is an attempt to extend control over her world. James's characterization of Mrs. Newsome as "all cold thought," as an agent who operates via an understanding which simply "doesn't admit surprises," sets her in direct opposition to his understanding of art and life (22:220). James's famous formulation is that the novel, if it is to be a good novel, "lives upon exercise, and the very meaning of exercise is freedom" ("Art of Fiction," 49). How far Mrs. Newsome falls from James's ideal is apparent in Strether's description of her.

"It's a fact that, I think, describes and represents her; and it falls in with what I tell you – that she's all, as I've called it, fine cold thought. She had, to her own mind, worked the whole thing out in advance, and worked it out for me as well as for herself. Whenever she has done with that, you see, there's no room left; no margin, as it were, for any alteration. She's filled as full, packed as tight, as she'll hold, and if you wish to get anything more or different either out or in – ... you've got morally and intellectually to get rid of her." (22:222)

To be sure, Mrs. Newsome's closure is indicative of what Gadamer would say is a refusal to acknowledge the claim upon one that experience makes. To be able to "work the whole thing out in advance" suggests Mrs. Newsome deals with knowledge as though it were a quantifiable thing with which she is filled to the brim. And this is exactly how Mrs. Newsome approaches the world, not just as though reality were a finite quantity one could contain, but that mastery depends upon containment, depends, that is, on eliminating life itself. The reduction to the absurd here is Sarah Pocock's testament to closed-mindedness. When Madame de Vionnet offers herself as a guide through Paris, Sarah tartly responds: "As you know I have been to Paris. I *know* Paris" (22:91). Strether's final realized picture of Mrs. Newsome is thus galvanic. Despite his multiple and fluid descriptions of Chad, of Madame de Vionnet, of Paris, he is unable to penetrate Mrs. Newsome's interpretive fortifications: "I haven't touched her. She won't *be* touched. I see it now as I have never done; and she hangs together with a perfection of her own ... that does suggest a kind of wrong in *any* change in her composition" (22:222). For Mrs. Newsome, one has a certain number of experiences that matter and then understanding of "the world" comes into sharp focus. Life, like the ideology of realism James found such a masquerade, is itself a process of strict control, of stasis.[7]

Numerous James characters match this rather mercenary description: we think immediately of the early Christopher Newman, of Caspar Goodwood, of Henrietta Stackpole, Mona Brigstock, Waymarsh, Sarah and Jim Pocock, Adam Verver, Mrs. Costello, to mention only a few. One defining characteristic of these characters is that their worldly and, to varying degrees, mercantile successes spring from their ability to visualize the world as unalterably black and white, good and bad. James continually critiqued this forced dualism which he saw as a powerful and debilitating force that transformed reality so as to meet the requirements of a commodifying ideology which accumulated experience as though it were capital. Attitudes such as Mrs. Newsome's served further to displace what James felt to be the broadening value of experience and, by extension, art, by a narrow reification which had as its aim the reduction of life itself to some quantifiable thing. The comic version of Sarah's obdurate response comes from Strether's "travelling" companion, Waymarsh, who moves through Europe completely insulated from any sense of actually being there; as he says "I don't seem to feel anywhere in tune" (21:29). James exaggerates the Waymarsh phenomenon by having the "exile from Melrose" turn down the opportunity of a play because, having seen two and a circus, he feels he has seen about all there is (21:49).

For James, Mrs. Newsome's refusal to recognize that "Experience is never limited . . . never complete" belies the very responsibilities of consciousness and sets such restrictive limits on the role of art as to make art irrelevant ("Art of Fiction," 52). James battled the threatened reduction of art to play, to diversion from the real business of living his entire life. For instance, the Preface to *The Golden Bowl* ends with the oft-quoted "art is nothing if not exemplary" (1341). In other words, Strether characterizes Mrs. Newsome as distinctly unJamesian, as a prosaic anti-novelistic individual who neither involves herself actively in life nor engages actively in perception, but instead sits magisterially atop the whole affair, where, as Rivkin notes, "her fixity of purpose makes it impossible for her to imagine any shift or deviation" ("Logic of Delegation," 824). To shift or deviate is to question, to question to suggest error, and to admit error is to bring the whole edifice of understanding toppling over.[8]

Readers of James must bear in mind the full import of James's critique of closed-mindedness such as Woollett's. It is not just that these characters' reduced perceptual horizon artificially constrains life for themselves (and that this constraint makes for interesting fiction), their imposed constraints have a more violent and socially realized force when they similarly imprison everyone and everything they encounter. As a writer of travel literature, and as a master of international fiction, James was acutely aware of the dangers in any form of public or private ethnocentrism. His novels in the broadest possible sense are an attempt to overcome cultural and personal postulations. What is worth further consideration with *The Ambassadors*, is that in large measure the situation of the novel reverses the focus he followed in his 1877 novel *The American*. Where for the most part Parisian rigidity is the antagonist in the earlier novel, in the latter it is America's moral obduracy. Examined from this perspective *The Ambassadors* can be read as an episode in social history, especially when one considers the novel's publication at the dawn of the twentieth century. Such a reading would foreground James's commitment to try and steer a powerful but young nation into its role as international figurehead for the twentieth century. What such a reading suggests is that James saw America as veering dangerously off course and that, taken with his late short-stories (most of which are set in America) and *The American Scene*, *The Ambassadors* is an elegiac lament not for some idyllic past, but for a present which has forgotten how to live and a future which will close itself off from all that comes down to it from the past. James makes this point most forcefully in his late, New York story "Crapy Cornelia," where his protagonist White-Mason comes up against a New York culture he finds "overwhelmingly alien" (*Complete Tales*, 12:335). James's disillusionment is given voice in White-Mason's observations of New York society:

This was clearly going to be the music of the future – that if people were but rich enough and furnished enough and fed enough, exercised and sanitated and manicured and generally advised and advertised and made "knowing" enough, *avertis* enough, as the term appeared to be nowadays in Paris, all they had to do for civility was to take the amused ironic view of those who might be less initiated. In *his* time, when he was young or even when he was a little less middle-aged, the best manners had been the best kindness, and the best kindness had mostly been some art of not insisting on one's luxurious differences, of concealing rather, for common humanity, if not for common decency, a part at least of the intensity or the ferocity with which one might be "in the know." (348)

White-Mason's reference to the general "ferocity" with which one's being "'in the know'" is demonstrated in his New York sounds like a remark about Mrs. Newsome's Woollett in *The Ambassadors*. And it is in the complexity of Lambert Strether's evolving subjectivity that *The Ambassadors* becomes more than an anthropological study of conflicting cultures. Though the novel is such a study, it is also, more importantly, a study of how one learns to live within and through cultures, and how one learns to release subjective constraints and begin to live *with* the world rather than *in* a world. That distinction in *The Ambassadors* is registered through the development of Strether's ability to understand.

However before James allows us to see Strether as a challenge to Woollett's propensity to reification, he shows us how Strether too can be seen in Mrs. Newsome's reifying light. The difference between the pair is that Mrs. Newsome has orchestrated her life around rigorous principles of management which thwart any disruptive incursions.[9] Strether, on the other hand, has assumed the status of produced object. In other words, for Mrs. Newsome there is only *one* way to live, and she has mastered it. But her mastery has its limitations, one of which is its limited ability to respond to life, particularly, as Strether has it, the enjoyment of life.[10] Joy's attendant is play, and play's lack of control, which is precisely why Chad's bohemian behavior not only elicits such fantasies of depravity in the Woollett consciousness – Chad being a "young man a wicked woman has got hold of" – but why Woollett remains oblivious to Madame de Vionnet's positive influence and persists in characterizing her as "base, venal – out of the streets" (21:54–55). This can also be seen as the reason behind Sarah Pocock's ringing condemnation of Strether's expansive and open opinion of Madame de Vionnet as a woman. Sarah recoils at Strether's suggestion by asking him whether he

"can sacrifice mothers and sisters to her without a blush, and can make them cross the ocean on purpose to feel the more, and take from you the straighter, *how* you do it? ... Do you consider her even an apology for a decent woman?" (22:200, 202)

James's presentation of the violence of Woollett's condemnation of Marie de Vionnet leads one to believe that it is not the woman's threat of corrupting Chad which has raised Mrs. Newsome's concern, but the abandon she surely evokes in Woollett's son. It is as though what Woollett sees in the Parisian woman is a threat to their need for limits, for when limits are questioned (as Madam de Vionnet's affair with Chad suggests they are) the concept of control is challenged, and with the challenge of control comes the breakdown of moral and interpretive order.

It is perhaps for this reason that nurturing maternalism is only notable for its absence in the Woollett doyenne. What is more at issue is the disruptive threat Paris, and particularly Madame de Vionnet, pose to the managed order of things in Woollett. This is not to say that James was employing once more the stereotype of the Old World corrupting the innocence of the New. On the contrary, *The Ambassadors* makes it particularly clear that the corrupting force resides in the New World's suspicion of experience as a way to understanding. It is not with some small degree of irony that *The Ambassadors*, which takes place completely in Europe, is one of James's most probing autopsies of American culture. Leon Edel has commented effectively on this aspect of *The Ambassadors*. "America," he says, "is Mrs. Newsome, an implacable, immobile force, intransigent and exigent: she is there, in Woollett, or in a hundred cities where values are unambiguous, and where everyone pays a price – the price of muffled feeling, the conventional, the prescribed" (*The Master*, 76). Thus, despite being the prisoner of her own bad marriage, her own cultural and religious imperatives, Marie de Vionnet, in the most threatening way, represents the possibility of disagreement introduced by a questioning consciousness. This is exactly the defense of her Strether offers Sarah Pocock, who arrives in Paris as Mrs. Newsome's incarnation: "She has struck me from the first as wonderful ... she would probably have represented even for yourself something rather new and rather good" (22:202). Something new is precisely what Woollett does not want. Mrs. Newsome's Woollett has been characterized by unquestioning obedience, by a cultured understanding that restraint is the only governing principle. James reveals Mrs. Newsome's postulation as indicative of a conviction that her "personal sense" is synonymous with the objective sense, a point she displays when she severs her relations with Strether.

III

In an excerpt dealing with "The Study of Philosophy" in his *Prison Notebooks*, Antonio Gramsci makes several introductory observations

that offer a particularly good window onto the nature of the
negativity of Strether's experience in *The Ambassadors*. Gramsci
argues that one acquires a conception of the world through being a
member of "a particular grouping" of people who "share the same
mode of thinking and acting" (*Selections*, 324). This "conformism,"
Gramsci shows, is an inescapable mode of existence. The question
here, as Gramsci notes, is not whether the subject is socially
constructed, but what is the nature of the social construction. That
question being, as Gramsci notes, "of what historical type is the
conformism, the mass of humanity to which one belongs?" (324).
The answer necessarily leads one to an examination of self. In
relation to *The Ambassadors*, Strether's critical understanding of the
worlds of Woollett and Paris leads immediately to a relentless
examination of Strether himself. In James's words from the Preface,
Strether's interpretive "revolution" is the result of his experience of
being "thrown forward, rather, thrown quite with violence, upon his
lifelong trick of intense reflection" (1312). Thus, as though speaking
of Lambert Strether, Gramsci notes how the "starting-point of
critical elaboration is the consciousness of what one really is, and is
'knowing thyself' as a product of the historical process to date which
has deposited in you an infinity of traces, without leaving an
inventory" (*Selections*, 324).

How much James and Gramsci understand the self and one's
conception of the world as stratified composition is apparent in the
following juxtaposition. For Gramsci, our conception of the world is
"a response to certain specific problems posed by reality." These
problems are invariably "specific and 'original' in their immediate
relevance." The task of the interpreter is the attempt to try and
understand the present situation, the "quite specific present, with a
mode of thought elaborated for a past which is often remote and
superceded" (324). This, of course, is exactly the predicament of the
Woollett Strether trying to find his way in Paris. Already in London
Strether notes how those "before him and around him were not as
the types of Woollett," being that the restrictions of Woollett
consciousness allow for only two types – "the male and the female"
(21:53). The situation of Paris upends completely Strether's default
mechanism, as though Paris, so other-worldly, so like a "vast bright
Babylon," functions as an objective correlative that destabilizes
Strether's Woollett conformity and forces him to interrogate his
established hermeneutic practice. Paris, in other words, allows

Strether to question the nature of the conformism to which he has been subject.[11] James says as much directly in the Preface: "the false position for him ... was obviously to have presented himself at the gate of that boundless menagerie primed with a moral scheme of the most approved pattern which was yet framed to break down on any approach to vivid facts; that is to any and all liberal appreciation of them" (1311).

Strether's predicament, then, is to find a way of considering his present situation in Paris by either applying a mode of thought based on former experiences of Woollett, an interpretive paradigm now superseded by the active present of Paris, or to scrap his past and learn to live through his present experience by submitting to its own particular terms. To choose the former, James suggests, is to succumb to Woollett's prosaic safety and the pressure of Mrs. Newsome's interpretive demands; the latter choice is to grasp "an opportunity lost," revel in the ambiguity of Paris and allow experience to unravel and reconstitute Strether's understanding. One last note from James's Notebook comments on *The Ambassadors* brings the point home:

> my vague little fancy is that he "comes out," as it were (to London, to Paris – I'm afraid it *must* be Paris; if he's an American), to take some step, decide some question with regard to some one, in the sense of his old feelings and habits, and that the new influences, to state it roughly, make him act just in the opposite spirit – make him accept on the spot, with a *volte-face*, a wholly different inspiration. (*Notebooks*, 227)

IV

What about this *"volte-face"* James speaks of? As anyone who reads *The Ambassadors* quickly notices, sudden decision-making is not one of Strether's shortcomings. But *The Ambassadors* is about change, about the difficulty of reaching an understanding of anything, and about the danger of attempting to impose understanding on any situation. As we have seen, imposed understanding is Woollett's hermeneutic, a "method" which depends upon the removal of the interrogative.[12] James sets Strether at odds with his Woollett origins with the first sentence of the novel, a question, the first in what becomes an unceasing flow of questions – "Strether's first question, when he reached the hotel, was about his friend" (21:3). His next question is implied, but has to do with reflexive interrogation, with his mission of rescue, with the awakening sense not just of why he is in Europe, but who he is in the most fundamental sense. Strether's gaze is adjusted inward in the novel's second paragraph, revealing his amazement at "such a consciousness of personal freedom as he hadn't known for years; such a deep taste of change and of having above all for the moment nobody and nothing to consider" (21:4). James accentuates the sense of escape, of release from constraints, as the prevailing attitude Strether demonstrates in the initial stages of his European experience. Almost upon disembarking Strether breathes deep and revels in the sense of having "stolen away from every one alike," of giving himself over to "uncontrolled perception" (21:4, 50). Strether's strength, James explains in the Preface, is that he has "imagination galore" (1307), a quality that sets him apart from the Woollett crowd who have none – Sarah, Mrs. Newsome, and even Chad, as Strether points out.[13]

The atmosphere of release which suffuses the first pages of *The Ambassadors* deserves close scrutiny. That Europe provokes such a vision of freedom, such a sense of bounty for Strether, suggests more about Woollett and who or what Strether was there than what he is on the other side of the Atlantic. James accentuates the reader's sense that Woollett is a center of manipulative power by fore-grounding Strether's sense of release. On his first walk about Paris Strether pauses in the Luxembourg Gardens and gives way to "the plenitude of his consciousness." The chain of thought James drama-tizes in Strether's mind as he relaxes in the Gardens establishes once and for all Woollett's ideology. As Strether loses himself in the moment he finds it is "the difference, the difference of being just where he was and *as* he was, that formed the escape." However, escape brings with it the bewilderment "of his finding himself so free," so "young," so alive, which provokes an intrusion in Strether's picture of his Woollett image. Later, James similarly interrupts one of Strether's raptures with an intrusion of something from another reality Strether is trying to come to understand when he has Chad and Madame de Vionnet float into Strether's country idyll. This early rupture, like the boating scene, forces Strether to confront what cannot be done away with – in the Gardens' case the reality of his Woollett life: "poor Lambert Strether washed up on the sunny strand by the waves of a single day, poor Lambert Strether thankful for breathing-time and stiffening himself while he gasped" (21:81–82). The surprise of the intrusion, however, involves not just

the worn-out Woollett man, but the principal reason for his feeling
"so distinctly fagged out" (21:83).

There was nothing in his aspect or his posture to scandalize: it was only
true that if he had seen Mrs. Newsome coming he would instinctively have
jumped up to walk away a little. (21:82)

The progress of Strether's Luxembourg Gardens idyll is important:
Paris evokes a sense of escape, escape freedom, freedom a sense of
having done something wrong, something that would lead Mrs.
Newsome to extend a scolding finger across the Atlantic to wave in
Strether's face. The sense of the pathetic in Strether is evident in his
reaction to the thought of Mrs. Newsome seeing him in the Gardens.
"He would have come round and back to her bravely, but he would
first have had to pull himself together" (21:82). Indeed, this fixation
on, or willing submission to, the power of surveillance as well as the
unacceptable use of cultural certitudes as a way of manipulating and
monitoring behavior was something James detested in convention
and in the political astringency he saw as characteristic of America.
His novels such as *The Ambassadors* or stories like "Daisy Miller" are
full of episodes in which a governing hegemony feels no need even to
hide its assumptions of supremacy and openly articulates as a truism
the belief that there is a right way and a wrong way to behave. In
exposing these principles as thinly disguised mechanisms of control
James can be seen as using the novel as a liberating device and not,
as Mark Seltzer has argued, as a "relay of mechanisms of social
control" (*Henry James and the Art of Power*, 149). More specifically,
James exposes the shaky foundations upon which hegemonies are
always built, and in exposing those structural defects allows his
audience an opportunity to contest if not deconstruct the way things
are.

The atmosphere of release Strether finds in Europe is also a
characteristic which sharply demarcates him from his Woollett
origins. James highlights Strether's transition from Woollett to
European consciousness by having him openly admit his own
attempted reauthorization, as though the prepared script is rendered
obsolete when confronted by the scene of Europe. "Nothing could
have been odder," James tells us, "than Strether's sense of himself as
at that moment launched in something of which the sense would be
quite disconnected from his past and which was literally beginning
there and then" (21:9). However, though the idea of reauthorizing

oneself is a persistent theme in James, and is especially apparent in *The Ambassadors*, one should not understand Strether's attempt to gain control of his interpretive framework as a successful overthrow of Mrs. Newsome's restrictive hermeneutic. James, like Gramsci, was well aware that one's past always leaves behind a footprint of its presence. For Strether this means that reauthorization demands revaluation. In other words, in order to become someone new, Strether has to admit to what he has been, which, invariably, means an examination of Mrs. Newsome as well. His attempt to reconcile these competing versions of his identity, the remembered youth, the forgettable middle period, and the sudden efflorescing maturity constitutes the principal action of *The Ambassadors* and is the general focus of what we could call the experience of Jamesian hermeneutics.

To say one is the product of one's past experiences is one thing, to understand how one has been produced by those experiences, as Gramsci noted, is another. For Strether the double-edged interrogation forces him to confront not only the extent to which Mrs. Newsome has manufactured him, but the degree to which he is an accomplice in her designs. If Strether's life has been "an opportunity lost," as he admits, James makes it particularly clear that the lost opportunity was part of a bargain Strether (like Isabel Archer) entered of his own accord. To foreground the sense of lost life which floods Strether's consciousness in the initial sequences of *The Ambassadors*, James provides a glimpse of his protagonist's youth. He tells us the young Strether was a man of ambition and vision. How closely he matches James's prescription for an artistic sensibility is apparent in the explanation of Strether's honeymoon in Europe.

It had been a bold dash, for which he had taken money set apart for necessities, but kept sacred at the moment in a hundred ways, and in none more so than by this private pledge of his own to treat the occasion as a relation formed with the higher culture and see that, as they said at Woollett, it should bear a good harvest. He had believed, sailing home again, that he had gained something great, and his theory – with an elaborate innocent plan of reading, digesting, coming back even, every few years – had been to preserve, cherish and extend it. (21:85–86)

It is not by accident that Strether's youthful vitality is reflected in language that calls to mind James's own narrative descriptions of art, particularly of the writing process. What are the *Notebooks* but bold dashes meant to bear a good harvest, collections of ideas – "germs," as James called them, to which he returns again and again in an unceasing process of literary extension. An excerpt from James's *Notebook* bears relevance to this argument. In making notes for *The Princess Casamassima*, James is suddenly moved to apostrophize his vocation: "Oh art, art, what difficulties are thine; but at the same time, what consolation and encouragements, also, are like thine? Without thee, for me, the world would be, indeed, a howling desert" (*Notebooks*, 68). Like James's testimonial to the power of art, Strether's youthful plans aim at finding solace in the fertility of experience, particularly experience of art. James seems to suggest the youthful Strether tried to assure his survival by bringing back a collection of "lemon-coloured volumes" from his first visit to Paris. That these texts sit neglected, "stale and soiled and never sent to the binder," is an indication of the fate of art in the sterile world of Woollett (26:86–87). And, perhaps by extension, as James's late short story "Crapy Cornelia" suggests, these neutered texts reveal the fate of art in a country whose "music of the future" has not, "for common humanity," hidden its preferences for pure mercantile advancement over any measure of artistic enhancement (*Complete Tales*, 12:348).

The language Strether employs in describing the failure of his theory to bear fruit solidifies James's sense of the connection between vitality, art, and intellectual growth. It is almost as if James were reversing, or at least blurring, the relation between art and life so that we cannot so easily say life gives rise to art, but vice versa: art is not purely or solely mimetic – it is originary. Art and Nature, in James's formulation here, have changed places. In looking back over his intentions Strether finds it "a marvel that he should have lost account of that handful of seed." But what is lost comes back, James suggests, if given the right opportunity. "Buried for long years in dark corners at any rate these few germs had sprouted again under forty-eight hours of Paris. The process of yesterday had really been the process of feeling the general stirred life of connexions long since individually dropped" (21:86). "Germs" and "seeds" are the kernels of life in James's literary machine. To describe as mislaid seeds Strether's failure to make theory praxis, and its efflorescence as germs newly sprouted, is not just to establish Strether's (thwarted) artistic sensibility, but to make an implicit connection between the process of art and the process of life. In particular, by linking Strether's return to life through "sudden flights of fancy in Louvre galleries, hungry gazes through clear plates behind which lemon-colored volumes were as fresh as fruit on the tree" is to suggest an interanimation between desire and the aesthetic and how the dynamic between these drives puts one on the path toward personal understanding (21:86). Understanding, James suggests through Strether's sense of fascination and bewilderment in Paris, is a (pro)creative process, a constant flow between past, present, and future.[14] America, on the other hand, is, as Simmel's argument shows, a culture of money which has only one, fixed gaze, and that is directed to future profits. The culture's single-minded attention to making money, to material acquisition, effectively dissolves the natural bond between art and life James sees as a special obligation of the body politic to promote. More specifically, the American emphasis on mercantilism prevents the temporal dynamic Strether comes to experience from occurring at all and instead condenses everything into the profitability of the moment which, by extension, limits the field of enterprise to those things whose success or failure can be predetermined. In other words, real creativity, which includes artistic creativity as well as the creative responsiveness to life James advocated, is prematurely excised as a negative investment possibility. This fixedness, of course, is exactly what Woollett wants, and is what Strether initially comes to Paris to achieve.

v

The Luxembourg Gardens scene we have been examining provides a particularly helpful way of looking at James's presentation of Strether's developing hermeneutics. Here James shows how Strether's environment catalyzes conscious thought by forcing him to break free from his traditional lines of interpretation and come to understand himself, as though from a third person perspective, in the actual activity of thought. Like Christopher Newman's sudden insight before the comical duchess, Strether finds in his newly defined and liberating point of view that "the cup of his impressions seemed truly to overflow" (21:80) in such a way that his present impressions radiate beyond the scene before his eyes and lead his consciousness to examine his past and the multifold manipulations which have imprisoned him up to this moment of emancipation. James's narrative method in this scene is as important as what and how Strether thinks. It not only imitates Christopher Newman's moment of insight, it also follows the structural architecture of Isabel

Archer's famous midnight vigil in chapter forty-two of *The Portrait of a Lady*. James uses the Luxembourg Gardens idyll as a structural apperception through which the past is juxtaposed against the present in such a way as to bring about an awakening. But that enlightened understanding of the past is most important for Strether in its liberating force. By showing Strether *at* thought, James shows us not just what Strether is thinking, but how thought is always embedded in the historical forces which have contributed to the individual subject. The first step to real understanding, James thus shows, is to learn how to think. To this extent James presents Strether – "not a man to neglect any good chance for reflexion" – in just this process (21:89–90). While in the Gardens Strether looks over his life as though from the outside, as though watching a character enact the drama of his life. Strether speaks of the various " 'movements' " which have constituted his life, of "sequences he had missed and great gaps in the procession" (21:88). He looks at various scenes through his past and notes how he "had failed ... in everything, in each relation and in a half a dozen trades," how he "hadn't had the gift of making the most of what he tried," and, most importantly, how he "appeared to himself to have given over his best years to an active appreciation of the way [things] didn't come" (21:83, 85, 82). This final insight is crucial for Strether because it is what allows him to begin the active dissociation of his past from his present reality, from imposing an understanding to being engaged in the active process of living through situations and emerging on the other side of those experiences with an understanding that reflects one's own conscious attempt *to come* to understanding.

Of course Strether's expressions of independence come at a price. That question of cost resonates throughout *The Ambassadors* and functions as a powerful force either of punitive or remunerative value. In trying to come to an understanding of Strether, the reader should not underestimate his role as a paid functionary, a representative of a larger force – Mrs. Newsome. Money, like an invisible hand, shapes *The Ambassadors*'s plot. In fact the entire plot of the novel is set in motion by money matters. After all, Strether is sent to Paris to rescue Chad Newsome so that the family business will remain in the family's control. Chad, as Strether explains, stands to gain "a handsome 'part,' a large share in the profits" should he be on hand to take advantage of the possibility (21:70). And Strether, too, stands to gain a handsome remuneration upon the successful execution of his ambassadorial mission, a fact of Woollett business not lost on Waymarsh who points out, "if you get him you also get Mrs. Newsome" (21:110). The supremacy of capital, at least in Chad Newsome's mind, is most apparent at the novel's conclusion where Chad, unable to free himself from "the money in it" throws over his "love" for Madame de Vionnet in favor of the financial rewards offered by Woollett servitude. Despite Strether's passionate outburst that Chad "damn the money in it," one can recognize in Chad's final decision James's poignant critique of the dehumanizing forces of mercantilism (22:317). As a budding capitalist, a member of the next generation of buccaneers, Chad's seeming cavalier disposal of his "relationship" for capital gain reminds us of Simmel's argument that the distinguishing interpersonal consequence of a money culture was that human values, human relationships were measured in cash-value terms. One could say Chad's decision rings in "the music of the future" James decried in *The American Scene* and the late short stories such as "Crapy Cornelia" (*American Scene*, 348).

Furthermore, in a direct way it is the invisible hand of capital which brings Strether to the Luxembourg Gardens and introduces his idyll. James tells us that on this second morning in Paris Strether hastens to call "on the bankers of the Rue Scribe to whom his letter of credit was addressed" (21:76). The absence of the letter leaves Strether "disconcerted" and initiates a long contemplative walk that winds up in the Gardens. It is on this walk that the reader really gets an opportunity to get to know who Strether is and how he came to be that way. Strether's being "disconcerted" at not having proof of credit brings up one of the most crucial determining forces in his life, his lack of capital. Indeed, in the midst of his reverie Strether points to the source of his failure as "his want moreover of money" (21:87). James uses Strether's financial failures to reflect his character's failure to measure up to what America expects of men, as Dawidoff has argued (*Genteel Tradition*, 135). That Strether winds up in Paris a paid functionary of a woman whose power masculinizes her in the commercial culture which regulates America is a testimony of his failure as a man and a telling point in *The Ambassadors*, especially given the similarities between Strether and Henry James. Like Strether, James was not a participant in business or industry and one who also felt pinched by a want of capital. For both men, this monetary lack was seen as the consequence of having given their life over to aesthetic contemplation rather than some more materially productive occupation. Not surprisingly, criticisms of James at the time and well into the twentieth century, including recent commentaries, often characterize him as an effeminate dandy expatriate along the lines of the aesthetes burlesqued by George Du Maurier's *Punch* cartoons.[15] The point of these critiques is to highlight the un-American and "unmanly," in William's words, aspects of the career James had chosen. But what James exposes in Strether's experiences here in the Luxembourg Gardens scene and throughout the course of *The Ambassadors* is how the enforced conscription of America's mercantile machinery often set an individual at odds with him- or herself. Dawidoff comments on this culturally produced estrangement and argues that *The Ambassadors* reveals how the "upper-middle-class American cultural orthodoxy propounds understandings of sexual, economic, aesthetic, and moral life that do not necessarily serve the inside needs of the people in whom they are inculcated" (*Genteel Tradition*, 1135). To some extent, the hostility James faced from his public upon his infrequent returns, and the hostility Strether evokes from Sarah Pocock, is rooted in these individuals' willingness to address, contest, and finally refuse the cultural controls which fix roles and behaviors as narrowly as, to paraphrase Mrs. Newsome, right and wrong. In challenging these orthodoxies James was, as Dawidoff says of Strether, "not the kind of man America trusts" (136). The cost of this challenge, though, is profound. Strether's ruminative ambulations show a man undergoing a crisis of consciousness. The suggestion in *The Ambassadors*, at least in the early descriptions of Strether and Maria Gostrey, is that being out of the business loop, short-handed financially, demands a resignation of freedom.[16] Strether, we see, can only preserve the dream of his youth by allowing it to become something else as long as he tries to conform to the principles of acceptable behavior in Woollett.

The corollary, of course, is that in order to be that young man, Strether has to become someone else: Mrs. Newsome's indentured servant. How much James wants us to see Strether's sense of indebtedness to Mrs. Newsome reveals itself through the nature of the language Strether uses to describe her. James has Strether retreat to abstract concepts so as to accentuate a sense of avoidance rather than an attempt to represent someone. Thus Mrs. Newsome is "wonderfully able," "handsome," "admirable," "a swell," "genuine," "grand," "perfection." What is telling in Strether's choice of terms is how little they reveal, as though the Woollett doyenne were unapproachable, even through language. Furthermore, the abruptness of Strether's response to any inquiries about Mrs. Newsome suggest more about Strether than the object of his description. To the reader, as to Maria Gostrey, the immediate platitudes which fall from Strether's mouth whenever the question of Mrs. Newsome comes up suggest more the self-consciousness of the oppressed than the picture of beatitude and largesse Strether aims to evoke. We have already noted how Strether feels immediate shame when he imagines himself caught in the Luxembourg Gardens by Mrs. Newsome. This pervasive sense of the magisterial gaze becomes more pronounced when Sarah Pocock arrives in Paris in a judiciary form. Strether's sense of Mrs. Newsome's power becomes manifest with the arrival of Sarah. Where he earlier felt Mrs. Newsome's long approbative arm figuratively reach across the Atlantic, he now finds Sarah the metonymic extension of Woollett judgment. Strether, James tells us, "saw himself, under her direction, recommitted to Woollett as juvenile offenders are committed to reformatories" (22:61). In commenting on this aspect of *The Ambassadors* Paul Armstrong likens the psychological dynamics of Strether's consciousness to the characteristic of the master-slave relationship as described by Hegel. It is true, Strether has been "slave to ... many masters" as Armstrong suggests, and that like the master/slave relationship described by Hegel, Strether has undergone "a doubling of consciousness" in order to reconcile the distinction between his private and public conception of self, but there is more to Strether's recoil at the thought of being observed from Woollett (*Challenge*, 99). What *The Ambassadors* relentlessly shows is that Mrs. Newsome's coercive force is so powerful that it has completely overwritten Strether's consciousness and effectively erased whatever individuality he had and replaced it with her (America's?) type. Not until he is in Europe tasting freedom does Strether even begin to perceive how pervasive Mrs. Newsome's influence has been. The intended cultural ramifications again point up the degree to which James saw America as a place of such commercial astringency, as a culture so focused on getting and spending, that it could no longer even muster the intellectual or emotional energy to entertain the idea that art or any innovative aesthetic intentions had any culturally remunerative value whatsoever.

If the master-slave analogy is too strong a one for the relationship between Mrs. Newsome and Strether, then one could alternately choose the patron and dependent artist. The Woollett "Review" plays a particularly interesting role in this aspect of Strether's character. In describing the undertaking to Maria Gostrey Strether reveals more about himself than the project: "Certainly, Woollett has a Review – which Mrs. Newsome, for the most part, magnificently pays for and which I, not at all magnificently, edit. My name's on the cover" (21:64). When Maria Gostrey asks if Mrs. Newsome's name graces the cover as well, Strether pauses before explaining: "She's behind the whole thing; but she's of a delicacy and discretion – !" (21:64). James's juxtaposition of attributed magnificence and his having Strether momentarily pause foreground the sense of discontinuity between the patron and the servant. Mrs. Newsome's name need not be on the cover because Mrs. Newsome and the Review are synonymous, the Review stands as testimonial to her magnificence, in Strether's words "It is her tribute to the ideal," with "the ideal," of course, being measured according to "her book" (21:66, 22:224). Strether's name on it is simply an advertisement of his relative insignificance and indebtedness to his patron, a fact not lost on him as he makes clear through his pejorative use of "magnificent" to describe his role in the editorial undertaking. James indicates the disparity between Strether's sense of the aesthetic and how far from it Mrs. Newsome's conception of "the ideal" falls when Strether admits the Review's hollowness is attributable to its concentration on mercantile discourse.

The green covers at home comprised, by the law of their purpose, no tribute to letters; it was a mere rich kernel of economics, politics, ethics that, glazed and, as Mrs. Newsome maintained, rather against *his* view, preeminently pleasant to touch, they formed the specious shell. (21:87–88)

This attempt to dissociate himself from the Review calls attention to an important aspect of Strether's experience of identity and how that identity has been rigidly constructed by Woollett. The link between the putative editor and the publication, the forced conformity of both to Mrs. Newsome's conception of the ideal, allows James to confer metonymic status upon the Review. As metonym, the Review then functions in the text as yet another embodiment of Mrs. Newsome's power, and as a public picture of Strether's abjectness. The similarity between the Review – a specious shell that reflects Mrs. Newsome's magnificence – and Lambert Strether – a similarly specious shell that reflects Mrs. Newsome's influence – must not be lost. James makes the point directly when he has Strether attempt to explain why he puts his name on the cover: "It is exactly the thing that I'm reduced to doing for myself. It seems to rescue a little, you see, from the wreck of hopes and ambitions, the refuse heap of disappointments and failures, my one presentable little scrap of an identity" (21:65). Again, the sense of displaced authority is foregrounded. The Review offers Strether a moment of insight. His editorial control there is a reflection of the editorial control exerted over his own life, a lack perhaps better understood in what would be the Review's and its culture's economic language. In those words Strether's editorial responsibilities, he understands, have no value-added significance, just as his life or what he's "accomplished" with it has, in his commercial culture, no value-added significance.

His name on the green cover, where he had put it for Mrs. Newsome, expressed him doubtless just enough to make the world . . . ask who he was. He incurred the ridicule of having to have his explanation explained. He was Lambert Strether because he was on the cover, whereas it should have been, for anything like glory, that he was on the cover because he was Lambert Strether. (21:84)

Strether's consciousness is, as James reveals through the Luxembourg Gardens idyll and Strether's descriptions of his role in the Woollett Review, both fractured and discontinuous. James characterizes Strether as an individual who, because of disappointments and relative poverty, has resigned all claim to autonomy. Indeed James foregrounds the idea of a controlling determinism in Strether's understanding of life. In the midst of his oft-quoted injunction urging Little Bilham to live, Strether makes the following curious digression:

"The affair – I mean the affair of life – couldn't, no doubt, have been different for me; for it is at the best a tin mould, either fluted and embossed, with ornamental excrescences, or else smooth and dreadfully plain, into which, a helpless jelly, one's consciousness is poured – so that one 'takes' the form, as the great cook says, and is more or less compactly held by it; one lives in fine as one can. Still, one has the illusion of freedom; therefore don't be like me, without the memory of that illusion." (21:218)

The character displacement, the new Strether yearning for freedom and the former man who gave up his chances, forces a destabilizing indeterminacy upon Strether. Not able to be the man of his youth and not willing to accept the man he has become in his maturity, Strether seems to exist in between identities, in a perpetual interstice.

VI

This feeling of displaced presence, of voyeurism, permeates James's novels and is accentuated by his refinements in point of view. Ross Posnock has shown that the narrative architecture of *The Ambassadors* mirrors the lack of fixity in Strether's identity. Posnock points to the prevalence of balcony scenes in the novel as telling examples of how the margin often offers the best point of view. As Posnock argues, "James makes margin one of the novel's pivotal motifs, embodying it architecturally in the image of the balcony, which Strether first gazes up at and eventually will gaze down from" (*Trial of Curiosity*, 226). Posnock's point here is important, for the balcony, which is simultaneously part of and adjunct to a building, is a neat variation of that novelistic vantage James speaks of as "the house of fiction" in his Preface to *The Portrait of a Lady*. In *The Ambassadors* the balcony scenes – the first with Little Bilham looking down upon Strether first looking up, another, late in the novel, showing Strether gazing over Paris, looking at himself – are perfect examples of the voyeuristic eye. So too, we might add, are the numerous garden scenes. The garden shares adjunct status with the balcony, and like the balcony, the garden offers refuge and perspective from the margin. It is no surprise then that Strether's famous outburst to Little Bilham occurs in Gloriani's garden, where Strether, invited to observe the party but not to really participate in it, retreats to collect his thoughts.

The oft-cited garden scene in which Strether makes his impassioned speech to Little Bilham brings to the forefront of *The Ambassadors* James's concerns with the nature of experience and understanding. Understanding, for James, was never something one arrived at, but, rather, something one was forever moving along in, as though in a continuous process of revision. The place of observation in such a hermeneutic is obvious, as F. O. Matthiessen noted in his study *Henry James: The Major Phase*. In his examination of *The Ambassadors*, Matthiessen concentrates on the dynamic between observation and understanding in Strether's developing awareness of his relationship to his self and the nature of relations between Chad and Madame de Vionnet. For Matthiessen, Strether, like James, "keeps emphasizing the importance of seeing" (30). In this way Strether approximates his creator, something Matthiessen remarks upon when he reminds us of our knowledge "that James himself lived in large measure by his eyes" (30). But, as I have suggested, *The Ambassadors* is about more than seeing what is happening before one's eyes, as Little Bilham quickly points out to Strether. When pressed by Strether to divulge what he knows about Chad and Marie de Vionnet, Bilham explains he can only tell Strether "what they pass for," and warns Strether of attempting to assume much more based on appearances: "What more than a vain appearance does the wisest of us know?" (21:202–3). Often the visually inapparent, what Strether comes to understand by reconstructing past events and juxtaposing them against present experiences, is what drives understanding forward. By highlighting the way understanding constantly builds and rebuilds itself from experiences observed or contested, hidden and eventually revealed, James anticipates an important aspect of the theory of truth in his brother William's pragmatism. Little Bilham seems an embodiment of William's understanding of how "New truth is always a go-between, a smoother-over of transitions. It marries old opinion to new fact so as ever to show a minimum of jolt and a maximum of continuity" (*Pragmatism*, 35). It is the sense of inbetweenness captured by Little Bilham's remark on "appearances" and William's notion of truth as a bridge that James's fiction examines. The sense of inbetweenness warns against closure, against the projection of interpretation and the assumption of epistemological certitudes such as those which characterize Mrs. Newsome, and, in an attenuated degree, Sarah Pocock. For Henry James, that shadowy area in between moments, in between words and actions, was the area we could "not possibly not know, sooner or later, in one way or another" (Preface, *The American*, 1062–63). And while the understanding which emerged from that shadowy area was always being revised, at least in being open to revision it suggested a vital connection with the world absent from the imposed and manufactured sureties of, say, Woollett. The theoretical structure of this aspect of James's hermeneutics becomes the focus of James's writings from *The Portrait of a Lady* on. In *The Ambassadors*, just as in *The Portrait of a Lady*, understanding is constantly in a dialectic between a present situation which always remains partially hidden but requires action and a retrospection which often brings what was

hidden into focus and allows one to complete the picture, at least for
the moment. Lambert Strether, however, marks a distinctive shift in
the focus of what I have described as James's method. The process of
interpretive revision which plays a central role in both novels
becomes in *The Ambassadors* much more internal. In this later novel,
James shows understanding to be a far more complicated event.
Where Isabel Archer is shown to arrive at an understanding through
one particular scene, *The Ambassadors* suggests Strether's illumination
– his understanding – cannot be represented in a single scene, a vigil
in which everything becomes clear all at once, but comes of a piece .
in which every event is constantly causing a shifting and reshuffling
of the whole and the end picture is always in the process of coming
into sharp focus.[17]

Furthermore, in *The Ambassadors* James adds to Isabel Archer's
critique of material experience a large measure of subjective reappraisal. Strether not only revises his understanding of what he sees
or believes he sees, but is continually revising his vision of himself.
This change in focus comes as a result of a refinement of James's
conception of experience. We can say that experience in *The American*
or *The Portrait of a Lady* means primarily what the perceiving subject
encounters in the material world and how that subject constructs an
understanding of those experiences. In *The Ambassadors*, however,
experience comes to mean something much larger as James adds a
level of psychological complexity to Strether's consciousness. Fred
Kaplan picks up on this widening of James's focus in his recent
biography on James. Like Matthiessen before, Kaplan finds a close
connection between Strether and his creator.

Like James, Strether, who is about the same age as his creator, has the
ambivalent satisfaction of being an observer observing himself making
observations rather than a participant. He embodies James's heightened
sense, at the beginning of the twentieth century, of looking over his own
shoulder at where he has come from and where he is now. (*Henry James*,
468)

The sense of Strether looking over his shoulder is already
apparent in the Luxembourg Gardens scene where he examines not
only his past, but literally looks over his shoulder in expectation of
meeting Mrs. Newsome's reproving eye. The Strether in Gloriani's
garden is brought up to date, so to speak, by James. The object for
this Strether is the present man. His impassioned, Paterian, injunc-

tion to Little Bilham to grab hold of life and live is produced directly by his responsiveness to his present experiences and the sense they invoke of an opportunity lost.

"Live all you can; it is a mistake not to. It does not matter so much what you do in particular, so long as you have your life. If you haven't had that what *have* you had? ... Do what you like so long as you don't make *my* mistake. For it was a mistake. Live!" (21:217)

The tone of Strether's outburst is as important as its content. The language's urgency and the directness of the appeal are indicative of someone fully open to the possibilities of life's presentness. No reader has ever doubted that Strether's impassioned speech is made as much for himself as for Little Bilham's benefit. Moreover the force of Strether's language seems a purposeful tactic by which James surrounds and opposes the question of determinism as it comes up in the midst of this appeal to seize life. One can overcome, or at least have the illusion of overcoming, determinism, the "illusion of freedom," James seems to be suggesting, by cultivating an openness to experience (21:218). This is exactly what Strether learns to do in Paris and what sets him at such odds against Woollett. James measures the distinction between Mrs. Newsome and Strether ultimately through a comparison of each's ability not only to *see*, but to be willing to revise all prejudices based on the experience of new phenomena that transcend the subject's pre-established interpretive paradigm. In one of his final assessments of the Woollett doyenne Strether admits "I have been interested *only* in her seeing what I have seen. And I have been as disappointed in her refusal to see it as she has been in what has appeared to her the perversity of my insistence" (22:220–21).

James never really overcomes Strether's admission of deterministic forces operating in life, but neither is that his intention. More to the point is James's idea that the illusion of freedom is dependent upon the individual subject's ability to remain open to experience and to resist the idea that one can use interpretation to fix events and thereby control them. What Strether comes to see through his experience is that understanding is incompatible with fixity and control. Determinism, James suggests, like any other construct which tries to project meaning and to corral experience within a pre-established paradigm, is always going to be limited by its own boundaries. As such the determined life, or at least the life given over to determinism, will always be exceeded by experience, by that which "cannot be done away with" (Gadamer, *Truth and Method*, 320).[18] One way to develop such an openness, James suggests through Strether, is to be forever engaged in a process of revision.[19] Strether's garden soliloquy marks a change of focus from James's earlier presentation of this scene, Strether in the Luxembourg Gardens, where Strether gives the reader a view of a man more attuned to his past, to what he had become rather than what he is. The latter scene, despite its origin in a vision of the past, is rooted in the present and directed toward the future. As he winds up his speech Strether brings home the point when he says more to himself than Little Bilham, "what am I to myself?" (21:219).

VII

Strether's asking the question, "what am I to myself?" is the first step in the process of changing his present. For James understanding is always a process, always a movement of response, in the sense of responding to the requirements of ever changing situations. Strether's question is what Gramsci meant when he said the "starting point of critical elaboration is the consciousness of what one really is, and is 'knowing thyself' as a product of the historical process" which has been in your making (*Selections*, 324). Daniel Mark Fogel has commented effectively on the importance of visualizing the self in *The Ambassadors*. According to Fogel, when what Strether sees does not "accord with his preconceptions,"

he feels it incumbent upon him to change his views, to reassess his objectives, and to revise his plans of action. Since moreover, the capacity to see and judge and the desire to do well are not sufficient to account for moral heroism of the sort Strether attains, one must add that James does not limit the imperative to see to objects outside the self: the most difficult requirement for the Jamesian hero is that he must see truly into himself, must recognize his own limits and possibilities so that he may act conscientiously within them. (*Romantic Imagination*, 25–26)

James's familiar statement about the nature of reality from "The Art of Fiction" provides a particularly helpful insight into James's sense of how experience and revision operate in someone like Strether. We recall James says "[t]he measure of reality is difficult to fix ... Humanity is immense and reality has a myriad forms" (51–52). The difference between Mrs. Newsome and Strether, between closure and openness, lies in the reading of reality in James's formulation. It is important to note that it is not "reality" which needs to be fixed, but the "measure" of it. For Mrs. Newsome, as we have seen, reality can be reduced to some brute fact, something given. Consequently, rather than understanding her need to grasp, to "measure" reality, Mrs. Newsome instead operates by fixing, imposing constraints upon reality so as to privilege her own self-serving certitudes and ratify herself as stabilizing authority. Thus, rather than standing before a situation in a stance open to its possibilities, Mrs. Newsome remains closed off and refuses the situation any opportunity to tell her anything she does not already know. For James, Mrs. Newsome's refusal to understand is in the most basic sense, then, a refusal or rejection of hermeneutics.

In contrast, *The Ambassadors* shows, as James himself presents through his house of fiction metaphor, reality to be a matter more or less of (a never stable) perspective. For Strether the struggle to understand goes on *within* reality, in the sense that his attempt to divine what is going on between Chad and Madame de Vionnet and, more to the point, what he should think about it, is part of the reality of his situation and is not, as Sarah Pocock neatly decides, external to it. Strether accentuates the shift in focus as he becomes more and more capable of living through and experiencing the social nature of reality and interpretation and, thus, less and less dependent upon Maria Gostrey. As he says, "the rush of experience" has allowed him to develop his own ability at coping with experience: "It was the proportions that were changed, and the proportions were at all times, he philosophized, the very conditions of perception, the terms of thought" (22:49). James's larger point here is that the perceiving mind is not external to the world, trying to distinguish between the real and the not real, the good and the bad, categorizing so as Mrs. Newsome does. Rather, the interpreting subject is inside reality, and of course therefore cannot grasp the whole of it but must construe the whole from the part, from the perspective within the limits of a *real* situation. James sets the tone for this struggle with Strether's first description of Paris.

His greatest uneasiness seemed to peep at him out of the imminent impression that almost any acceptance of Paris might give one's authority away. It hung before him this morning, the vast bright Babylon, like some huge iridescent object, a jewel brilliant and hard, in which parts were not to be discriminated nor differences comfortably marked. It twinkled and

trembled and melted together, and what seemed all surface one moment
seemed all depth the next. (21:89)

James's simile underscores the sense of multiplicity Strether finds
himself having to move through in his effort to construct a mental
picture of what is going on about him. As a metaphor for reality,
James's description of Paris calls attention to the impossibility of ever
putting one's finger down and saying "this is it," or, in keeping with
the language of the novel, "there you are." The counter-simile
involving Woollett would be to compare Woollett to a transparent
sheet of glass where the possibility of distortion is absent. And this is
exactly Mrs. Newsome's line of vision. James complicates the
geographic contrasts by personifying Paris's complexity in Madame
de Vionnet. She challenges Strether's initial interpretive closure, his
adherence to Mrs. Newsome's rigorous realism, by presenting herself
as multiple, as defying description.[20] Upon first meeting her, for
instance, Strether "felt *his* character receive for the instant a smutch
from all the wrong things he had suspected or believed" in accord-
ance with Woollett's expectation, i.e. that she be a "wicked woman,"
who could only be "base, venal – out of the streets" (21:237, 55).
Marie de Vionnet embodies James's challenge to the tendency to
confine vision and reality to expectation. Rather than conform to
Woollett's and Strether's expectations, Madame de Vionnet explodes
them, as Strether notes amazedly, "she had taken all his categories
by surprise" (21:271). Of course the point is that categories are
necessarily limited, the province of Woollett's interpretive paradigm,
and are restricted by their very status as categories. Marie de
Vionnet, for the most part, transcends description and the fixity of
categorization, a fact that not only enchants Strether, but bewilders
Waymarsh and excites the hostility of Sarah Pocock. Unlike Mrs.
Newsome who books Strether "by her vision" and commands that
what he finds " 'suit' her book," Marie de Vionnet adopts a Jamesian
voice and informs Strether that "*any* truth – about us all – that you
see for yourself" is acceptable (21:253). The accent on "*any*" is a
testament to the multiplicity of truths and why revision must needs
play an important role in understanding.

Priscilla Walton takes Marie de Vionnet's textual function one
step further by suggesting Marie not only teaches Strether to
recognize multiplicity, but how he can take an active role in the
construction of reality.

By offering herself as a text for Strether to read ... she, like the polyvocal mode of reading that she signifies, inspires him to co-create texts with her. In her effort to teach him about co-production, or the active role of the reader, she demonstrates to him that writing cannot be confined. (*Disruption of the Feminine*, 116)

The question of co-creation and co-production, Walton suggests, raises a crucial point in *The Ambassadors*, that whenever the viewing subject attempts to construct meaning the construction at some point is made to match the mental expectations of the constructing subject. The pitfalls associated with this type of projection are apparent throughout James's work. Woollett's limited perceptivity is an example. Christopher Newman makes the mistake of projecting his values upon the Bellegarde family and winds up on the outside as they close ranks. Isabel Archer constructs a fanciful image of Osmond and winds up the victim of his psychological brutality. Hyacinth Robinson creates an image of himself as gentleman and commits suicide when the reality of his life destroys the fiction. In each of these cases James foregrounds the internal process of consciousness as it attempts to create meaning. The failure for each character lies exactly at the point of projection, the point at which they fill out and attempt to act in the world in accord with their image of it, or on the basis of the desire they project onto it. Invariably what these characters create and impose explodes as the "real thing" looms up larger or altogether different than what had been anticipated. Paul Armstrong calls this crucial moment the challenge of bewilderment through which James dramatizes "the act of interpretation as a process of composition." As Armstrong explains, James's "larger hermeneutic point" is in how the moment of bewilderment "shows the extent to which we expect the world to conform to our habitual interpretive schemes – the extent to which they pattern our perception in ways we do not notice until ... they break down" (*Challenge*, 6).[21] For Strether the sudden realization that Chad "was none the less still Chad" represents one such moment (22:284).

VIII

In *The Ambassadors*, James dramatizes the danger projection presents to understanding by exposing the discrepancy between what the character thinks is going on, and what the reader sees is actually the case. The most obvious and well-documented example is Mrs. Newsome's attempt to imprison Marie de Vionnet by imposing upon her a particular Woollett-produced conception of the *femme du monde*. But Lambert Strether too is guilty of a creative projection which leads him to misread his situation as much as Mrs. Newsome does hers. More specifically, Strether is guilty of a double projection, the second of which builds upon the exploded image of the first. Strether is guilty first of projecting an image of Chad Newsome as a vulgar youth who has fallen into the clutches of a base and venal woman. When this turns out not to be the case, Strether immediately overcompensates by making Chad an idealized image of his own youthful and morally circumspect self. Both interpretive projections, as we shall see, debilitate Strether's capacity for understanding, and, in doing so, underscore James's artistic concerns with what he saw as the limitations of imposing any ready-made form of mediation upon what is strange.

Gadamer's analysis of how foreconceptions and projections operate in understanding are helpful in coming to understand the hermeneutic trap Strether lays for himself. In examining Heidegger's description of how understanding inevitably takes place in a herme-neutical circle, Gadamer refers to Heidegger's insistence that "what we call 'Thrownness' belongs together with that which is projected" (*Truth and Method*, 232). To summarize briefly, this means that our being "thrown," in Heidegger's sense of the word, means accepting and understanding the limits of the "ground" we have been "thrown" upon.[22] The "ground" includes all the conditions of our existence, all that has gone into the construction of our consciousness and character, all that we know of ourselves, and all that operates below the level of what can be directly known. In short, Heidegger's "thrownness" means being always already situated in regard to external phenomena. Strether's "thrownness" involves the whole nature of relations with Woollett, his status as Mrs. Newsome's factotum, and his awareness of his youthful desires. Both Heidegger and Gadamer show how one's "thrownness" or, in Gadamer's language, one's foreconceptions and prejudices can have a contam-inating effect on interpretation. As Gadamer explains, "All correct interpretation must be on guard against arbitrary fancies and the limitations imposed by imperceptible habits of thought ... which originate in [the interpreter] himself" (*Truth and Method*, 236). Gadamer's point here is important in relation to Strether and to the reader of James's texts. For Gadamer, "a person," let us say Strether or a reader of *The Ambassadors*, "who is trying to understand a text," let us say Chad, or Madame de Vionnet, or *The Ambassadors*, "is always performing an act of projection" (236). The reader always projects forward, building meaning "as soon as some initial meaning emerges" which allows him to revise his earlier expectation. This, of course, is what it is to be open to the possibilities of the text.

If I can stick with Gadamer a few moments longer, his assistance in our understanding of Strether and *The Ambassadors* will become evident. Throughout his analysis of understanding Gadamer repeatedly warns that the possibility of true understanding can occur only when the interpreting subject is aware of "the tyranny of hidden prejudices" which invariably prevent the text (or other person) from "assert[ing] its own truth against one's own fore-meanings" (239, 238). The only requirement, Gadamer explains, is our remaining "open to the meaning of the other person or of the text" (238). This, to be sure, runs exactly contrary to Woollett's understanding of interpretation. Mrs. Newsome, as we have seen, is not particularly open with respect to things that exist beyond her influence. As I have said, ideologically Mrs. Newsome is a representative of the narrowly realistic tradition James believed limiting to fiction because its covert ideology masquerades behind protestations of realistic representational strategies. For James, as for Gadamer, the failure of hermeneutics occurs when the interpreting subject refuses to acknowledge the requirements of revision so as to modify understanding in light of newly-acquired knowledge. An individual – Mrs. Newsome as Realist author – who remains essentially sealed off from life seeks to extend control over the world by confining life's fluidity within a method of perception based on a strict management of reality.[23]

A final word from Gadamer brings the point home, especially if we think of someone like Sarah Pocock's interpretation of Madame de Vionnet, and, as I will show, Strether's interpretation of Chad. As Gadamer points out:

If a person is trying to understand something, he will not be able to rely from the start on his own chance previous ideas, missing as logically and stubbornly as possible the actual meaning of the text until the latter becomes so persistently audible that it breaks through the imagined understanding of it. Rather, a person trying to understand a text is prepared for it to tell him something. (238)

The applicability of this formulation to Sarah Pocock is made apparent by Strether in a passage already referred to. Sarah, of course, has been commissioned by Mrs. Newsome to find Chad and Madame de Vionnet exactly as Woollett had originally projected – a wayward son caught in the web of a base and venal woman. Woollett, to paraphrase Gadamer, is not prepared to be told anything else. And that is exactly the response Strether meets with when he pleads Madame de Vionnet's case with Sarah Pocock. When Strether says, "She has struck me from the first as wonderful. I have been thinking too moreover that, after all, she would probably have represented even for yourself something new and rather good," Sarah's response is as quick as it is predictable. Woollett does not need anything new: "a 'revelation' – to *me*: I have come to such a woman for a revelation?" (22:202). Ironically, Sarah's refusal to be open to the possibility of newness here reminds us of Strether's reference to Mrs. Newsome's "perfection" of "composition", in both cases what James underscores is the essential closedness of these interpretive subjects (22:222). With the reaction Strether's praise of Madam de Vionnet provokes, James dramatizes Woollett's manipulative power – its "ferocity" of being "in the know" – by bringing Strether under the fixed, unblinking gaze of Woollett ("Crapy Cornelia," *Complete Tales*, 12:348). In an interesting use of the *ficelle* James allows us a glimpse into Woollett's projected image of Strether's Parisian identity. Jim Pocock assumes the role of *ficelle* and allows the reader to see what Woollett believes has happened to Strether. Pocock's crude sensualism, his perverse nudge and wink conversations with Strether – "oh you, you – you *are* doing it!" – are textual clues James provides of the moral dissolution Woollett assumes has overtaken her first ambassador. To ensure we get what "it" means to Jim, James follows the statement with the explanation that Jim's "doing it" was "charged with rich meaning" (22:78). Jim, James repeatedly tells the reader, "had come for a good time" and would leave the "moral side to Sally" while he "availed himself" with "recreation" (22:83–84, 81). For Woollett, Strether's failure to carry out his embassy and his praise of Madame de Vionnet is indicative of only one thing – that, as Sarah asserts, "of thinking this person here so far superior to her" (22:203). In James's larger hermeneutic explorations, Sarah's and Mrs. Newsome's closed-mindedness is analogous to the narrowly realist and often lifeless fiction he felt constrained art within coercive or forced limits. As his fiction repeatedly shows, James waged a constant struggle against subjectivities such as Sarah's and her mother's for the sake of his readers and his belief in art's living qualities. In James's critique, petty orthodoxies would impose a static form upon what he saw as a fluid and ever-modulating reality. The Sarah Pococks, Mrs. Newsomes, and Gilbert Osmonds of the world gain their power over others by taking away any medium in which understanding can take place. What James shows in *The Ambassadors* and throughout his career is how works of art and ways of interpreting which mirror Sarah's and Mrs. Newsome's conceptual horizon are actually a denial of life, and should be seen as a denial of interpretation, since such rigid formulations undermine what James saw as the protean and destabilizing power of mimesis.

Each of the interpretive projections we have been examining is an example, in varying degrees, of the hermeneutic circle. James used this process to show how interpretation is always already influenced by one's expectations. He suggests throughout his novels that one's expectations invariably lead to a moment of destabilizing bewilderment in which what was anticipated to be turns out to be altogether other, and that all attempts to fix reality, to make it conform to a preestablished picture, lead one to accept the counterfeit for the real thing, or the shadow for the substance. To this extent, James's hermeneutics anticipates Gadamer's own understanding of the hermeneutic circle.[24] Gadamer thinks of the hermeneutic circle not so much as an interpretive procedure, but as a way of describing the rationality of everyday life, where understanding as a mode of being requires openness and flexibility precisely because the singularity and unpredictability of experience necessitates that our judgments be in a process of constant revision. James too, as we have seen, understood that flexibility and openness are part of this quotidian rationality. James's attention to *how* his characters understand as much as *what* they understand adds another dimension to his texts in that the reading subject is invariably drawn into the text and led to examine along with the perceiving character the whole process of understanding. While the character projects hypotheses in an attempt to grasp the whole of reality, the reader is carried along and invariably led to participate through either questioning these hypotheses or by projecting his or her own.

James's theoretical aim here is worth commenting upon. *The Ambassadors* is the first novel in which James relied solely on the complex indirection which characterizes his late phase. The novel's limited omniscience underscores James's conviction that one could never know everything without contaminating the "reality" of what is known.[25] As Leon Edel explains, James chose limited omniscience over the old tradition in which the novel disclosed everything precisely because the removal of an omniscient authorial voice allowed the reader to assume an active role in relation to the text. Rather than hand meaning over, James "allowed his readers to know only as much as one learns in life. And he developed for the first time on so consistent a scale shifting angles of vision. In terms of old-fashioned story-telling this resulted in a novel without action. The excitement was intellectual, the pleasure resided in the unfolding of little details" (*The Master*, 77). Furthermore, by taking the authorial voice off stage, so to speak, James creates the distance necessary for the reader's own involvement in the generation of meaning. This dynamic of living forward and understanding backward charac-terizes all of James's late style and lends itself particularly well to analysis from a phenomenological perspective. Edward Casey makes a point about the "specifically phenomenological method" which sheds light on the nature of James's narrative method. Phenomen-ology, Casey explains, "places special stress on firsthand or direct description thereby minimizing recourse to ... highly mediated constructions ... What is sought in the implementation of such a method is an accurate description of a given phenomenon *as it presents itself to one's own experience,* not an explanation of its genesis through reference to antecedent causal factors" (emphasis added, *Imagining,* 8–9). Thus, what the reader discovers as *The Ambassadors* unfolds and Strether's understanding of things is increasingly called into question is the degree to which he or she is authorially involved in constructing expectations of Chad, of Madame de Vionnet, of Strether, expectations based on what has been presented, and what we assume or project to be the case. In this way James's late narrative refinements foreground the degree to which what we already believe or what we want to be the case shapes our understanding of what is.[26]

Reading James's narrative experiment through Gadamer's under-standing of foreconceptions and prejudice allows us to get to the bottom of James's own hermeneutics. By explaining the degree to which understanding (if it is properly to be called so) always involves an interpretive crisis and demands an ongoing conceptual reconstruction, Gadamer offers a way of reading which succeeds in elevating the typical James text, such as *The Ambassadors*, to a fully live and active work of art. (After all, James's characters experience interpretive failures, and James's hermeneutics depends upon interpretive failure since the breakdown of one's interpretation – i.e. one's prior view of things, one's expectations, the meaning one has at the outset – is a condition of successful interpretation for the character as well as the reader.) As such, the Jamesian text's fundamental openness can be finally expressed. Such a text, James realized, demands a reader's participation, but rewards that effort by allowing the reading subject to carry over into the world the aesthetic experience not as an escapist abstraction, but as a meaningful event which has an immediate and direct application to reality as measured in the reader's expanded and active understanding. In Gadamer's formulation, this means allowing the text to open itself before the reader and "begin to speak." Only then, explains Gadamer, as though commenting on a text like *The Ambassadors*, can understanding begin, for to "understand a text is to come to understand oneself in a kind of dialogue."[27] Here again Gadamer's analysis of understanding captures exactly James's narrative method. For what is it to read a James text if it is not to read oneself in a dialogue? Thus, James's narrative strategy in texts like *The Ambassadors* is to diminish authorial power so as to liberate the reader's mind. The benefits of such a liberation extend beyond the boundaries of literature itself. Rather than accepting passively the author's version of things, the reader finds James's texts a place where active minds meet and change. To understand Jamesian hermeneutics along these lines is to see how James's aesthetics works toward giving art an active voice which demands an enlightened engagement from its audience. Sadly, it is perhaps because of this demanded and threatening requirement that so many readers find James so easy to avoid or so easy to misunderstand.

James accentuates the tension between imposition, adaptation, and revision in his hermeneutics by having Strether's interpretive categories come under pressure the moment he disembarks in Europe. Strether's initial interpretive failure resonates throughout *The Ambassadors* and comes when he projects an image of what he expects Chad to be like. Strether's embassy is to rescue Chad from the clutches of a "base" and "venal" woman of the streets. James makes clear that Strether departs Woollett and arrives in Paris with this anticipation intact. In this way Strether's point of view is no more than an extension of Woollett's, a fact not lost on Maria Gostrey as she reminds him that one "can only judge on the facts," not, that is to say, on hypotheses hatched in another culture (21:54). That Strether has such a strong impression of who and what Chad is, even before he sees him, ultimately is reflective of who and what Strether is, at least at that moment. James's description of Strether's anticipated impression marks the shift in narrative focus from Chad's care to the ambassador's own. When Maria Gostrey suggests Strether's mission is to lure Chad away from the corrupting woman with "a lot of money," Strether partially agrees but goes on to say "I'm acting with a sense for him of other things too. Consideration and comfort and security – the general safety of being anchored by a strong chain. He wants, as I see him, to be protected. Protected I mean from life" (21:71). Of course, this is an exact description of Strether, and his projection of his identity upon Chad is a perfect example, James would say, of how the perceiving subject, unless actively aware of his interpretive prejudices, will always be manipulated by the constraining and determining categories of his or her (pre)history.

James shows the difficulty of remaining free of interpretive prejudice and open to experience by having Strether find "himself blindly, almost wildly pushing forward" from impression to impression (21:115). But showing Strether acquiring a surfeit of impressions is also a narrative ploy. Moving Strether through an unending series of refined impressions is a tactic by which James is able to trick the reader into accepting and joining with Strether's understanding of those things he experiences. James manipulates the reader by first developing the reader's sympathy for Strether as an elderly man who missed his chance at life and who lives in virtual imprisonment in Woollett, and then by catching us up in the "assault of images" that celebrate Strether's return to life (21:196).

Strether, in contact for the first time with that element [the romantic glory of Gloriani's world] as he had never yet so intimately been, had the consciousness of opening to it, for the happy instant, all the windows of his mind, of letting this rather grey interior drink in for once the sun of a clime not marked in his old geography. (21:196–97)

However, when Strether first confronts Chad he is brought up short by the overthrow of what is by that which he believed would

be. The consequences of this bewilderment are double: for Strether
his preconception of Chad is torn away and the whole idea of his
embassy comes to an abrupt halt. Furthermore, this marks the first
real moment in the novel where the reader is set adrift. The
alarming disparity between Chad as he appears in the opera box
and the image we have been led to expect by Woollett's absolutist
interpretation initiates our distrust in Strether's ability to take the
measure of things. James accentuates our developing skepticism with
regard to Strether's interpretive skill through the presentation of a
detailed description of the ambassador's bewildered reaction to
Chad.

What he might have shown, had he shown at all, was exactly the kind of
emotion – the emotion of bewilderment – that he had proposed to himself
from the first, whatever should occur, to show least. The phenomenon that
had suddenly sat down there with him was a phenomenon of change so
complete that his imagination, which had worked so beforehand, felt itself,
in the connexion, without margin or allowance. It had faced every
contingency but that Chad should not *be* Chad, and this was what it now
had to face with a mere strained smile and an uncomfortable flush.
(21:136–37)

What James shows here through the development of Strether's
reaction to the unexpected Chad is how much we are dependent
upon prior conceptions in order to understand at all. As Strether
struggles for ground on which to construct a revised theory of Chad,
he projects, once again, an image of himself. This time the image is
that of "the pale figure of his real youth," the spirit Paris has evoked
and which has been wandering about, so to speak, looking for a
body to inhabit since being brought back to life. Strether admits as
much in an earlier scene when, in the midst of thoughts about Chad,
he begins to think about not only what he wants out of the Parisian
visit, but what he would have done had he been afforded Chad's
"privilege."

He wasn't there to dip, to consume – he was there to reconstruct. He
wasn't there for his own profit – not, that is, the direct; he was there on
some chance of feeling the brush of the wing of the stray spirit of youth.
(21:94)

This projection of an idealized image of his youthful self onto Chad
is a crucial moment of transference in *The Ambassadors* as it offers an
insight into Strether's developing impercipience, of his almost

incredible inability to see the nature of Chad's and Madame de Vionnet's intimacy when it is apparent to everyone, including the reader. Only at the end of his adventure does Strether come to see that they are "intimate" and that Chad "was none the less only Chad," a perception which, ironically, returns both Strether and the reader to the earlier bewilderment at Chad's not being Chad (22:278, 284).

The second and more devastating projection Strether builds upon the exploded image of his first – the vulgar Chad – has to do with the *volte-face* Chad's altogether other than anticipated appearance evokes. When the metamorphosed Chad thwarts Strether's ability to know by imposition, Strether experiences a hermeneutical crisis, and responds by falling back on yet another preconception. As his critical skills, his ability to respond perceptively to the situation abandon him, Strether fills his gap in understanding with an already produced image. The rapidity with which Strether moves from a mild contempt for Chad to aesthetic enchantment with him catches the reader by surprise. The shift in Strether's perception is partially "represented by the fact that Chad had been made over" (21:150). However, it is not just that Chad has been made over by others; Strether himself completes the make over when he ascribes to Chad his own moral uprightness. James makes the reader aware of this transference when he has Strether answer the question "whom should I enjoy being like" with the following sudden recognition: "It was the click of a spring – he saw the truth. He had by this time also met Chad's look; there was more of it in that; and the truth, accordingly, so far as Bilham's enquiry was concerned, had thrust in the answer. 'Oh, Chad!' – it was that rare youth he should have enjoyed being 'like' " (21:220). The result of Strether's transference is crucial for it is what disables him from taking the true measure of Chad and Madame de Vionnet and forces not just Strether but the reader into yet another hermeneutic circle. That is, when Strether overwrites Chad's identity with the fantasized image of his own youthful self, he effectually removes the original Chad Newsome from his interpretive horizon and takes away any ground on which understanding can take place for the reader as much as for Strether.

The consequences of this transference are far-reaching for everyone involved in *The Ambassadors*, reader included. Once Strether has transferred to Chad his own moral character, he cannot help but see the relationship as "virtuous." Strether becomes like a character in a play who actually believes the roles all the other players are inhabiting to be their real identities. Indeed, not only do metaphors of drama and the stage permeate *The Ambassadors*, the text is filled with direct references to drama and to Strether's imagined impression of himself as a playwright or author. For instance, the entire country scene is an example of how Strether transfigures reality by overwriting what is there with what he imagines the scene should look like according to his textual experiences of such a "reality." To this extent, the country scene is a microcosm of Strether's whole Parisian experience. Strether talks of "the spell of the picture" which helped create "the scene and a stage," and that the "very air of the play was in the rustle of the willows and the tone of the sky." Then, as though commenting directly on his experience of Parisian social reality, Strether says the "play and the characters had, without his knowing it till now, peopled all his space for him, and it seemed somehow quite happy that they should offer themselves, in the conditions so supplied, with a kind of inevitability" (22:253).[28] And since his is the center of consciousness through which all experiences are mediated, everyone and everything involved is artificially ennobled. And this is exactly what happens. After all, Strether's elevated belief in the people involved does not just condition his understanding of them, it also influences their understanding of themselves, a point brought into sharp focus when Marie de Vionnet breaks down into uncontrollable sobs during her final conversations with Strether (22:285–87). For, despite their additional qualities, Chad is a womanizer, Madam de Vionnet an adulteress, and Little Bilham a liar. Maria Gostrey calls Strether's attention to his power over reality when she remarks "that you dressed up even the virtue" of it all (22:300). How readers make their way through the elements of fancy and reality in Strether's experience is directly proportional to their ability to understand Strether better than he does himself. That readers become unavoidably caught up in and then suspicious of Strether's ability to understand what is going on testifies to the novel's success at inducing an epistemological crisis in its reading audience. James's intended provocation of such a crisis in *The Ambassadors* elevates the text to the status of a practical hermeneutics and makes apparent literature's direct application to reality. In other words, the reader's reaction to Strether's self-coerced understanding is an empirical demonstration of how the James text first refuses to be constrained within a typical reading experience, and second, how that text goes so far as to interrupt and then revise the reader's own interpretive process.

IX

How Strether winds up the only one involved in *The Ambassadors* unable to see the truth of Chad's and Madame de Vionnet's relationship is an interesting study in how easily one can fall victim to what Gadamer called the "tyranny of hidden prejudices." When Strether looks closely at Chad he is won over by the (at least superficial) change. By showing the way Strether constructs reasons for his new conviction, James highlights the degree to which all understanding is necessarily composed and therefore suspect. Strether reasons from Chad's improved appearance that the woman involved must be good, since "the product of her genius" appears so impressive (22:116).

> The moment really took on for Strether an intensity. Chad owed Madame de Vionnet so much? What *did* that do then but clear up the whole mystery? He was indebted for alterations, and she was thereby in a position to have sent in her bill for expenses incurred in reconstruction. (21:336)

Once Strether arrives at his assumption that the affair is virtuous, every experience is filtered through a distorting medium which serves more to corroborate than illuminate his preconceptions. Part of the novel's irony is that the more apparent the affair's adulterous nature becomes for the reader, the more Strether seems determined to believe in its platonic quality. When pressed by Little Bilham, Strether admits to attributing "a very high ideal of conduct" to Chad (21:285).

Strether's misperception of Chad dramatizes again the mistake of closing the hermeneutic circle prematurely. The deeper Strether falls into his projected image of Chad, the more impressive Chad appears, and the more impressive Chad becomes for Strether, the more Strether finds him the envied realization of his own youthful desires. Strether makes explicit the transference of his identity in explaining his perception of Chad and Marie de Vionnet to Maria Gostrey. Strether admits the couple is his "surrender," his "tribute, to youth," and that they offer him a chance to make "up late for what I didn't have early." As Strether asserts, "the point is they're mine. Yes, they're my youth; since somehow at the right time nothing else ever was" (22:51). Strether's remark, of course, extends itself beyond the text with the reader's ineluctable query: "what are they to me, and why?" Two passages from *The Ambassadors* warrant observation in how they illuminate the process of Strether's self-imposed deception. The first comes as Strether marvels at Chad's ability to socialize during Gloriani's party:

He was as easy, clever Chad, with the great artist [Gloriani] as with his obscure compatriot, and as easy with every one else as with either ... Chad accordingly, who was wonderful with both of them, was a kind of link for hopeless fancy, an implication of possibilities – oh if everything had been different ... Our friend hadn't come there only for this figure of Abel Newsome's son, but that presence threatened to affect the observant mind as positively central. (21:197–98)

The second, toward the end of the novel, comes immediately following Strether's break with Sarah Pocock and shortly before Strether discovers the full extent of Chad's relations with Marie de Vionnet. Like the above passage, the one which follows reveals Strether's desire and his tendency to experience life vicariously through Chad.

And if many things moreover passed before them, none passed more distinctly for Strether than that striking truth about Chad of which he had been so often moved to take note: the truth that everything came happily back with him to his knowing how to live. (22:231)

Once Strether abandons what we could call a hermeneutics of suspicion[29] and allows a mentally produced image to stand between him and a more complete understanding of his experiences, he becomes susceptible to the very modulations of perception James saw as simultaneously wondrous and hazardous. What James drama-tizes through Strether's attempt to struggle his way toward under-standing is how easy the situation of reality can change with a subtle shift in the perceiver's perspective. Once again James's house of fiction metaphor is an apt explanation of what goes on in life. Since Strether sees Chad as the embodiment of his own youth and Madame de Vionnet as the magnificent artist whose hand has wrought the change in Chad, every action which involves these characters is conditioned within Strether's interpretive paradigm. Strether's interpretation of his encounter with Madame de Vionnet in Notre Dame shows this hermeneutic persuasion at work. As far as

Strether is concerned, Marie de Vionnet's presence in the church proves the extraordinary nature of her relationship with Chad.

This attitude fitted admirably into the stand he had taken about her connexion with Chad on the last occasion of his seeing them together. It helped him to stick fast at the point he had then reached; it was there he had resolved that he *would* stick, and at no moment since had it seemed as easy to do so. Unassailably innocent was a relation that could make one of the parties to it so carry herself. If it wasn't innocent why did she haunt the churches? – into which, given the woman he could believe he had made out, she would never have come to flaunt an insolence of guilt. She haunted them for continued help, for strength, for peace – sublime support which, if one were able to look at it so, she found from day to day. (22:10)

The interrogative dynamic reveals the depth of James's analysis of the circular character of understanding here. Strether makes a question-begging assumption about the nature of the relationship, then posits that Marie de Vionnet's presence in Notre Dame proves the relationship's virtuousness, and finally concludes from his premises that she would not be in the church to begin with were the relationship different from what he thinks.[30]

However, it would be incorrect to suggest James condemns Strether. On the contrary, though Strether's interpretive wanderings dramatize what both James and Gadamer agree are the pitfalls associated with the attempt to hypothesize about or project meaning upon reality, so too do they make manifest the need to be ever and always open to the possibility of contradiction, perplexity, and, to the refusal of reality to be confined within an interpretive paradigm. The stance of openness James presents here dramatizes a way beyond what ends up as the pathological deformities portrayed by, say, *The Sacred Fount*'s narrator, whose hermeneutics is determinately rooted in control and closure. Accordingly, as much as Strether's own mind dupes him with regard to Chad and Madame de Vionnet, so too does it allow him to escape the blind and unforgiving rigor of Woollett's restrictive vision. Throughout his Parisian experience Strether surrenders his imagination and opens to the possibilities of Paris. Indeed Strether's giving his imagination free rein and his misreading of Chad and Marie de Vionnet are complementary, for from the moment he sees Chad as the manifestation of his youth his free-floating imagination takes care of the rest and enables him, ultimately, to get a much better understanding of the affair than does

Sarah Pocock, who merely equates it with a cheap adultery and condemns it accordingly.

Martha Nussbaum has characterized this shift in Strether's consciousness as a willingness to surrender, to be passive, to revel in the particularity of life: "a willingness to surrender invulnerability, to take up a posture of agency that is porous and susceptible of influence, is of the highest importance in getting an accurate perception of particular things in the world" ("Perceptive Equilibrium," 71). Strether's willingness to accept "particularity," Nussbaum goes on to say, "involves a willingness to be incomplete, to be surprised by the new" (71). In this way, Strether's experience of reality, that is to say of other people and, of course, of himself, matches the structured dialectic of bewilderment and enlightenment, where one is the condition of the other's possibility. This is how James understood our experience of reality. It might not be too paradoxical to say that the failure of understanding becomes the medium of understanding, but Jamesian hermeneutics comes down to something *like* that. James makes this point repeatedly through the course of his career. For instance, in the Preface to the *Princess Casamassima* he claims it "seems probable that if we were never bewildered there would never be a story to tell about us" (1090). Strether's own celebration of life's bewildering multiplicity echoes James's statements to the same.

"It isn't playing the game to turn on the uncanny. All one's energy goes to facing it, to tracking it. One wants, confound it, don't you see?" he confessed with a queer face – "one wants to enjoy anything so rare. Call it then life" – he puzzled it out – "call it poor dear old life simply that springs the surprise. Nothing alters the fact that the surprise is paralysing, or at any rate engrossing – all, practically, hang it, that one sees, that one *can* see." (21:167)

Strether's celebration of the uncanny, of course, flies in the face of Woollett's paradigm of interpretive confinement and is precisely what Gadamer means by the hermeneutical experience. For Gadamer, such an experience brings about a release from constraints and makes possible a condition of openness. That Strether recognizes "the fact that the surprise is paralysing" but also responsible for his new-found ability to see, parallels exactly Gadamer's sense that the hermeneutical experience involves a breakdown of one's conceptual framework and leaves one suddenly naked with respect to the world.

For James the difference between the interpretive stance of Sarah Pocock and that of Lambert Strether was the difference between a narrowly referential realism and the type of more openly ambiguous, psychologically complex, and, James would have it, *real* novel he saw as valuable. Ross Posnock has noted that "James's technical achievement and imaginative engagement with the groping motions of curiosity is a tribute to fallibilism, to loss of control, and to the hazards of accident" (*Trial of Curiosity*, 246). James says as much in an essay on Guy de Maupassant. The "novel," he explains, "is simply a vision of the world from the standpoint of a person constituted after a certain fashion," and "it is therefore absurd to say that there is, for the novelist's use, only one reality of things." In developing this line of thought James also explains that though the novel is "a direct impression of life ... the impression will vary according to the plate that takes it, the particular structure and mixture of the recipient" ("Guy de Maupassant," *Literary Criticism*, II, 522–23). Sarah Pocock's competing vision dramatizes James's understanding of reality's tendency toward multiplicity, or at least reality's tendency to "conform" to the perspective of the individual perceiver. But one should not interpret Strether's condition at this stage of his development as James's advocacy of a simple open-mindedness. For James's *laissez-faire* disengagement is every bit as much a form of mediation as is the rigidity of Sarah Pocock's conceptual apparatus. The former is forever in danger of being overrun and disabled by the latter, a point James makes when he has Strether's sense of things challenged by Sarah Pocock's constrictive vision. Unlike Strether's, Sarah's interpretive paradigm is unable to accommodate particular modulations of reality. While Strether waits for Sarah to confirm his impressions, to whisper "You're right; we haven't quite known what you mean, Mother and I, but now we see. Chad's magnificent; what can one want more?", Sarah of course sees an altogether different picture, a change that is "hideous," and a woman who is nothing but a vulgar adulteress (22:80). Sarah's refusal to see Chad and Madame de Vionnet as Strether does so astonishes the latter that he is led not only to question his ability to understand but to ask about the nature of reality itself.

However, there is more at stake in the stand-off between Strether and Sarah than competing modes of vision. James makes a larger point about experience and interpretation in general. Rather than merely privilege the beginnings of Strether's openness, James goes so far as to suggest that openness is the most nearly natural state and that prejudice is a learned behavior that must be unlearned if understanding is to occur at all. James dramatizes this idea through Sarah's experiences in Paris, particularly the development of her "virtuous affair" with Waymarsh. Maria Gostrey and Strether imagine Waymarsh making love to Sarah: "Floating her over in champagne? The kindness of dining her, nose to nose, at the hour when all Paris is crowding to profane delights, and in the – well, in the great temple, as one hears of it, of pleasure?" (22:137). To be sure, Sarah's relationship with Waymarsh is important because through it James suggests the line between virtue and adultery is not so easily drawn, that there are degrees of each. In fact, as James shows, it takes the "fixed eyes of their admirable absent mother fairly [to] screw into the flat of [Sarah's] back" to remind her that she needs to find Paris a Babylon and everything in it vile (22:162). The crux of the conflict between Sarah and Strether comes when Sarah leads Strether to question the whole idea of his understanding of reality.

Was he, on this question of Chad's improvement, fantastic and away from the truth? Did he live in a false world, a world that had grown simply to suit him, and was his present slight irritation ... but the alarm of the vain thing menaced by the touch of the real? Was this contribution of the real possibly the mission of the Pococks? (222:80–81)

The stand-off between these ambassadors is made more difficult for the reader because both share in the truth, so far as the reader is able to determine. In having the reader want to modify Sarah's judgment and see Chad and Madame de Vionnet as more than adulterers, James shows the insufficiencies of interpretive categories when applied to particular circumstances.

x

Through the course of *The Ambassadors* everything builds to a powerful moment of bewilderment: the famous country scene in which Strether feels himself moving about within a Lambinet painting. Nowhere in the novel is Strether more responsible for transfiguring his impressions to suit his mental landscape, or more oblivious to the solipsism James exploited in developing his center of consciousness technique, and nowhere in James's fiction (other than,

perhaps, Isabel Archer's searching night vigil) does James so effectively highlight the epistemological crisis Gadamer sees as yoked to
the hermeneutical experience. Strether's experience of reality in this
scene has more to do with what he brings to it than what it gives to
him. James tells the reader how Strether does not "once overstep the
oblong gilt frame" within which he experiences the French country-
side: "The frame had drawn itself out for him, as much as you
please; but that was just his luck" (22:252). The moment of bewilderment occurs when something from outside his framed vision intrudes
and transcends his ability, momentarily, to absorb and make sense of
the event. Only when Chad and Marie de Vionnet drift into
Strether's picture, when "at the very moment of the impression ...
their boat seemed to have begun to drift," does Strether realize the
full extent to which he has been mistaken about the larger reality of
their affair (22:256). The sudden explosion of Strether's frame of
reference matches exactly James's understanding of reality as an
unfixable, ever-expanding horizon, what William James referred to
as a "multiverse."[31]

Strether demonstrates the creative nature of consciousness by first
absorbing the boating couple into his picture, "as if these figures, or
something like them, had been wanted in the picture, had been
wanted more or less all day, and now drifted into sight with the slow
current, on purpose to fill up the measure," and then by being
thrown back on his earlier experiences in an effort to understand
and assimilate this unexpected event. In a scene reminiscent of
Isabel Archer's night vigil, Strether returns at the end of the evening
to Paris and spends the night awake in a "vain vigil" (22:256, 266).
The internal structure of Strether's vigil is identical to Isabel's.
Strether's vision of Chad and Madame de Vionnet in the country
constitutes an apperception which impresses itself upon his present
frame of reference and allows him to reconstitute his understanding
in light of a reinterpretation of past experiences. Not only do the
boating couple prove, James would say, that the "real represents to
my perception the things we cannot possibly *not* know," but their
unexpected appearance accentuates the very reason why a fixed
determination of reality is impossible: "it being but one of the
accidents of our hampered state, and one of the incidents of their
quantity and number, that particular instances have not yet come
our way" (Preface, *The American*, 1062–63). What Strether finds by
his own admission, "as he was afterwards to remember," is that he

has been the unwitting victim of the tyranny of hidden prejudices: "He recognized at last that he really had been trying all along to suppose nothing. Verily, verily, his labour had been lost. He found himself supposing innumerable and wonderful things" (22:260, 266).

To answer why Strether does not recoil at the sudden realization of the affair's adulterous component is to get at the role attunement (what Rivkin calls the "logic of delegation") plays in Jamesian hermeneutics ("Logic of Delegation," 829). To be sure the recoil is expected by all, including the reader. James makes these concerns apparent through Maria Gostrey's observations of Strether at the time of his disabusement: "the difference for him might not inconceivably be an arrest for his independence and a change in his attitude – in other words a revulsion in favor of the principles of Woollett. She had really prefigured the possibility of a shock that would send him swinging back to Mrs. Newsome" (22:296). That Strether does not retreat to "the principles of Woollett," despite the high personal cost of his break with Mrs. Newsome, explains how far he has moved the other way, toward a celebration of the uncanny. To accept the uncanny is to accept bewilderment as a condition for understanding, to accept reality as a continually enlarging horizon. And in coming to accept and possibly even welcome the possibility of bewilderment as a condition of understanding Strether learns, as Rivkin has argued, that "experience, the truth of life" which he believed was stable, is more correctly to be understood as "something detached from any fixed ground" and not only "revisable" but even "multiple" (828). This revision of consciousness seems to be James's larger point in *The Ambassadors*. We recall James's remark in his preliminary notes for the novel that the "idea of the tale" centered on "the revolution that takes place in the poor man" (*Notebooks*, 227). Strether's capacity to respond to the situation, his being able first to assimilate it and then revise his understanding in a way that acknowledges his respect for Madame de Vionnet and his commitment to her relationship with Chad as a good thing, shows how much Strether has learned to be open to the probability of bewilderment. Strether's enlarged capacity to understand the multifoldness of reality reminds us, once again, of Foucault's remarks about the need to forcefully escape the imprisonment of interpretive systems:

what would be the passion for knowledge if it resulted only in a certain amount of knowledgeableness and not, in one way or another and to the extent possible, in the knower's straying afield of himself? There are times in life when the question of knowing if one can think differently than one thinks, and perceive differently than one sees, is absolutely necessary if one is to go on looking and reflecting at all. (*Use of Pleasure*, 8)

For Strether, the sudden shock that "the couple thus fixing his attention were intimate" tests his ability to think about adultery in a way inaccessible to his Woollett self. That he succeeds demonstrates James's idea that understanding and interpretation, if they are to occur at all, demand action, in the sense that Strether is given a choice between falling back on Woollett's narrowly correct interpretation and his recent, more ambiguous and indeterminable understanding of the affair.

Strether's epiphany comes not in his realization of the simple truth of the couple's intimacy, nor in his refusal to revert to Woollett's principles, but in his determination to "absolutely prevent" Chad "from so much as thinking of" abandoning Marie de Vionnet (22:311). The reader should not underestimate the remarkable reversal Strether undergoes during the course of his Parisian experience. How Strether responds to Chad and Madame de Vionnet is as much a surprise to himself as to all observing him. Sent on an embassy to force Chad's return to "the general safety of being anchored by [Mrs, Newsome's] strong chain," Strether winds up doing his best to break the chain at the very moment he finds all of Woollett's expectations of baseness verified (21:71). James underscores Strether's *volte-face* by having Strether implore Chad to remain with Marie de Vionnet in the same language he first used to make Chad aware of his filial duties. A juxtaposition of Strether's earlier and later injunctions to Chad brings James's point home with clarity. The first, imploring Chad's return to Woollett, is as follows:

"Well, we want you to break. Your mother's heart's passionately set upon it, but she has above and beyond that excellent arguments and reasons. I have not put them into her head – I needn't remind you how little she's a person who needs that. But they exist – you must take it from me as a friend both of her's and yours – for myself as well. I didn't invent them, I didn't originally work them out; but I understand them, I think I can explain them – by which I mean to make you actively do them justice, and that is why you see me here. You had better know the worst at once. It is a question of an immediate rupture and an immediate return." (21:148)

The second, imploring Chad to remain, echoes the first, but with an ironic twist. In counseling Chad to remain, Strether deploys the severe moralist's language of Woollett for what can only be seen as the anti-Woollett position and pleads for fidelity within adultery:

"let me accordingly appeal to you by all you hold sacred ... You'd not only be, as I say, a brute; ... you'd be a criminal of the deepest dye ... You owe her everything – very much more than she can ever owe you. You've in other words duties to her, of the most positive sort; and I don't see what other duties – as the others are presented to you – can be held to go before them." (22:311–13)

The determination of his insight is crucial for Strether because it is what allows him to begin the active dissociation of his past from his present reality. Rather than live by projection, Strether begins his engagement with life by learning to live through his experiences individually and coming to understand those experiences on their own ground. It is in this way that Foucault's explanation of this process fits Strether's experience particularly well, especially as James depicts Strether in the act of freeing thought from interpretive routine in an effort to wrest some measure of interpretive freedom. "The object," Foucault points out, is "to learn to what extent the effort to think one's own history can free thought from what it silently thinks, and so enable it to think differently" (*Use of Pleasure*, 9). The degree of Strether's successful transformation can be measured in three phases. First in his recognition of, and subsequent refusal to fall in step with, Mrs. Newsome's systematic, fixed hermeneutic. Second, in his rigorous and selfless defense of Madame de Vionnet, especially when he could either remain silent or acquiesce to Sarah Pocock's condemnation of her (22:203). And, third, by his final refusal to pass judgment on Madame de Vionnet and Chad, even when he becomes aware of how he has been manipulated into complicity with the pair: "that his intervention had absolutely aided and intensified their intimacy, and that in fine he must accept the consequence of that" (22:278).

But it is not enough for James to show that Strether has learned to think differently. Understanding in James's hermeneutics always takes the form of action. Once again Gadamer's conception of insight, as something which "always involves an escape from something that had deceived us and held us captive," can teach us much about James's concerns with the role of understanding in his work. Strether's revaluation of what it means to be faithful, to be obligated, indeed to be ethical, "involves an element of self-knowledge" and is an important and enabling aspect of understanding, especially if any understanding of things or between people is to take place (*Truth and Method*, 310–20). The experienced person, Gadamer tells us, is not someone who "knows everything and knows better than anyone else," like Mrs. Newsome, but is someone who is "radically undogmatic" because life has taught him to remain open to the possibility that things may be different than they appear, they have been, or than one would like to believe (219). This experienced person is what, for example, Isabel Archer or Lambert Strether come to be. And by experienced I do not mean the more simple notion of worldliness (where experience is the opposite of innocence). Nor do I mean the sense captured by some of James's Europeans who become impervious to experience. These characters are fazed by nothing, nothing reaches them. What I see as more central to James's experiment in *The Ambassadors* (hence my recourse to Gadamer) is the emphasis on how the product of experience is not knowledge but openness or *phronēsis*, where experience leads to a kind of practical wisdom. An experienced person in this sense is responsive, capable of acting in the sense of carrying through in a situation and doing what is called for. Strether's actions at the end of *The Ambassadors*, his refusal to align himself with the Pococks or to bend under Mrs. Newsome's pressure, reveal his final openness and ability to cope with and make sense of everyone, including himself. It is to this extent that *The Ambassadors* can be seen as a *vade mecum* for James's hermeneutics.

James demonstrates how completely Strether meets the requirements of the experienced person in his final conversation with Marie de Vionnet. Fully expecting condemnation, Marie de Vionnet acknowledges how she must appear "[s]elfish and vulgar" to Strether (22:281). However, rather than criticize her, Strether demonstrates his sensitivity to her role in the affair and his understanding not only that the particular often outweighs the "universal," but that ethical values themselves must be fluid if they are to have currency in life. In examining this aspect of Strether's developing understanding of contingency Armstrong argues that *The Ambassadors* "suggests that the choice of an interpretive attitude is itself an ethical decision," and that as "an international drama *The Ambassadors* explores how conventions institutionalize ways of being with others. It suggests that there are as many possible forms of personal relations as there are cultural codes" (*Challenge*, 100, 102). This recognition of the need for subjective and cultural openness is the intended outcome of James's notion of experience and captures exactly the structure of Jamesian hermeneutics. In such a hermeneutics, one's capacity for understanding is directly proportionate to one's ability to get out of one's self. Again, the similarity between James's and Gadamer's notion of understanding is illuminating. As Gadamer explains, "the person with understanding does not know and judge as one who stands apart and unaffected," like Mrs. Newsome or Sarah Pocock, for instance, but stands, rather, "as one united by a specific bond with the other, he thinks with the other and understands the situation with him" (*Truth and Method*, 288). Thus, far from categorizing Madame de Vionnet as an adulteress, as Woollett's restrictive paradigm demands, Strether finds her situation much more complex and alive, larger than the simple facts Sarah throws in his face (22:203–4). Strether completes his ethical and interpretive revolution by offering Madame de Vionnet praise and support: "You've been making, as I have so fully let you know I have felt, . . . the most precious present I have ever seen made" and "[t]here's something I believe I can still do" (22:283, 288).

However, Strether's proposal of aid raises an important question about the conclusion of *The Ambassadors*. That Strether has become experienced in the way Gadamer describes being experienced is evident. James goes to great lengths to reveal the degree of change. But experience, in order to be properly called experience, is always disruptive, always takes away something we heretofore had accepted as understood. For instance, Chad's and Madame de Vionnet's intimacy presents Strether with a new and better understanding of their affair, a revelation which then brings about a reassessment of his entire interpretive system. Gadamer, as we have seen, explains the sea change experience brings as a productive negativity, since by characterizing something as an experience, what we really mean is that we have encountered an object in a way that takes our interpretive categories by surprise and "that we have not seen the thing correctly hitherto and now know it better. Thus the negativity of experience has a curiously productive meaning" (*Truth and Method*, 317).

The immediate comparison, of course, is Strether's experience of the affair. But several others give an indication of how deep and complete they become. He once again reevaluates Chad, bringing him back to earth as "none the less only Chad" (22:284) and he finds himself able more fully to understand Mrs. Newsome as imperme-able, like "some particularly large iceberg in a cool blue northern sea" (22:223). Strether's metaphor is important as it not only calls attention to the hardness of Mrs. Newsome's understanding, but also how much of her had remained hidden beneath her quiet surface.[32] Maria Gostrey focuses our attention on Strether's more complete understanding of Mrs. Newsome's influential power when she compares her to a block whose size is difficult to determine: "Little by little it looms up. It has been looming for you more and more till at last you see it all" (22:223). Gostrey's depiction captures exactly James's belief that since the interpreting subject is inside reality, any attempt to grasp the whole of it is thwarted by the limits of the interpreter's perspective. Mrs. Newsome so completely made up what Strether had understood as his reality, his life in Woollett, that only a shift in perspective, a view from the other side of the Atlantic gave him sufficient distance to see the whole of her influence. Strether's last word on his understanding of the Woollett doyenne is, as he explains to Maria Gostrey, that "She's the same. She's more than ever the same. But I do what I didn't before – I *see* her" (22:323).

We have seen that experience, its productive negativity as Gadamer has described the process, has consequences in James's hermeneutics, especially so at the conclusion of his novels. And we have seen how the end for James's characters like Christopher Newman, like Isabel Archer is indeterminate. So too are the consequences Strether must face as a condition of his experience. The point of this indeterminacy, I have suggested, is that James takes his characters through a series of experiences which refine their consciousness so that they finally approach mirroring his own, but that he ends their development there, as though to be responsive in the Jamesian sense means being dissociated from a fixed, localized world and aware that subjective identity is an ongoing project of negotiation between self and others, and between what is inside and what is outside. The parallel between the characters and James is clear, for James too belonged to no particular country or no particular world. Indeed, James celebrated his expatriatism as an example of his cultivated alien and nonidentity posture, as yet another way of breaking down boundaries. In his words: "I aspire to write in such a way that it would be impossible ... to say whether I am at a given moment an American writing about England or an Englishman writing about America ... and so far from being ashamed of such an ambiguity I should be exceedingly proud of it, for it would be highly civilized" (*Henry James Letters*, 1, 142). In *The Ambassadors* Marie de Vionnet calls Strether's attention both to the consequences of his experiences and how they have left him disconnected from the world. As he leaves her for the last time, supposedly before his return to Woollett, Madame de Vionnet forces Strether to recognize the impossibility of returning to the Woollett he left behind: "Where *is* your 'home' moreover now – what has become of it? I have made a change in your life, I know I have; I have upset everything in your mind as well; in your sense of – what shall I call it? – all the decencies and possibilities" (22:282). The question is so important for James's strategy in *The Ambassadors* that twice in the novel's last scene he has Maria Gostrey ask Strether "[to] what do you go home?" (22:325).

The answer to this question has involved readers of James from the moment of *The Ambassadors*'s publication. It is perhaps enough to say that Strether goes home to nothing, or that the first step in the direction of Woollett brings about the completion of his life, so far as James was interested in it. Strether, for his part, agrees that the return to Woollett will "amount to the wind-up of his career" (22:294). "Career" here is unmistakably to be read as "life," a connection James establishes by having Strether imagine what the future holds now that he is fully aware of social relations in Paris and his complicity in their development.

He had been great already, as he knew, at postponements; but he had only to get afresh into the rhythm of one to feel its fine attraction. It amused him to say to himself that he might for all the world have been going to die – die resignedly; the scene filled him with so deep a death-bed hush, so melancholy a charm. That meant postponement of everything else – which made so for the quiet lapse of life; and the postponement in especial of the reckoning to come – unless indeed the reckoning to come were to be one and the same thing with extinction. (22:293)

"Extinction" is one of the consequences of experience in James's hermeneutics. Extinction in the sense of being unable to inhabit the world one had heretofore known, unable to be the person one had heretofore been. Strether, as James mentions in *The Ambassadors*'s "Project," has "come so far through his total little experience that he has come out on the other side" (390). The "other side" here

seems to be the other side of fiction. For one thing that happens at
the end of almost all of James's major novels, to characters like
Strether, and Isabel Archer, and Maggie Verver, and Christopher
Newman, and, interestingly, Hyacinth Robinson, is that the characters are no longer containable within any plot or story. This is
perhaps why Strether backs away from Maria Gostrey's offer.
Resolution of his life is still premature, old as he is. He is no longer a
character in a novel. Viewed from this perspective *The Ambassadors*'s
famous final "Then there we are!" can be read as a coda for all of
James's work (22:327). "Then there we are!" is James's injunction to
readers to carry the dialogue they have been having with the text out
into the world at large. " 'Then there we are!' " is simultaneously the
beginning and the end of a spell, for as the reader puts down the
book and adjusts his or her enhanced gaze upon the world it is
almost as though James reaches out and draws back a curtain to
reveal a world which has been sufficiently altered as a result of the
reading experience. For James, who felt strongly "that the province
of art [was] all life, all feeling, all observation, all vision," art could
be no less ("Art of Fiction," 59). For James this was what "the high
and helpful ... civic use of the imagination" amounted to (Preface,
"Lesson of the Master," 1230). It is perhaps enough to say that
beyond that James did not care to go.

CHAPTER 5

Recovery and revelation: the experience of self-exposure in James's autobiography

> We shall not cease from exploration
> And the end of all our exploring
> Will be to arrive where we started
> And know the place.   T.S. Elliot, "Little Gidding"

I

By his own admission Henry James was not a passive reader. In a letter to Mrs. Humphrey Ward of June 17, 1899 James confesses "I am a wretched person to *read* a novel – I begin so quickly and concomitantly, *for myself,* to write it rather – even before I know clearly what it is about! The novel I can *only* read, I cannot read at all!" (*Henry James Letters,* IV, 110–11). This is a rather remarkable statement from a writer who has been persistently accused of being a passive aesthete more content with guarding the past than facing the present, more comfortable seated on life's sidelines as a passive observer than involved as an active participant. Granted, those who make an argument for the passive and detached formalist can and do call James's autobiographical admissions to their aid, but that enlistment is rather selective. Thus the James who says "I seemed to be constantly eager to exchange my lot for that of somebody else," or that "Pedestrian gaping" was "prevailingly my line," brings the weight of his own voice behind the school which has, as John Carlos Rowe suggests, determinedly fixed James as a "high-modernist" who "has been mythologized as the master of a life-denying estheticism" (*Theoretical Dimensions,* 28).[1] But James's comment about his reading or, more exactly, his appropriation of texts raises an aspect of James's relationship with art and life that cannot easily be accommodated within the "James the Aestheticist" school. In saying "I begin so quickly and concomitantly, *for myself,* to write it rather," James

185

explains something central about his understanding of experience, something which not only goes far beyond passive reception, but suggests that one reevaluate what James meant when he explains how he wanted to step into other subjectivities or found himself transfixed before the human shuffle. In fact, what James's confession to Mrs. Humphrey Ward points to is a writer whose tremendously subtle and transformative consciousness innately seeks both to over-write other texts and, as the fiction and autobiography dramatize, overwrite other subjectivities, including his own. To read James this way is to find him an active and transformative agent whose aesthetics is focused on the interactive quality of experience and must be read in terms of action, and whose perception is fundamentally destructuring and recreative.

Such a reading of James's autobiographical as well as his fictional work seeks to reexamine more traditional and deep-seated notions of Jamesian subjectivity. Posnock's *The Trial of Curiosity* is the most recent, and perhaps most sustained examination of this active and engaged side of Jamesian aesthetics. In a chapter focusing on James's autobiography, Posnock recovers James's notion of the self as active and goes so far as to suggest that James's operative question in the autobiography is "What does it mean for the self to have form?" (*Trial of Curiosity*, 169). What Posnock goes on to show is how completely James "equates intersubjectivity with representation" (172). Rather than document a fixed subject, the autobiography, from the opening sentence which blurs the distinction between biography ("the attempt to place together some particulars of the early life of William James" [*Autobiography*, 3]) and autobiography (Henry's memories), reveals James's understanding of the self as "permeable" and goes from there "to destabilize identities in order to reopen the question of how self and other are related" (168, 170). It is by paying attention to these lines of James's recollection that the autobiography, from start to finish, can be seen as dramatizing the development of an aesthetic which has transformed observation and contemplation into a form of participation and which relies on the cultivation of an active perceptual discrimination.

As Posnock argues, "nonparticipation," in Jamesian parlance, "is not a refusal of action and submission to passivity but commitment to a particular mode of practice called 'discrimination'" which, contrary to conventional belief, "is not an elitist mechanism of exclusion but an instrument of individual and cultural replenishment that propagates the 'more' – what James calls the 'margin'" and "enlarges possibilities of perception and hence of experience" (180–81). Thus, at the level of his autobiography, James adjusts his fine-tuned discrimination not only toward his past in an effort to squeeze the most possible out of his memories, but to examine those memories in such a way as to show how they reveal the same dialectic of bewilderment and enlightenment which forms the principal content of his fiction. *A Small Boy and Others*, as well as the remaining two volumes of the autobiography, build up then, as Leon Edel explains, "the development of an artistic sensibility and the education of an imagination, and that capacity for observing 'by instinct and reflection,' with irony 'and yet with that fine taste for the truth of the matter which makes the genius of observation'" (*The Master*, 456). It is in this sense, in how James lives through and appropriates memory open-endedly, that the autobiography demonstrates the full measure of Jamesian experience and its role in the development of an appropriative and endlessly open subjectivity which, by its very constitution, thrives on active, perceptual participation.

If, as I have argued throughout this book, an understanding of James's hermeneutics comes down to an understanding of his conception of experience as a fundamentally negative process through which one's subjectivity is constantly being breached and reconstructed anew, then James's autobiographical writings should reveal this dialectic of bewilderment and enlightenment as an ineluctable aspect of self-representation. Such an argument would require some demonstration that in looking back over his life James not only reexperienced events, but that he began, once again to quote his remark to Mrs. Humphrey Ward, "quickly and concomitantly" to rewrite the prior text, where "text" would simultaneously refer to those memories he summons and the self he finds embedded in the past and observing from the present. James would say it was impossible to do anything else since he possessed "an imagination to which literally everything obligingly signified," even himself (*Autobiography*, 449). This active, one could go so far as to say enlivening, aspect of James's relationship with writing is precisely what he focused on when he explained his *Notes of a Son and Brother* to Henry Adams in a letter of March 21, 1914. In response to what James refers to as Adams's "melancholy outpouring," James says:

the purpose, almost, of my printed divagations was to show you that one *can*, strange to say, still want to – or at least can behave as if one did [want to talk and live]. Behold me therefore so behaving – and apparently capable of continuing to do so. I still find my consciousness interesting – under *cultivation* of the interest ... I still, in the presence of life, ... have reactions – as many as possible – and the book I sent you [*Notes of a Son and Brother*] is a proof of them. It is I suppose, because I am that queer monster the artist, an obstinate finality, an inexpressible sensibility. Hence the reactions – appearances, memories, many things go on playing upon it with consequences that I note and 'enjoy' ... noting. It all takes doing – and I *do*. I believe I shall do yet again – it is still an act of life." (*Henry James Letters*, IV, 705–6)

In referring to his "printed divagations" as an experience which provokes "reactions" and stimulates his consciousness to such a degree that he can quantify the autobiographical text as "an act of life," James foregrounds what I have referred to as the principal aspect of his hermeneutics – the sense of experience as an event which destructures only to recreate subjectivity and promotes the cultivation of an essential openness to the possibility of experience itself. Furthermore, even the internal dynamics of the prose here solidify James's notion of art, at least insofar as he was a practitioner, as synonymous with an active engagement with the world around him. Note, for instance, how James moves from an explanation of the behavior of his consciousness – "interesting – under *cultivation* of the interest" – to equate that curiosity with "the presence of life," and, finally, to link both his consciousness and life at large with artistic sensibility. The notable lack of distinction between the private and public, as the similar refusal to divide the aesthetic from the everyday, foregrounds James's conception of art as "an act of life," and "life" as a complex of "reactions – appearances, memories, [and] many things" which require, as does art, a degree of receptivity which cannot be accommodated by a fixed subjectivity.

It should be noted here that the extent of what I have referred to as James's active engagement with the world is not to be confused with a critique of more conventional forms of activism, but nor is it to be interpreted as a valorization of passivity. James does not mean by active engagement a call to the barricades, as I have mentioned, but a perceptive grasp of the interanimating process by which all forms of interpretation and understanding, private and public, historical and immediate, imprint themselves upon our consciousness and shape the way we see the world. Active engagement means a level of perception which treats reality as fluid and not something either given and fixed, or something created by the imposition of an imperializing will. This is the position James takes as an artist. Since the world always presents itself as a mirror to art, the artist's chore, James says, is not merely to capture that image – as a naturalist – or to duck it – as an aesthete – but to make it more clear by offering a point of view which documents the drama of a "perspectival realism" (to borrow Rowe's phrase, *Theoretical Dimensions*, 188). Such a distillation of experience can be successful only if the artist actively collects, forges, and shapes a representative work which not only gives the impression of life itself, but makes life seem understandable to the reader through the protagonist's hermeneutic struggle. This is James's victory in his hermeneutics. The artist could be a "man of action in art," one who presents life in the form of a possibility only art can yield.

We can see the basic structure of this position being worked out in James's novel *The Princess Casamassima*. When Lionel Trilling remarks that the novel's protagonist, Hyacinth Robinson, carries a death summons which is indicative of James's "demonstrative message, to the world in general, to his brother and sister in particular, that the artist quite as much as any man of action carries his ultimate death warrant in his pocket," he indicates the path James follows to worldly engagement through artistic creation ("Princess," 84). Granted, James would agree the artist is quite as capable as any other individual of forceful and worldly action. But the death warrant Trilling describes suggests an additional, larger danger; that presented by an understanding which attempts to corral the bewildering quality of experience within a restrictive consciousness and to assume from that perspective either an illusory control over reality or, if in the realm of art, to create works whose mimetic force is stunted. In *The Princess of Casamassima* James dramatizes this escapism through Hyacinth's devotion to an art divorced from the world. Such an art, James argues, is lifeless; those who produce it impotent, those who digest it in danger of enchantment. To view the world thus, James demonstrates, is to live behind a mask. So it is with Hyacinth, who despite desiring "to go through life in his own character," opts instead "to go through life in a mask, in a borrowed mantle," behind which "he was to be every day and every hour an actor" (5:86). But what James says of Hyacinth is applicable more generally to society as a whole. Role playing is a condition of the mind's buckling under the pressure of reality's refusal to be confined.

The role is a retreat from the requirements such pressure places on one's imagination. The death warrant is issued when we accept the *image* of the real, the confinement offered by the role, *as* the real thing. The thing itself, James demonstrates, can never be known since reality is always larger than any attempt to capture it. The artist's willingness to confront this threat openly is a risk, James would say, spared the rest of humanity. To take *that* risk is to carry the ultimate death warrant in one's pocket.

James was so convinced of the need to avoid the trap of preestablished interpretive paradigms that he embedded the idea of interpretive openness in the beginning passages of his autobiography. For instance, in the first moments of *A Small Boy and Others* James remarks upon what he sees will be some the "consequences of [his] interrogation of the past" (3). One aspect of the trip James finds particularly compelling is something all autobiographers necessarily confront, that to "recover" any memory is "at the same time to live over the spent experience itself" (3).[2] But rather than attempt to recapture that past from the small boy's perspective and thus offer up a documentary autobiography, James projects his present consciousness back and lives through from that perspective the recreated experiences of his young self. The difference is crucial because it allows James first to show how writing is, to quote his letter to Henry Adams, "an act of life," second, to find in his childhood experiences the seeds of his mature, examining consciousness, and third, to find in his developing response to himself and other people a complete manifestation of the Jamesian consciousness.[3]

This peculiar dynamic at work in the autobiography is what leads Edel to suggest that "if the old man pacing the narrow room superimposed himself on the bright-eyed small boy or the meditative youth, it was through insights into stages of his growth, the process that had made him artist and ultimately Master" (*The Master,* 457).[4] This explains the often confusing confluence of recovery, reliving, re-experiencing, and recreation presented in the autobiography. James catches himself in the act, so to speak, when he observes, via the autobiographical gaze, how he can "at any rate watch the small boy dawdle and gape again" (*Autobiography,* 16–17). What is provocative about this observation is how, one paragraph later, at the start of the next chapter, the gaze seems to change focus as James, employing the words he just used to document his memory, redeploys the phrase as part of a more purely creative gaze. To this extent, the second appearance of the phrase "dawdle and gape" takes on a whole new resonance by being linked directly to terms James used repeatedly to describe the specifically artistic process. In this sense the autobiographical flows into the fictional as though both were or, at least in James's case, will be the same: "But I positively dawdle and gape here – I catch myself in the act; so that I take up the thread of fond reflection" (*Autobiography*, 17). To be sure, rather than chronicling the past, James gives himself over to a "soft confusion" in which he can freely "reconstruct and reconstruct" in such a way as to excuse himself from the need for historical verisimilitude so as to get at a deeper level of understanding, which includes, as Edel has suggested, an understanding of what made James the small boy become James the Master (8, 79).

One of the first readers to notice the recreative composition of James's autobiography was his nephew Henry James III, William's son. In answer to his nephew's being offended by Henry's unauthorized revisions of William's letters, Henry explains that "documentary exactitude, verbatim ... or pedantic conformity" were not "in the least what I felt my job" to be (*Henry James Letters*, IV, 800). Rather, James explains, "when I laid hands upon the letters to use so many touches and tones in the picture I frankly confess I seemed to see them in a better, or at all events in another light, here and there, than those rough and rather illiterate copies I had from you showed at their face value" (802). James's literal and metaphorical revision of the letters, coupled with his invocation of William's ghost lamenting "Oh but you're not going to give me away, to hand me over, in my raggedness and my poor accidents, quite unhelped, unfriended, you're going to do the very best for me you *can*, aren't you," seems a gloss on his own recreative architecture in the autobiography. The difference in vision, of course, is that between the putative autobiographer, the person William's son expected to see, and James's uncontrollable need to control and recreate life and memory, to *make* his autobiography "a tale of assimilations small and fine" and thus avoid the "sundry expressions of life or force" he called "art without grace" (*Autobiography*, 105, 128). As Edel notes of the uncle's exchange with his nephew, James was convinced that some of the "family history" could only "be written as art: life in its raw state was inartistic" (*The Master*, 457). Towards the end of this letter James underscores the real issue at work in his reauthoring of the letters and authoring of the autobiography. One makes a mistake, James suggests, to believe that "my whole bookmaking impulse is governed by... any mere merciless transcript" quality.

I have to the last point the instinct and the sense for fusions and interrelations, for framing and encircling... every part of my stuff in every other – and that makes a danger when the frame and the circle play over too much upon the image. (*Henry James Letters*, IV, 803)

Read as a comment upon the entire autobiographical project, James's answer to his nephew assumes a heightened importance because it reveals, as Ross Posnock has argued, first, how James's fictional impulses problematize "the possibility of a 'mere ... transcript'" and, second, how Henry's "closeness to his brother William makes problematic the bourgeois norm of identity as *homo clausus*," the "encapsulation," Posnock, quoting Norbert Elias, explains, "of the self within in the self" (*Trial of Curiosity*, 172, 169). Thus the letter to his nephew, like the autobiography, becomes an arena in which James foregrounds and explains the need for the self to be fluid and open to the possibility of new experience and demonstrates how art was for James, as Millicent Bell infers, "*both* being and doing,... an endless receptivity as well as a mode of acting upon others" ("Fiction," 472). In short, James could no more refrain from acting on the text of William's letters than he could on the text of his memories, and, by extension, upon the text of his subjectivity. Any attempt at a transcript or verbatim account would introduce a reification through which a fixed subject – the past – would pre-empt the fluid, living subject of the present. And as James's fiction reveals, stasis is the enemy of art since all it can produce is dead copy as opposed to "an act of life" (*Henry James Letters*, IV, 706). There is however a darker underside to Henry's seemingly imperialistic editorial practices. Given his need, as he admits, to rewrite everything he comes into contact with, one questions here whether the appropriational and transfigurative quality of his consciousness has moved beyond Posnock's notion of permeability and become the very thing he sought to eliminate throughout his life, an acquisitorial faculty bent on accumulating experience in a programmatic, systematic manner rather than through a receptively open one. Yet, while this charge may seem accurate initially, when we see that what James is doing with William's letters is best understood as a transfigurative display in which what was William and what was Henry become some kind of hybrid subject which, in its creation, reveals the multiplicity of things both Henry and William advocated, then an accusation that Henry has become Mrs. Newsome or Adam Verver is somewhat premature.

So while the appropriational aspect William's son accuses his uncle of recalls James's remark about his transformative reading habits, it also points toward one of the most important aspects of Jamesian consciousness – its ability to assert a vital agency through its transformative power. For James the extent to which the mind is able to transfigure reality equals the degree to which that mind is, as Sharon Cameron has argued, "dynamic" and alive (*Thinking*, 68).[5] For this reason it is incorrect to equate the transfigurative aspect of Jamesian consciousness with passive observation or the subtle manipulation of reality so as to afford the perceiving subject a place in a superimposed or make-believe world. One need only recall James's belittlement of Hyacinth Robinson in *The Princess Casamassima* to appreciate the difference between transformational consciousness and the mere creation of simulacra. Rather, as Cameron shows, James's cultivation of active perception was a mode of empowerment. This seems what, in his way, James is getting at when he explains his being content to watch rather than directly to participate in life as most others did.

There was the difference and the opposition, as I really believe I was already aware – that one way of taking life was to go in for everything and everyone, which kept you abundantly occupied, and the other way was to be as abundantly occupied, quite as occupied, just with the sense and image of it all, and only on a fifth of the actual immersion: a circumstance extremely strange. Life was taken almost equally both ways – that, I mean, seemed the strangeness; mere brute quantity and number being so much less in one case than the other. (*Autobiography*, 164)

What is it that makes up the difference between the two modes of being James refers to here if it is not the ability of his consciousness first to appropriate, then to transfigure, and, ultimately, to control his perceptual encounter with reality? And it is worth mentioning here, if only because of the general tendency to misread this oft-quoted passage from *A Small Boy and Others*, that the "way of taking life" is, in the end, exactly the same for both modes of being. Nowhere does James say the "life" which he experiences on only "a fifth of the actual immersion" is any less or different than the "life" experienced by the more physically involved participants. The distinction resides, once again, in the difference between a purely critical and a creative consciousness, between the James who complains of his uncle's unauthorized reconstruction of text, and the James who confesses his inability just to read and transcribe. And, for James, that distinction is where one either registers or resigns control of self. William Goetz has explained this ambiguous tension between passivity and activity in the Jamesian consciousness by pointing up James's tendency to use terms like critical and creative synonymously. Rather, what James shows, Goetz argues, is a refusal to

accept any clear contrast between a faculty of receptivity and one of activity; ... Consequently, the imagination need not be seen as a power of pure creation *ex nihilo* in opposition to the merely passive or reproductive mental faculties. In line with the romantic conception of the imagination, James tends to see the imagination as a co-agent in the emergence of reality itself, or as a power that re-creates, and maintains in existence, the *données* of experience. Instead of being the absolute creator of an alternative, vicarious, and imaginary world, the imagination participates in the coming-into-appearance of the real world. (*Darkest Abyss*, 70)

One other important aspect of James's explanation of his stream-lined participation is that the dynamic quality of James's consciousness is able to extend control over external phenomena, as opposed to being confined solely to internal experience. Cameron explains the full ramifications of this projective aspect by examining James's *The American Scene* and showing how James's cultural observations employ the same transfigurative power in relation to his native land as we find in his autobiographical memory. As Cameron shows, in surveying American society James reveals power to be "a consequence of the ability of consciousness to dominate objects, which are repeatedly subordinated to its interpretive reassessment" (*Thinking*, 7). Again, the four-fifths disparity between modes of being in the above quote from *A Small Boy and Others* seems made up for through a dialectic of subordination and reassessment, something James refers to elsewhere as the difference between "[l]ife being all inclusion and confusion," capable of "nothing but splendid waste," and "the sublime economy of art" which, through "discrimination and selection, ... rescues" and "saves" the "hard latent *value*" (Preface, *Spoils of Poynton*, 1138–39).

In light of Cameron's argument, the opening of James's *A Small Boy and Others* – "To recover anything" is "to live over the spent experience itself" – takes on a more profound resonance (*Autobiography*, 3). Read through the filter of Cameron's remarks on Jamesian consciousness, the autobiography becomes an exercise of power and mastery to the extent that it simultaneously foregrounds the permeable and the appropriational aspect of James's subjectivity. On the one hand, James reveals, as Posnock describes it, his "extreme commitment to the self as social process" by examining the influence his very public childhood had on the configuration of his unique identity (*Trial of Curiosity*, 182). And on the other, he offers a rendering of the fully-matured Jamesian consciousness which boldly asserts, as Paul Eakin has argued, "that all experience is subjective, and that what 'really happened,' autobiographically speaking, is what the self perceived" (*Fictions*, 115). In this way James's autobiographical volumes become an even more subtle exercise of power. To the reader who comes to the autobiography through James's corpus, and to the reader who comes to James through the autobiography, these volumes are an active rendering of the power available to "'one of the people on whom nothing is lost!'" ("Art of Fiction," 53). Furthermore, as a demonstration of what his mind was capable of, the autobiography is, in what it accomplishes, James's most profound creation. For as the texts unfold, *A Small Boy and Others*, *Notes of a Son and Brother*, and *The Middle Years* revise our conception of memory, of imagination, and, perhaps, as Sharon Cameron has suggested, of Jamesian consciousness in general, "what thinking is" (*Thinking*, 20).[6] The *Autobiography*, then, is something more than a record of one's lived experiences, rather, James inverts normal autobiographical practices and develops what one could only call a genre of life-writing wherein what is recounted is not the traditional record of, as I say, lived experiences, but instead a fully enlivened experience of life. For James autobiography becomes the creation, not the accounting of, a life. And for James, the unrelenting artist, autobiography could be nothing less than an exemplary mode of self-construction which fuses the human and the aesthetic so as to get behind and beyond both.

Furthermore, just as the dive into memory offers James an opportunity to "live over the spent experience itself," so too does the reader of James live over the experience of reading the fictions which precede James's autobiographical account. To this extent, the autobiography affords the reader a first and final vision of the authentic Jamesian consciousness which seeks to transform our understanding of that faculty and to instruct us in the responsive development of our own perception. As such, we could say that the autobiography speaks to us as Parisian architecture and aesthetic culture did to the young Jameses: "Art, art, art, don't you see? Learn, little gaping pilgrims, what *that* is!" (*Autobiography*, 191).

II

"And what is the title of the book?" asked Don Quixote.
"*The Life of Ginés de Pasamonte.*"
"Is it finished?"
"How could it be finished," said Ginés, "when my life is not finished as yet?"

(Cervantes, Don Quixote, 173)

If it is correct to say that in his fiction James takes his protagonists through a series of experiences which ultimately bring them to the point where their consciousnesses approximate but fall short of the author's own, the autobiography can then be seen as the completion of what James calls in his *Notes of a Son and Brother* "a man of imagination at an active pitch" (*Autobiography*, 455). The parallels between the fictional rendering of a Jamesian consciousness and James's autobiographical version become apparent when one juxtaposes the texts' final representations of these protagonists' consciousnesses with James's depiction of his own. In *The American*, for example, Christopher Newman concludes his European experience by reaching a type of practical wisdom which allows him to "accept the unchangeable" (358). In his Preface to the novel James suggests that "one's last view of [Newman] would be that of a strong man indifferent to his strength and too wrapped up in fine, too wrapped up above all in *other* and intenser, reflexions for the assertion of his 'rights' " (1055). Isabel Archer, we have seen, also achieves a measure of practical wisdom: "She was a person," the narrative explains, "of great good faith, and if there was a great deal of folly in her wisdom those who judge her severely may have the satisfaction of finding that, later, she became consistently wise only at the cost of an amount of folly which will constitute almost a direct appeal to charity" (3:144–45). And Strether, James tells us, comes "so far through his total experience that he has come out on the other side," where the "other side" means what lies outside interpretive categories and subjectivities ("Project," 390). What each of these characters finally grasp is the need to be actively and attentively engaged with the requirements of life. The irony of their eventual hard-won openness to the possibilities of experience is that, in a sense, the openness comes too late. In relation to these characters' texts, James dramatizes this final receptivity by forestalling any sense of traditional closure, suggesting as he does, that the characters' lives have developed beyond the confines of a text. Readers who want to see how these characters embrace their encounter with life once they have attained the ability to become attuned with what is, have to look elsewhere in James. That place, I suggest, is James's autobiography.

Two passages in the *Notes of a Son and Brother* make explicit the connection between James's fictional characters and the "reconstructed" vision of how his consciousness developed its uniquely Jamesian capacities. The first links James explicitly to Lambert Strether and explains James's conception of "a man of imagination." The second, in an uncanny manner, sums up the larger argument I have been making about the negativity of experience in James's hermeneutics. In his Preface to *The Ambassadors*, James admits that Strether finally offered him the long-sought "opportunity to 'do' a man of the imagination," an opportunity which led James to rejoice "in the promise of a hero so mature, who would give me thereby the more to bite into" (1307). What is of particular interest in the Preface's explanation of Strether's mental capacity is that James only goes so far as to accord Strether the status of being a "comparative case," that the "luxury" of doing an "imagination in *predominance*," a "study of the high gift in *supreme* command ... would still doubtless come on the day I should be ready to pay for it; and til then might, as from far back, remain hung up well in view and just out of reach" (1307). Not until he was in the midst of his *Notes of a Son and Brother* did James finally feel "the principle of response to a long-sought occasion ... for making trial of the recording and figuring act on behalf of some case of the imaginative faculty under cultivation."

The personal history... of an imagination, a lively one of course, in a given and favourable case, had always struck me as a task a teller of tales might rejoice in, his advance through it conceivably causing at every step some rich precipitation – unless it be rather that the play of strong imaginative passion, passion strong to *be*, for its subject or victim, the very interest of life, constitutes in itself an endless crisis ... The idea of some pretext for such an attempt had again and again, naturally, haunted me; the man of imagination, and of an "awfully good" one, showed, as the creature of that force or the sport of that fate or the wielder of that arm, for the hero of a hundred possible fields – if one could but first "catch" him, after the fashion of the hare in the famous receipt ... Meanwhile, it no less appeared, there were other subjects to go on with, and even if one had to wait for him he would still perhaps come. It happened for me that he *was* belatedly to come, but that he was to turn up then in a shape almost too familiar at first for recognition, the shape of one of those residual substitutes that engage doubting eyes the day after the fair. He had been with me all the while, and only too obscurely and intimately – I had not found him in the market as an exhibited or *offered* value. I had in a word to draw him forth from within rather than meet him in the world before me, the more convenient sphere of the objective, and to make him objective, in short, had to turn nothing less than myself inside out. What was *I* thus, within and essentially, what had I ever been and could I ever be but a man of imagination at the active pitch? – so that if it was a question of treating *some* happy case, any that would give me what, artistically speaking, I wanted, here on the very spot was one at hand in default of a better. (*Autobiography*, 454–55)

That James acknowledges that his ultimate subject came "belatedly" suggests the autobiography marks some sense of completion,[7] as though the late phase of Strether's life (that time James refers to in his "Project" for the novel when Strether "has come so far through his total experience that he has come out on the other side" [390]), for instance, could be captured and represented only when James did nothing less than turn himself inside out. And is not this exactly what autobiographical writing is, the turning of oneself inside out so as to represent in narrative form one's internal subjectivity?[8] However, this prescription for autobiography sounds very much like a description of James's own narrative method in his fictions. By locating his narrative point of view in a fictional center of consciousness, and then carefully depicting the vibrations of that consciousness as it comes into contact with the world, is not James turning someone like Isabel Archer, or Christopher Newman, or Lambert Strether inside out? Once again, James found himself confronted with the impossibility of maintaining a clean line between fiction and fact.[9] That James so easily crosses this boundary underscores the inherently autobiographical aspect of his fiction as much as it does the fictional aspect of his autobiography. And in fluctuating so naturally between his fictions and his autobiographical text, James succeeds in focusing the reader's attention on one of the principal aspects of all his work, that preestablished interpretive constructs will always come up short in their attempt to impose meaning on a reality which we "cannot possibly *not* know, sooner or later" (Preface, *The American*, 1063). The reader who attempts to wrest meaning from either type of text is forced to perform an intertextual hermeneutics through which James's fiction and his autobiography prove engaged in a dialectic of bewilderment and enlightenment. In this way the autobiography mirrors the internal dynamics of the fiction, and taken together, these texts force an interpretive engagement whose end product is the reader's heightened perceptual acuity. Thus, like a character in a Jamesian text, the reader is taken by James to a point of perceptual awareness where his or her consciousness can approximate James's and, consequently, the better appreciate his fiction. It is this interactive quality of James's work, a process amply demonstrated in the autobiography just as it is in the fiction, which John Carlos Rowe refers to when he claims that James, "[m]ore than any other modern author ... helps shape an esthetic of experience, which by means of its characterization as the 'reader's experience' helps in the difficult recuperation of the vanishing subject as well as the battered claims of literature for some truth and reality" (*Theoretical Dimensions*, 228–29).

A further complex and theoretical component of James's reference to Strether as a "comparative case" of an imagination at an active pitch and himself as the real thing, so to speak, is of deep significance to our understanding of the entire autobiographical project and how that project relates to or, perhaps, acts as a culmination of James's literary career. It is no surprise that in his *Notes of a Son and Brother* James redeploys the language he used to describe Lambert Strether in his "Project" for *The Ambassadors* fourteen years earlier. James's point, I take it, is, as Millicent Bell has shown, that *The Ambassadors* is "James's greatest plea for the worth of the kind of man *he* was, the justification of that inner vitality by means of which he had made his writing doing that rivalled the participation of others" ("Fiction," 465). Taken in the context of James's entire oeuvre, the metonymic connection between the character Strether and James is the author's attempt to show how carefully he took his characters to a point of perceptive and experiential development, to a point, that is, where their consciousnesses approximate, but finally fall short of duplicating, his own. In this way the reader finds the full realization of the former, the fictive, bodied forth in the latter, the autobiographical. And for James's larger battle with mimesis, with observation and participation and where the limits of art are, in the sense of where art and life become the same thing, the possibility of representation offered James in his autobiographical works allowed him the opportunity to put before the reader a vision his fiction – because it was fiction – was only allowed to gesture toward. The upshot of such a demonstration was to elevate the Jamesian sense of life and art to a level which extended beyond mimesis and opened for itself a new and expanded realm of understanding which united both reader and character in what Charles Feidelson has referred to as "a quest for meaning and for the meaning of meaning" ("Man of Imagination," 351). And that quest, the autobiography tirelessly shows, was rooted in a fundamentally open embrace of experience and understood through an aesthetics which was originary and productive precisely because it situated itself at that place where the unmediated and the aesthetic, where life and art meet. In the James corpus, the autobiography marks that intersection.

Strether's falling short of a fully manifested Jamesian consciousness raises a further question about James's own concerns as to the limits of art and what he perceived as the need to resolve the conflict between two modes of experience: the lived and the aesthetic. Strether's falling from the ideal is exactly the condition of fiction. That is, in coming up short, Strether demonstrates the inherent limits of textuality. For almost by definition a text is bounded by its covers. Thus the beginning and the end point up the limitations of whatever comes between, that is, the experiences of a textual representation are circumscribed by the limitations inherent in textual confinement. Really, what happens to characters after the text ends is a meaningless question because it is based on something that simply does not exist. Nevertheless, it is exactly this question which so often provokes furious debate between readers who want to share their reading experience. James's novels in particular were, as Marianna Torgovnick has amply demonstrated, often the instigators of debates about the "after-history" of characters like, say, Isabel Archer (*Closure*, 134). James himself noted this concern with a work's extra-textual life in a notebook entry on what he anticipated would be readers' dissatisfaction with *The Portrait of a Lady*'s ending:

The obvious criticism of course will be that it is not finished – that I have left her *en l'air.* – This is both true and false. The *whole* of anything is never told; you can only take what groups together. (*Notebooks*, 18)

Ironically, James's remark about the novel can equally well be applied to his unfinished autobiographical project. The third volume – *The Middle Years* – ends with James similarly left *en l'air*. James's problem was that within his own aesthetics, closure and confinement or completion were the very enemies of art, as Gilbert Osmond so amply demonstrates. To finish the autobiography would be to turn it into a static artifact, something altogether different than "an act of life."

How James confronted this paradox in his fiction is worth examining more closely, as his manner of resolving the apparent tension between the human and the aesthetic offers a key to unlocking Jamesian hermeneutics. On the surface it seems as though James was at a crossroads whenever he put pen to paper. Nevertheless, he felt convinced of the ability to employ art so as to make sense of life. We recall here his notorious dispute with H.G. Wells in which James concluded by asserting "[i]t is art that *makes* life, makes interest, makes importance, for our consideration and application of these things, and I know of no substitute whatever for the force and beauty of its process" (*Henry James Letters*, IV, 770). In this sense, Strether enters the debate as a representational figure through whom James attempts to show the development of a consciousness which responds to the pressure of experience by first overthrowing a preestablished (Mrs. Newsome's Woollett) interpretive paradigm and then learning to live beyond paradigms altogether, as though responsive and open to the flow of life. The paradox, of course, inheres in the very fictionality of the account. In using art to make sense of life, or, more precisely, in embodying a sense-making artifact within what invariably is a fixed text, James undercuts the very vitalism the art supposedly promotes. James's resolution was two-fold: 1) to develop a narrative method which by its very formal features drew the reader into the text and forced the reader to become an active participant in the search for meaning; and 2) to develop an aesthetics which had open-endedness as a formal feature. By so doing James was able to forestall his characters' final, textually-confined development and not only allow them an "after-history," but simultaneously, through his readers' coerced partici-pation, actually challenge his readers to try and glimpse his char-acters as they reach a final degree of development which takes both them and the reader beyond the boundaries of fiction.[10]

By doing away with traditional authorial narrative power and locating the reader's point of view in a center of consciousness, James was able to force the reader's participation in a way which re-invested his fiction with the openness he promoted. The reader of a James text struggles with the character's ability to understand and, invariably in opposition to the character, finds himself imposing or projecting his own meaning upon the fictional experience. And just as the typical Jamesian text ultimately exposes the dangers of interpretive projection through its characters' interpretive failings (Isabel's imposition of an identity on Gilbert Osmond, Strether's artificially ennobling of Chad Newsome and his relationship with Marie de Vionnet), so the reading experience similarly exposes the reader's own interpretive failings. By forcing the reader's engage-ment, and through that, the "larger hermeneutic point" as Paul Armstrong explains, "James shows the extent to which we expect the world to conform to our habitual interpretive schemes – the extent to which they pattern our perception in ways we do not notice" (*Challenge*, 6). And it is in this moment of bewilderment, when the world suddenly reveals itself to be altogether other than imagined, that the reader, like the character, recognizes the inherent need to embrace an interpretive openness and to accept life's essential fluidity. In preparing the reader to accept this position of openness, Jamesian hermeneutics reveals a notion of subjectivity which is socially constituted and is also, through its very cultural engage-ments, open to individual changes and developments. This is the full measure of Jamesian hermeneutics, and this is how James's fiction recovers a notion of subjectivity which is neither the blind victim of institutional power nor the unwitting agent of an unfixed, completely open-ended and disabling freedom. In bringing readers to this awareness James reinvests the notion of subjectivity with interpretive power.

Furthermore, it is in the very disruption of the reader's projected understanding that James recaptures art's vitalism and underscores, by example, what I have referred to earlier as, to paraphrase Gadamer, the negativity of experience. James returns to this fundamental aspect of his hermeneutics in one of the autobiography's most poignant moments. Early in what would become the final and unfinished installment – *The Middle Years* – James explains exactly the consequences associated with experience, which includes, by extension, the experience of self and others, as well as the experience of art.

I remember really going so far as to wonder if any act of acquisition of the life-loving, life-searching sort that most appealed to me would not mostly be fallacious if unaccompanied by that tag of the price paid in personal discomfort, in some self-exposure and some none too impossible consequent discomfiture, for the sake of it. Didn't I even on occasion mount to the very height of seeing it written that these bad moments were the downright consecration of knowledge, that is of perception and, essentially, of exploration, always dangerous and treacherous, and so might afterwards come to figure to memory, each in its order, as the silver nail on the wall of the temple where the trophy is hung up? (*Autobiography*, 561–62)

If this is a statement about the consequences of James's encounter with life, it can also be a read as a comment about what happens in the encounter with a work of art, and can be seen as a testimonial to an aesthetic which understood art to be a form of doing. For though the reader of any work emerges on the other side of the reading experience somehow changed, an experience James called "the great anodyne of art," the movement through a James text is a far more explicitly self-referential experience ("London Notes," 1400). Applying terms like "personal discomfort," "consequent discomfiture," "self-exposure," and the "consecration of knowledge" to describe the experience of James's characters is by no means an exaggeration, but nor are they an exaggeration of the reader's own experience. Again the furor over the conclusion to either *The Portrait of a Lady* or *The Ambassadors* supplies ample proof. Thus, by forcing the reader into the text, by enabling the text to become a means through which the reader's own consciousness becomes an object of observation, James is able to force both the text and the reader's subjectivity to open their boundaries and enable art to make a direct application to reality.

And this is exactly what the autobiography so fully and carefully demonstrates. In his Preface to *The Ambassadors* James claims autobiographical writing assumes "the double privilege of subject and object" (1316). As a reader of his personal and cultural history James demonstrates his own attempt to live through the ultimate Jamesian narrative and emerge on the other side of the experience. Along the way James shows the inescapable connection between lived and aesthetic experience, and how the latter is actively involved in our understanding of the former. In order to accomplish this exercise James represents his lived-experience as though it were a text the writing and reading of which brings about an enlarged understanding of his later self. In his recent biography of James, Fred Kaplan sees this movement between art and life as the internal architecture of the autobiography. Kaplan's point is that James was "[a]lways self-dramatizing" and saw the autobiographical project as one of "his daily imaginative ventures." For James, the writing was a chance to show how a man of the imagination came to be. To this end, as Kaplan notes, "[e]ach moment of the reconstituted past was given its place in the development of his artistic sensibility" (*Henry James*, 542). James alludes to this aspect of his project in *A Small Boy and Others* where he calls attention first to the difficulty of representing his consciousness, then to the possibility of the end product being meaningless to a reader, and concludes by giving voice to the ethical responsibility he feels in bringing the project to an audience.

One's record becomes, under memories of this order – and that is the only trouble – a tale of assimilations small and fine; out of which refuse, directly interesting to the subject-victim only, the most branching vegetations may be conceived as having sprung. Such are the absurdities of the poor dear inward life – when translated, that is, and perhaps ineffectually translated, into terms of the outward and trying at all to flourish on the lines of the outward; a reflection that might stay me here weren't it that I somehow feel morally affiliated, tied as by knotted fibers, to the elements involved. (*Autobiography*, 105)

Among other issues, what James reveals in the configuration of his memory is the confluence of aesthetic and lived-experience and how that experience itself invariably involves "personal discomfort," "consequent discomfiture," "self-exposure," and the "consecration of knowledge" (562). The effect of James's demonstration in this quote and the autobiographical text in general is to show how the aesthetic experience can carry over into the world and allow not for an escapist abstraction, but an active and aware participation.[11]

The autobiography's demonstration of the development of a "finely aware and richly responsible" consciousness is perhaps James's most sustained attempt at showing the connection between the aesthetic experience and the human experience. Ross Posnock has recognized this aspect of James's autobiographical project and differentiated it from an earlier "idealist phase," in which James tried to body forth his commitment to "the high and helpful ... civic use of the imagination" through the "idealism" of his characters (*Trial of Curiosity*, 189). The different tenor Posnock finds in the autobiography has led him to suggest that it was not "until the revisionary energies of his late nonfiction" that James created "a new matrix in which his efforts find their historicist and pragmatic consummation" (188). Citing James's connection with John Dewey, Posnock argues that James's project aimed at revitalizing contemporary existence and that his "civic campaign in his autobiography is an enlarging, not an elitist, act of discrimination." He goes on to explain how the autobiography "seeks to bridge what Dewey calls the 'chasm between ordinary and esthetic experience' that has been 'accepted as if it were normal,' as if the aesthetic possessed a private, 'merely contemplative character' " (189). To this extent, James's late non-fiction – *The American Scene* and the volumes of his autobiography – literally takes over from where his fiction leaves off, for these works demonstrate a real mind grappling with real, perceived phenomena in a real world, and they show, as the fictions ultimately do, how that mind comes to understand with such a high degree of empowerment only or precisely because it is open and permeable to the world it encounters. In Posnock's words, again quoting Dewey, "James's 'religion of doing' sponsors new forms of doing and being whose aim is to restore our capacity to see, hear, touch, and feel, as 'live creatures,' a capacity that the 'institutional life of mankind' has narrowed and dulled' " (189). Thus it would perhaps not be going too far to suggest that James's autobiography was recreative in the largest possible sense. In this way the work extends itself to encompass not just the personal history of Henry James, but the collective consciousness of James's public.

Why James never completed his autobiography is somewhat a mystery. He stopped work on the third volume, *The Middle Years*, when the war broke out in 1914 and never returned to it before his death in 1916. The intention of the third volume seems to have been, as F.W. Dupee suggests, "to embrace some portion of his early memory" ("Introduction," ix). But we cannot be sure, given that James's mode of creation at this stage was to dictate off the top of his head. Dupee cites Percy Lubbock, who observed that when James was "dictating *The Middle Years*," he "used no notes, and beyond an allusion or two in the unfinished volume itself, there is no indication of the course which the book would have taken or the precise period it was intended to cover"(x). One could speculate however, especially given James's commitment to open-endedness, that James came to understand, like *Don Quixote*'s Ginés de Pasamonte, the impossibility of completing an autobiography. And such a speculation fits well with the argument I have been making about James's work. On the one hand, one could say the autobiography had to remain open or "un-ended" if it was to be anything more than an incomplete vision of James, that is, yet another "comparative case." On the other, by leaving the text open, James once again, however inadvertently, demonstrated the fundamental permeability of his subjectivity. And perhaps most curious of all is the autobiography's stopping at just the moment James would have had to begin examining his life as a writer. I want to suggest that by stopping where it does, the autobiography irresistibly points the reader back to the fiction, as though where James's life is concluded is in his fiction just as his fiction is concluded in his autobiography. By doing so James was able to erase the boundaries of his self as well as his fiction and make available to all the full perceptual power of his consciousness.

Notes

I THE EXPERIENCE OF JAMESIAN HERMENEUTICS

1 One can imagine what a list of works which deal in some way or other with the concept of "experience" in James would look like. I have found Paul Armstrong's *The Phenomenology of Henry James*, which examines Jamesian consciousness and experience by way of phenomenologists such as Husserl, Heidegger, Merleau-Ponty, and Ingarden among others, the most helpful and extensive of recent arguments. Armstrong rightly concludes that to "understand James as a phenomenological novelist ... means to understand him as a novelist of experience" (205). See also Julie Rivkin, "The Logic of Delegation in *The Ambassadors*"; Michael Wutz, "The Word and the Self in *The Ambassadors*"; William Stowe, *Balzac, James, and the Realistic Novel*; Ross Posnock, *The Trial of Curiosity*; Mark Seltzer, *Henry James and the Art of Power*; Priscilla Walton, *The Disruption of the Feminine in Henry James*; Sheila Teahan, *The Rhetorical Logic of Henry James*.

2 Henry James, Preface, *The Princess Casamassima* (1091). References to James's Prefaces are from Henry James. *Literary Criticism*, II.

3 I have borrowed here Foucault's language from his "Introduction" to *The Use of Pleasure*. Despite the seemingly obvious ideological differences between Foucault and James, their conceptions of experience are remarkably similar. When Foucault explains his plan for a "history of the experience of sexuality," where "experience is understood as the correlation between fields of knowledge, types of normativity, and forms of subjectivity in a particular culture," he speaks in a language James understood and, in this instance, erases whatever ideological difference exists between them (4).

4 Henry James, *The Novels and Tales of Henry James*, 26 vols. (6:145). Unless otherwise indicated all references to James's novels will be to this edition.

5 Foucault refers to this releasement as an "analytic of finitude."

6 In his development of the international theme, and his theoretical purpose in bringing cultures into an interpretive clash, James antici-

pates Bakhtin's discussion of novelistic discourse in his essay "Discourse in the Novel." Note the similarity between James's novelistic practice and Bakhtin's theory of the novel's language in the following example from Bakhtin's essay: "In a word, the novelistic plot serves to represent speaking persons and their ideological worlds. What is realized in the novel is the process of coming to know one's own language as it is perceived in someone else's language, coming to know one's own belief system in someone else's system" (*Dialogic Imagination*, 365). Jamesians will think immediately of Lambert Strether when they read this passage.

7 In his "Art and the Construction of Community in 'The Death of the Lion'," Paul Armstrong similarly points out this limitation in Seltzer's argument. Armstrong explains James's awareness of power practices and that the "replication" in James's novels "of the communicative irrationalities of the public sphere in the realm of privacy does not mean ... that art necessarily reinforces mechanisms of social control it only pretends to evade" (99).

8 Because of the sweeping changes James made when he revised *The American*, and because my aim in this book is to give some sense of James's hermeneutics as it develops across his career, I have used the 1877 edition of this text (344).

9 Posnock's examination of the "permeable self" in James offers a powerful reading of James's conception of identity, especially given his assertion that James's characters often experience a resignation of will which leads to "an experimental venture to enlarge the self's range of modalities" (*Trial of Curiosity*, 168). But where I disagree with Posnock is in his suggestion that James promotes a "politics of nonidentity" because an absence of identity is the only way to freedom (16). Posnock wants to blur the distinction between a "permeable self" and a "politics of nonidentity," and what for James is perhaps better understood as a fluidity or flexibility of self. Understanding the self as fluid and flexible for James is what allows one to reach a condition of openness, where openness makes possible the receptiveness to experience. Posnock's argument for the resignation of self confuses openness with emptiness or vacancy. Furthermore, as Armstrong has pointed out, Posnock fails to consider "the negative possibilities of such a confusion" blurring creates, and "sees only its positive implications" ("Art," 107n.4).

10 For example, Walton suggests James promotes a straightforward, aggressive disruption of gender categories so as to destabilize the "referential Masculine Realist formulae" in favor of texts which are playfully open-ended and "offer plural and immeasurable possibilities" (*Disruption of the Feminine*, 163). But in claiming James's "texts are limitless precisely because in their polyvocality, they become Feminine creations themselves," Walton misreads the purposive flexibility inherent in James's conception of gender categories and underestimates his under-

standing of how relations are always involved in power plays of varying aggression (161). Walton's desire to read James's texts as examples of "'jouissance'" and as "polyvalent" reduces them to a deconstructive undecidability and ignores the author's own understanding of his art as a public effort to shape the civic imagination (163). To some extent Walton's reading of James winds up sounding very much like William James's accusations that his younger brother was nothing more than a Frenchified versifier.

11 In recognizing Chad's and Madame de Vionnet's relationship as something more than Woollett's categorically defined "adultery," Strether successfully escapes the traditional mode of reading which Scott sees as the "focus and the philosophy of our history,... one bent on naturalizing 'experience' through a belief in the unmediated relationship between words and things," and comes to realize that understanding requires a mode of perception which "takes all categories of analysis as contextual, contested, and contingent" ("Experience," 36).

12 James faults Anthony Trollope for ruining his fictions by making hamfisted claims about the text's fictionality and his own authorial control within the novels themselves. Trollope, James laments, "took a suicidal satisfaction in reminding the reader that the story he was telling was only, after all, a make-believe. He habitually referred to the work in hand ... as a novel, and to himself as a novelist, and was fond of letting the reader know that this novelist could direct the course of events according to his pleasure" ("Anthony Trollope," *Literary Criticism*, I, 1343).

13 In "The Lesson of Balzac" James picks up on this idea when he says the "most fundamental and general sign of the novel, from one desperate experiment to another, is its being everywhere an effort at *representation* – this is the beginning and the end of it" (*Literary Criticism*, II, 130).

14 In "The Lesson of Balzac," James makes a similar comment when he says Balzac "at all events robustly loved the sense of another explored, assumed, assimilated identity" (132). Of course, Balzac's robust pleasure is not unique. James similarly enjoyed this aspect of creation and of reading, and the subjective transference he refers to is also what he called the "great anodyne of art" in his essay "London Notes" (*Literary Criticism*, I, 1399). The point here is not just that an intersubjective transference takes place, but that following the transference, upon one's "return to the inevitable" we find ourselves changed, enlarged, somehow different from the person we were before the reading experience (1400). That we tend to forget this aspect of reading is a detriment to art, and a forgetting James tried to prevent by creating a narrative method which did its best to make readers forget they were reading. It is in this sense we should read James's famous remark to H. G. Wells that it is "art that *makes* life" (*Henry James Letters*, IV, 770).

15 Think of how Marcher's inability to understand becomes the medium

of his understanding in "The Beast in the Jungle." For instance, Marcher's epiphany before May Bartram's tomb: "It was the truth, vivid and monstrous, that all the while he had waited the wait was itself his portion. This the companion of his vigil had at a given moment perceived, and she had then offered him the chance to baffle his doom. One's doom, however, was never baffled, and on the day she had told him that his own had come down she had seen him but stupidly stare at the escape she offered him" (*Complete Tales*, 11: 401).

16 James's determination to cultivate a self which would be receptive to every modulation of observation and experience is a powerful demonstration of Merleau-Ponty's claims that "the system of experience is not arrayed before me as if I were God, it is lived by me from a certain point of view ... and it is my involvement in a point of view which makes possible both the finiteness of my perception and its opening out upon the complete world as a horizon of every perception" (qtd. in Armstrong, *Phenomenology*, 49).

2 THE EXPERIENCE OF DIVESTITURE: TOWARD AN UNDERSTANDING OF THE SELF IN 'THE AMERICAN'

1 The acquisition of a more full and historical understanding of life such as Newman arrives at in the closing pages of *The American* can be explained by referring to Gadamer's connection between experience in its most broad sense and the "historical nature of man." As Gadamer explains, "experience" is something one constantly acquires and from which one cannot be spared. Experience, of course, often brings disappointment, but it is often in these disappointments that one achieves greater knowledge and understanding – such as Newman does in his marital disappointment. As Gadamer would say, "the historical nature of man contains as an essential element a fundamental negativity that emerges in the relation between experience and insight" (*Truth and Method*, 319).

2 I am referring to Gadamer's expanded definition of the term as an explanation of the nature of "experience" as it operates in James's hermeneutics (*Ibid.*, 317).

3 Newman's suggestion that the idea of "nobility" can be claimed as one's own, though comic in *The American*, achieves a whole new level of magnitude with Adam Verver's idea of "American City" in *The Golden Bowl*.

4 See further Mrs. Tristram's early description of Madame de Bellegarde's authoritarian rule over Claire: "Her old feudal countess of a mother rules the family with an iron hand, and allows her to have no friends but of her own choosing, and to visit only in a certain sacred circle" (39).

5 The stagnation embodied in James's portrait of Europe, at least insofar

as it is evident in the Bellegardes' willingness to be "petrified in the past," has lead R.W. Butterfield to argue that they, and by extension Europe, "are simultaneously embodiments and dealers of death, their evil consisting chiefly in their simply not allowing life to take place, either in themselves or in others" (*"The American,"* 28).

6 Leon Edel, *Henry James. The Conquest of London. 1870–1881*, 270.

7 The connection here between Newman's constant deferral to literature as an interpretive and contextualizing device brings up again the question as to the degree of his reliance on guidebooks for knowledge.

8 It comes as no surprise that Valentin views Newman's suit with his sister, Claire, as a similar opportunity to enjoy the detached pleasures of observation. Valentin, who knows the suit to be impossible, tells Newman, "it will be entertaining" and that though he will be an "actor" insofar as he can help, he will also enjoy his more suited role as "spectator" (113). Valentin winds up telling Newman his chief interest in the affair lies in its amusing novelty. "After all, anything for a change. And only yesterday I was yawning so as to dislocate my jaw, and declaring that there was nothing new under the sun ... I won't call it anything else, good or bad; I will simply call it *new*" (114). In an interesting twist James shows Valentin's amused detachment to be mirrored by Mrs. Tristram, a thoroughly Parisianized American. She too finds curiosity the greatest interest in Newman's suit: "Curiosity has a share in almost everything I do. I wanted very much to see, first, whether such a marriage could actually take place; second, what would happen if it should take place" (349). The connection here between Valentin and Mrs. Tristram serves to accentuate James's point that European culture, as represented by people such as these, has lost the power of productive action.

9 Butterfield makes a similar, though more extreme comment about Valentin when he suggests Valentin suffers from "the ennui of the habitual spectator." Butterfield takes Valentin's disposition to its furthest manifestation when he claims that Valentin is "directed inexorably toward death," a direction the novel ultimately actualizes (25–26).

10 Although it is true Newman himself does not act to save Madame Dandelard, he does upbraid Valentin for his perverse " 'intellectual pleasure' " and claims "I don't in the least want to see her going down hill. I had rather look the other way." Newman concludes his visit by suggesting Valentin get his "sister to go and see her" (103–4). The point remains, nevertheless, that the scene strikes in Newman a need to act rather than observe and it is this impulse to act charitably that Newman owes to his "all-objective" disposition.

11 In his study of Newman's encounter with and failure to read Parisian social codes, William Stowe approaches such a view and suggests *"The American* functions as a model for misunderstanding, and a machine for

contemplating the nature of understanding itself rather than the object understood" (*Balzac, James, and the Realistic Novel*, 3).

12 It is perhaps for this very reason that James felt *The American* to be the best starting point for anyone seriously interested in understanding a selection of his "advanced" work. Roy Harvey Pearce begins his introduction to the novel by making reference to the response James sends to Fanny Prothero's inquiry on behalf of a young man from Texas requesting assistance in beginning a study of James. The more "advanced" list James suggested proceeded as follows: 1) *The American*, 2) *The Tragic Muse*, 3) *The Wings of the Dove*, 4) *The Ambassadors*, 5) *The Golden Bowl*. The full letter, dated September 14, 1913, appears in *Henry James Letters*, IV, 683–84.

13 John Carlos Rowe makes a similar point in discussing the intricate doubling James weaves throughout *The American*. In Rowe's argument, Newman's attendance of *Don Giovanni* is an example through which Newman is given the opportunity to view the "psychological significances of the allegorization" of the opera as it relates to his own circumstances. This, of course, passes beyond Newman and further causes the reader to question Newman's capacity to understand what he experiences. As Rowe points out, where "our previous perceptions had followed Newman's lead, our reading experience is now constantly at odds with Newman's impressions" ("Politics of the Uncanny," 85).

14 In her *Thinking in Henry James*, Sharon Cameron, following a different line of argument, makes a similar point about the Prefaces as a total project. The Prefaces, Cameron suggests, "attempt to revise, in the sense of redetermine, the reader's understanding of the central consciousness in the novel that follows" and that "the description of a novel, as James offers it up for our scrutiny in the Preface, changes the comprehension of it we would have without the benefit, or interference, of a preliminary, dictating perspective" (37, 38).

15 Newman's excessive reliance on the Bädeker is an indication of his willingness to resign his encounter with Europe to the authority of text and then to read Europe through an interpretive framework furnished by the pages of texts. The limitation of such a view, Said suggests, is "that people, places, and experiences can always be described by a book, so much so that the book (or text) acquires a greater authority, and use, even than the actuality it describes" (*Orientalism*, 93).

16 Edel explores this theme and concludes that Newman is ultimately a " 'Boor' " whose boorishness manifests itself in "the side of him which is at once pride in being a 'self-made' man and in his crass unawareness that there are things in the world which cannot be bought" (*Conquest*, 250).

17 See Carolyn Porter's "Gender and Value in *The American*" for a similar analysis of Newman's "remarkable misreading" of this introductory scene, and an excellent analysis of Newman's attempt to employ his

cash value in exchange for Claire de Cintré's "transcendent value" (108, 104).

18 Leon Edel makes no bones about stating that though he has some admirable and charming qualities, Newman "embodies also everything that Henry James disliked in the United States" (*Conquest*, 249).

19 Alwyn Berland makes a similar point about James's critique of the commercial rapacity with which individuals like Newman, or Adam Verver, or *Washington Square*'s Dr. Sloper approach cultural artifacts. As Berland points out, the "monuments and treasures of art for James are *part* of civilization as culture, and not detachable prizes. Removed from the atmosphere which generated them, they are always in danger of becoming either over-precious *objets d'art* or spoils" (*Culture and Conduct*, 221). What is particularly interesting in *The American* is how Newman approaches both art and Claire de Cintré by way of the same commercial proposition and how he reduces Claire to a "spoil" brought home from Europe.

20 When Newman tells Tom Tristram of his intention to "see the world" and perhaps "marry a wife," Tristram scoffs at the idea, citing the expense of it all, "especially the wife; unless indeed she gives it [money], as mine did" (18).

21 Newman's "fatality," suggests John Carlos Rowe, "is his stubborn refusal to take any event at more than its face-value" and "his utter failure to turn his experience into any kind of useful knowledge" ("Politics of the Uncanny," 85, 87).

22 As *The American* suggests, the origins of Newman's sense of superiority are diverse, but one place to look for a cause is certainly his patriotism. As Newman claims to Valentin, it is "the privilege of being an American citizen ... That sets a man up" (97).

23 On several occasions James remarks on Newman's democratic instincts. See, for example, Newman's "instinctive and genuinely democratic assumption of everyone's right to lead an easy life" (27–28).

24 Recall Newman's dismissal of Tom Tristram as "a very light weight," and then Newman's description of his proposed party to celebrate the announcement of his engagement (29). Newman aims to do the "grandest thing," which includes hiring "all the great singers from the opera, and all the first people from the Théâtre Française," as well as all his friends. Of course Newman's friends number among the wealthy elite. The element of conspicuous consumption in Newman's plan is evident, but it is Newman's understanding that putting on such an affair is what demonstrates grandeur of character that is most interesting in his plans.

25 Carren Kaston has explored this aspect of Claire's character in detail, noting that Claire's "sense of self is defined negatively, through refusals and resistances which appear assertive but actually consolidate her subjugation." Kaston goes on to note that Claire is for all intents and

purposes imprisoned "in her mother's imagination of her life," a point that accords with my claim that Newman's offered sanctuary winds up looking like a prison from Claire's side of the equation (*Imagination and Desire*, 29).

26 Readers of *The American* might throw up their hands at this point and accuse James of descending to gothic melodrama, an accusation James himself makes in the Preface to the novel. As James says, "the way things happen is frankly not the way in which they are represented as having happened, in Paris, to my hero." James's self-critique goes on as he admits "it is difficult for me to believe to-day that I had not, as my work went on, *some* shade of the rueful sense of my affront to verisimilitude" (1065, 1067).

27 See above, chapter one.

28 Gadamer describes *phronēsis* as practical knowledge which "means that it is directed towards a concrete situation. Thus it must grasp the 'circumstances' in their infinite variety" (*Truth and Method*, 21). *Phronēsis* thus means, as Gerald Bruns has put it, being responsive rather than controlling, "being responsive to what situations call for in the way of action." And since "situations are always made of other people, *phronēsis* in particular means responsiveness to others" (*Hermeneutics Ancient and Modern*, 259). Gadamer describes *techne* as knowledge of a particular skill – the "knowledge of the craftsman" (*Truth and Method*, 281). In *The American*, Newman's commercial skills, his manufacturing skills, can be characterized as *techne*.

29 James's depiction of America matches Simmel's characterization of the modern money culture in striking detail. Simmel argues that one of the things which "betrays the influence of money" in contemporary culture is the remorseless drive to regulate "individual and social relations as *calculative* functions," and the attempt to "conceive of the world as a huge arithmetical problem" (*Philosophy of Money*, 443–44). In language James would find interesting Simmel goes on to explain how the "money economy enforces the necessity of continuous mathematical operations in our daily transactions," absorbing the "lives of many people" in the process and reducing "qualitative values to quantitative ones." The outcome of this calculative process matches exactly what James came to see as endemic in America. "Gauging values in terms of money," Simmel explains, "has taught us to determine and specify values down to the last farthing" (444). The "superstructure of money relations erected above qualitative reality [will] determine much more radically the inner image of reality according to its forms" (445). Think again here of Newman explaining how he has not had time to feel, only to do and make himself felt.

30 *Aisthēsis* is what Aristotle calls perception, especially insofar as perception can be described as a faculty which aids, as Martha Nussbaum explains, in the judgment or discrimination involved in "ethical

matters." *Aisthēsis* is thus "a faculty of discrimination that is concerned with the apprehending of concrete particulars, rather than universals" (*Fragility*, 300).

31 Of course, lack of imagination is also a severely disabling quality in Jamesian hermeneutics. For instance, it is precisely because Woollett has no imagination that it will go on repeating itself within its own monad. And Owen Gereth becomes the witless victim of Mona Brigstock precisely because, as James suggests, "Owen had no imagination" (10:42).

32 Edel claims Christopher Newman's eventual understanding of the essential closedness of Parisian society mirrors James's own experience of the same. To this extent, at least, Newman "reflects, in a measure, some of [James's] frustration at not achieving entrance into this [the French aristocratic] world" (*Conquest*, 259).

33 For instance, it is Isabel Archer's ultimate knowledge that her reality is with Gilbert Osmond which brings her back to Rome so as to confront her fate in *The Portrait*; just as it is Hyacinth's insight into the inescapable realities of his own being that lead him to suicide in *The Princess Casamassima*; just as it is Strether's profound understanding of his past and present self that allow him to overcome the pressures of Woollett conformity and the lure of Maria Gostrey's offer to provide him a "haven of rest" in *The Ambassadors*. For Isabel Archer, Hyacinth Robinson, and Lambert Strether, as for Christopher Newman and a host of other readily available examples from James's canon, action initiates the process of understanding.

34 It is worth noting that Newman sails for Europe and leaves, as he does so, his former self behind, much as does Strether on his voyage. In *The American*, Newman is explicit about the change Europe brings: "I seemed to feel a new man inside my old skin and I longed for a new world" (23). Compare this with Strether who finds the "first 'note' of Europe" to evoke "such a consciousness of personal freedom as he hadn't known for years" and allows himself to be led "forth into the world" a new man (*Ambassadors*, 21:3, 13). Both men's experiences develop, as Daniel Mark Fogel argues, "as a reaction to [their] past [lives]" (*Romantic Imagination*, 167). For Newman, the nominal connection between himself and Christopher Columbus leads to another observation. Like Newman, Columbus set out to discover and conquer a new world – to "get the best out of it I can," in Newman's words. And like Columbus, who met with failure in his undertaking, who misunderstood completely the world he encountered, and who wound up unable really to return home, Newman too winds up displaced, dislocated, and distanced from his prior world. Both men undergo the negativity of experience: their understanding of the world was made immeasurably larger, but at the cost of having a world taken away.

35 James's remarks as to Newman's position at the end of the novel follow

a path quite similar to mine. "All that [Newman] would have left at the end," James explains, "would be therefore just the moral convenience, indeed the moral necessity, of his practical, but quite unappreciated magnanimity; and one's last view of him would be that of a strong man indifferent to his strength and too wrapped up in fine, too wrapped up above all in *other* and intenser, reflexions for the assertion of his 'rights'" (Preface, *The American*, 1055).

3 BONDAGE AND BOUNDARIES: ISABEL ARCHER'S FAILED EXPERIENCE

1　In "The Art of Fiction," James similarly claims: "It is the very atmosphere of the mind; and when the mind is imaginative – much more when it happens to be a man of genius – it takes to itself the faintest hints of life, it converts the very pulses of the air into revelations" (52).

2　Compare Charlotte Stant's description of the shopkeeper: "it isn't perhaps even at all – that he loves to sell [his things]. I think he would rather keep them if he could; and he prefers at any rate to sell them to the right people" (*Golden Bowl*, 23:106).

3　Collecott argues James felt empowered by his ability to contain Isabel and make her perform for his viewing pleasure. Despite granting Isabel a high degree of consciousness and despite suggesting she was free to take off on her own, James, in Collecott's view, still asserted his masculine authority by framing Isabel in his idea of her portrait: "all this perception and vivacity cannot give her a life beyond James's creation, not indeed, beyond his strictly artistic conception of her as a sensibility which happened, for reasons of *his* convenience, to be female" ("Framing *The Portrait*," 69). Again, Collecott seems to be advancing her own "submerged agenda," crossing the line between Isabel as character and real-life person (41).

4　Stephen Donadio explains the claim James felt upon him from the need to create art at greater length. Donadio explains that both Nietzsche and James saw "the power of art as the only activity capable of creating values and raising experience from insignificance" (*Nietzsche, Henry James*, ix–x). In his own artistic way Ralph Touchett uses Isabel as raw material for a work of art which will lend value and significance to his waning years. Dorothea Krook touches on a similar point when she suggests Ralph "contents himself with making Isabel's career the object of his detached and amused contemplation" (*Ordeal*, 28).

5　James's use of the delaying dash seems indicative of Ralph's mental pause between the enigmatic statements which usually characterize his conversations and a recognition that he must be honest and confess his real feelings for and involvement with Isabel.

6　I use Trollope as an author through whom we can highlight Ralph's comment about Isabel's possible "prosaic" career because James himself made such comments about Trollope in his 1883 essay about the author's career. James praises Trollope for being "safe; there were sure to be no new experiments" in one of his novels. Were Isabel to marry Warburton, her life would follow the "perceptibly mechanical process" James saw in Trollope's fiction ("Anthony Trollope," *Literary Criticism*, I, 1333, 1331).

7 Jonathan Freedman makes a convincing argument that *The Portrait of a Lady* can be read as a battlefield on which James "suggests that even the most noble, if naive, examples of the aestheticizing vision are fatally flawed" and thus attempts to "repurify the aesthetic" (*Professions of Taste*, 158). In Freedman's argument Ralph does not fare as well as he does in mine. Freedman paints Ralph as an aesthete who, though not as extreme as Osmond, still "falls into Gilbert's aestheticizing vision" (154). In so doing Ralph finds himself "forced by the very structure of his perception to reify and then aestheticize Isabel" (154). I prefer to see Ralph in a different light, as does Tanner, and find the freedom he allows Isabel to develop as she will needs also to be considered when assessing Ralph's sensibility. By treating Isabel as fluid and changeable Ralph cannot really reify her the way Freedman suggests.

8 In having Isabel blurt out her apprehensions at a "large fortune" and the onrush of "freedom" with its responsibilities and obligations, James captures an essential component of freedom as it develops and functions in a money culture. Simmel has argued that "each human fate can be represented as an uninterrupted alternation between bondage and release, obligation and freedom," and that "what we regard as freedom is often in fact only a change of obligations" (*Philosophy of Money*, 283). A fluctuation between bondage and release is an accurate way of describing the tempo of *The Portrait of a Lady* and takes us in a direction that allows for an interpretation of Isabel that foregrounds the extent to which American mercantile forces and the commodification of women, as well as the restrictions on female self-determination, are implicated in Isabel's tragedy.

9 Ralph's bewilderment is also an example of how James demanded his works be allowed to develop a certain living quality of their own, such as he claims Isabel to have acquired. Isabel presents the possibility of the unexpected, as Ralph realizes. James absolutely abhorred any formulaic method of novelistic and artistic production. To follow a rigid formula is to be prosaic like Trollope who "had reduced his admirable faculty to a system" ("Anthony Trollope," 1331). The sterility of the prosaic formula occupies as well a large part of James's critique of Besant in "The Art of Fiction," and enters *The Portrait of a Lady* through Gilbert Osmond, the "sterile dilettante" (4:71).

10 A. D. Moody argues Isabel's problem is largely that the world just is not as "she chooses to imagine it. Her folly is in choosing to cultivate the

proud ideal of things in defiance of the ordinary world, to which she is nevertheless inescapably subject, and which is likely to be deeply treacherous" ("James's Portrait," 26). Moody's argument bears weight given the treachery Madame Merle and Osmond are able to practice on Isabel; but one could push the premise further and include in it the treachery Isabel suffers from misreading and misinterpreting herself.

11 John Carlos Rowe argues that in James "there are no impressions that are not always already involved in complex semantic, social, and historical determinations," and characters like Isabel Archer are "impressionable naifs" who mistake interpretations for impressions because they "have not yet learned to read the codes with 'imagination'" (*Theoretical Dimensions*, 194).

12 Tanner finds the same habit in Isabel by examining her tendency to prefer enclosed places over the open landscape. Tanner sees her fantasies about the world beyond the door of her grandmother's Albany as expressive of "Isabel's whole attitude toward life: her theories and imagined versions of reality are generated behind closed doors and covered windows. Instead of venturing forth she sits and pours over books" ("Fearful Self," 76). I would take Tanner's point one step further and say that Isabel's choice of enclosed spaces is reflective of the tendency her mind has toward closure, in the sense that Isabel's attitude imposes itself upon a reality she constructs from the world about her.

13 Armstrong also argues for "James's interest in interpretation as an act of composition" in his *Challenge of Bewilderment* (91).

14 In the Preface James explains his conception of Henrietta as *ficelle* as one who "belongs to the subject indirectly" and whose role is to "run beside the coach" and allow Isabel to keep moving through the text (1081, 1082).

15 In the essay James sees "reversion to instinct" and a lack of openness as stances which will "block up the ingress" and leave one to "sit in stale and shrinking waters" ("The New Novel," 125). It is worth commenting that this is exactly what comes to happen to Isabel once she marries Osmond and that Osmond himself matches James's description here, for if anyone has been sitting in "stale and shrinking" waters Osmond has. And I wonder if James's elaborate water metaphor at the end of the novel wherein Isabel feels she is drowning after being kissed by Goodwood is a result of the sudden opening of "the ingress" the kiss prompts?

16 I do not want to belabor the point, but there are a number of interesting similarities between Bunyan's *Pilgrim's Progress* and Isabel's Roman encounter. I am not suggesting James had in mind an allegorical project such as Bunyan's, just that the parallels between Christian's need to learn his world and Isabel's need to learn hers afford a perspective on Isabel's plight in *The Portrait of a Lady*. For much of the novel from Rome

forward details the ramification of Isabel's failure to distinguish the real from the counterfeit, and the life made available to her as a result.

17 Isabel's change presents an example of how one's understanding of self, other, world, is always already the product of prejudices and expectations whose reality is continually subject to "particular instances" which "have not yet come our way" (Preface, *The American*, 1063). The most dramatic example of this type of revaluation in *The Portrait of a Lady* comes in the famous night vigil of chapter forty-two.

18 I am indebted here to Armstrong who explains his use of the phrase "gestalt shift" as descriptive of the change Isabel's manner of perception undergoes upon her seeing Osmond and Madame Merle in an anomalous position (see *Phenomenology*, 122–23). I use the term in connection with Isabel's decision to marry Osmond because the decision flies in the face of everything she has explained as her desire not only to avoid marriage, but to experience the world.

19 We are reminded here of *The American*, as Isabel assumes an almost identical role to Christopher Newman's during his first meeting with Claire de Cintré and her narrative an almost verbatim duplication of this earlier novel's parallel scene.

20 Freedman sees Isabel's production of Osmond's portrait as a "moment of mental *ekphrasis*" demonstrative of the degree of aestheticism through which Isabel sees the world. He points out how Isabel "adopts the attitude" of an artist admiring her work and then "proceeds to try to add it [Osmond] to her collection" (*Professions of Taste*, 156–57). The irony in Isabel's intentions here, as Freedman also notes, is that Isabel imposes these images on Osmond and then seeks to collect them, only to find "herself collected," an example of the consequences misreading can exact (157).

21 Carren Kaston argues "Foremost among the competing authorial acts and authorial visions which constitute the plot of *The Portrait* are those of Ralph Touchett and Gilbert Osmond" (*Imagination and Desire*, 42). Kaston rightly explains that Ralph's vision is what allows Isabel to create herself, while Osmond's is tyrannical, wanting "to discipline the subject in the house of fiction or to posses it from a window of the house" (42–43). What does not fall under the rubric of Kaston's argument, or Gass's or Holland's for that matter, is Isabel's reluctance to share in Ralph's authorial vision and her misunderstanding of and subsequent desire to appropriate Osmond's.

22 Leon Edel notes in his biography that James understood *The Portrait of a Lady* to be his artistic rebirth or coming of age. James responded to T. S. Perry's offer to write a monograph on his work to date (1880) with an injunction to wait for the publication of his forthcoming novel: "It is from that I myself shall pretend to date – on that I shall take my stand" (*Conquest*, 402).

23 I am referring of course to his comments about reality in the Preface to

The American (1063) and "The Art of Fiction" where he says "Humanity is immense, and reality has a myriad forms" (52).

24 Armstrong makes a similar point central to his argument about *The Portrait of a Lady* and James's understanding of understanding in general, claiming the vigil "is the narrative equivalent of the dialectical relation between the reflected and reflection," and reveals "in James a correlation between narrative structure and fundamental epistemological processes" (*Phenomenology*, 124– 25).

25 Iser's argument is as follows: "As the past fact is recalled against the background of its own observability, this constitutes an apperception, for the invoked fact cannot be separated from its past context as far as the reader is concerned, but represents part of a synthetic unit, through which the fact can be present as something already apprehended. In other words, the fact itself is present, the past context and syntheses are present, and at the same time the potential for reassessment is also present" (*Act of Reading*, 117).

26 Jurgen Habermas makes a somewhat similar theoretical point in his review of Hans-Georg Gadamer's *Truth and Method*. For Habermas "knowledge is rooted in the actual; it remains bound to contingent conditions." But like Iser here, and James and Isabel, Habermas understands "reflection does not wrestle with the facticity of transmitted norms without leaving a trace. It is condemned to be after the fact," and, as I mention, "in glancing back it develops retroactive power" ("Review," 358).

27 Freedman has shown how James created in Osmond an individual who shares "direct affinities with popular satires on aestheticism" (*Professions of Taste*, 146–53).

28 We are reminded here of George Osborne's vanity in *Vanity Fair*. There Thackeray's narrator mockingly refers to Osborne as a "hero among ... third rate men." Like Osborne, Osmond and, to be sure, this aspect of Isabel's character cultivate an image of superiority which passes for the real thing only within a circle of those who know no better. The absence of sensibilities such as Ralph's at the Thursday evening gatherings is remarkable given the hosts' proprietary attitude with respect to a guest list (199).

4 LAMBERT STRETHER AND THE NEGATIVITY OF EXPERIENCE

1 Maria Gostrey's pointing out how, with the "wonderful impressions you'll have got a great deal," suggests Strether will return to Woollett as a Proustian figure who will wile away the remainder of his days in remembrance of things past (22:326). This has been a traditional way of reading *The Ambassadors*. Indeed Strether goes so far as to make just this suggestion when he argues himself into believing America will offer the best vantage from which he can refine his skills at observation and

interpretation: "he was to see, at the best, what Woollett would be with everything there changed for him. Would not that revelation practically amount to the wind up of his career?" (22:294). But to condemn Strether to something so prosaic is to misread much of his own experience of the Parisian affair. To stick with the Proustian analogy for a moment longer, we can say that most of *The Ambassadors* is for Strether not just a remembrance of things past, but an experience of what might have been, and, in this sense, an experience of what actually *is*, a sort of bringing of himself up to date. But the final conversation never goes any further. And it cannot, for what James shows through the course of *The Ambassadors* is that Strether's experiences, like all experience in the true sense of the word, leaves one disconnected from the world one had heretofore inhabited.

2 Daniel Mark Fogel reaches a somewhat similar conclusion to mine when he suggests that Strether's Parisian experience brings about a character-building synthesis. In Fogel's argument the synthesis shows how "Strether's limited Massachusetts propriety has evolved into a higher order of rightness, informed and enriched by all that he has taken in since his arrival in Europe" (*Romantic Imagination*, 3).

3 Posnock's remarks about James's notion of a "permeable self," like mine about the roles of revision and permutation, see in *The Ambassadors* a logic of interpretation which offers a counter statement to Rivkin's "delegation" and "'supplementarity'." And while I find myself in agreement with much that Rivkin says of Strether's experience, I end up with a completely different sense of Strether's self and a conception of James's hermeneutics which Rivkin's "logic" would qualify considerably.

4 Martha Nussbaum has noted that Mrs. Newsome's presence in *The Ambassadors* is captured "vividly in her absence," and that she "articulates, by contrast, Strether's moral movement." Like Nussbaum I find "James's richly comic portrait of Mrs. Newsome lies at the center of his story of Strether's adventure" ("Perceptive Equilibrium," 66).

5 Catherine Gallagher has noted the connection between literary representation and political representation in such a way that seems applicable to *The Ambassadors*. Gallagher suggests that both literary and political representation "assume that the accumulation of facts automatically produces value, and each asserts that the value of a representation is directly proportional to the amount of detail it includes about observable social reality." The ambassador, like Strether for instance, is "determined by his likeness to those he represents, his membership in certain social categories" (*Industrial Reformation*, 222).

6 Posnock sees Mrs. Newsome's rigidity as an implacable attempt to fend off the possibility of difference. In his words, she is "a veritable fortress against difference, surprise, or alteration" (*Trial of Curiosity*, 225).

7 James's attitude toward the practice of literary realism in his time,

though often complicated by his own transumption of the mode, can be seen as one of frustration and impatience. Perhaps the most well known example of this attitude is James's dispute with Walter Besant in "The Art of Fiction." It is here that James argues for the slightly modified form of reality – "a reality ... coloured by the author's vision" – which should comprise the province of art. The primary quality of fiction, James explains, is directly correlative to the prismatic quality of the author's mind. For, though the production of art requires "the sense of reality" and "experience," how these ideas are "converted ... into a concrete image and produce [...] a reality" is what determines the quality of the product ("Art of Fiction," 52–53). For James the difference between a literary realism which simply transferred the author's observations from the world to the text, bypassing the writer's mind, and the mode of fiction which allowed the author's experience to pass through the filter of his or her imagination so as to produce "the illusion of life" was immense. "The cultivation" of the latter, "the study of this exquisite process, form," as James said, "to my taste, the beginning and the end of the art of the novelist" (53). James continued this argument throughout his career, returning to it with full force in his Prefaces, and foregrounding it in his discussion of "The Younger Generation" (1914) of novelists. Revised as "The New Novel," this late essay redeploys the language of "The Art of Fiction" as part of James's critique. For instance, he accuses Arnold Bennett's novels of being "a great dump of ... material" which "quite massively piles itself up." The conclusions of these novels, in James's opinion, "suggest to us fairly our first critical comment: 'Yes, yes – but is this *all*? These are the circumstances of the interest – we see, we see; but where is the interest itself, where and what is its centre, and how are we to measure it in relation to *that*?'" ("The New Novel," 124–59, 136, 133). See also John Carlos Rowe's study of James's struggle with and transumption of Victorian realism in *Theoretical Dimensions*, (58–83).

8 Nussbaum notes that what Paris brings Strether is a sense of life as an adventure, as an opportunity to encounter something new, "this is a sense of life already removed from that of Woollett, where dignity is preserved by keeping down the new, acknowledging it only insofar as it exemplifies some law whose sense is already understood" ("Perceptive Equilibrium," 70). In Strether's words, "Woollett isn't sure it ought to enjoy" (21:16).

9 Posnock makes an effective argument about Mrs. Newsome's "managerial prowess," noting her control of Woollett's industry, the Review, and Strether. As Posnock shows, "Mrs. Newsome embodies one of the 'master-spirits of management' that James would encounter in 1904" when he returned for a last tour of America (*Trial of Curiosity*, 226).

10 Strether says as much to Maria Gostrey in his first conversation with

her. "Woollett," he admits, "isn't sure it ought to enjoy. If it were it would. But it hasn't, poor thing... anyone to show it how" (21:16–17).

11 In an argument similar to mine, Armstrong notes that "Strether's bewilderment in Paris reveals that his earlier reality was only an interpretive construct, a framework of assumptions and hypotheses now cast into bold relief because they have been surprised" (*Challenge*, 67).

12 I am in agreement with Martha Nussbaum who notes that in "the style of Woollett, the interrogative, we feel, must play a small role" ("Perceptive Equilibrium," 70).

13 Strether and Maria Gostrey note the lack of imagination in the Newsomes in the concluding stages of *The Ambassadors*. First Strether tells Chad "you have, I verily believe, no imagination," and then Maria Gostrey notes the power being without imagination lends one. Speaking of Mrs. Newsome, she says "[t]here's nothing so magnificent – for making others feel you – as to have no imagination" (22:223).

14 I am making a connection here between James's hermeneutics and Gadamer's analysis of understanding. Gadamer suggests understanding "is not to be thought of so much as an action of one's subjectivity, but as the placing of oneself within a process of tradition, in which past and present are constantly fused. This is what must be expressed in hermeneutical theory, which is far too dominated by the idea of a process, a method" (*Truth and Method*, 258).

15 See for example Du Maurier's cartoon *Maudle on the Choice of a Profession* (1881) which, though burlesquing Oscar Wilde, matches the satirizations of James with equal force (qtd. in Freedman, *Professions of Taste*, 148).

16 To the extent that the frustrations of freedom and disposable capital are linked, *The Ambassadors* shares a similarity with *The Portrait of a Lady*. We recall Ralph Touchett wants to enable Isabel's freedom by making over to her a large inheritance so she can spread her wings. Ironically, it is the financial windfall Isabel finds constraining and it is Strether's attempt to secure financial security which similarly brings about the "resignation of his freedom."

17 James's method in *The Ambassadors* mirrors William's notions of experience as something "remolding us every moment, and our mental reaction on every given thing is really a resultant of our experience of the whole world up to that date" (*Principles*, 228).

18 In his biographical study of James, Leon Edel notes that James understood *The Ambassadors* to be a philosophical novel in which Strether gets a certain education through his discovery that "the flexible cosmopolites 'live' by being open to experience, while the New Englanders keep themselves closed" (*The Master*, 71).

19 Millicent Bell makes an argument similar to mine when she suggests that *The Ambassadors* tells the story of a man "who embraces the same opportunity as the author – in life rather than art – to revise and revise again, to rewrite his personal plot" (*Meaning*, 327).

20 That Madame de Vionnet embodies multiplicity has been noted by numerous critics. See for example Laurence Holland's *The Expense of Vision*; Maud Ellmann's "'The Intimate Difference': Power and Representation in *The Ambassadors*"; Julie Rivkin's "The Logic of Delegation"; and, more recently, Priscilla Walton's *The Disruption of the Feminine in Henry James*.

21 See also Armstrong's *Phenomenology*, 115–17.

22 See Martin Heidegger, *Being and Time*, 344–46. I am indebted here to Paul Armstrong's discussion of Heidegger's concepts of "thrownness" and "ground" (*Phenomenology*, 19).

23 How fully Mrs. Newsome follows a line of strict referentialism, cementing words and referents together in order to impose as opposed to work toward understanding, has led Julie Rivkin to see the Woollett doyenne as "almost a parody of the absent author" who is determined, through her proscriptive interpretive schema and ambassadorial delegates, to validate and thus universalize her "New England conception of identity as a stable reality" (824, 929).

24 Paul Armstrong has commented insightfully on James's use of the hermeneutic circle as a narrative technique. Though James obviously did not invent the hermeneutic circle, as Armstrong points out, "he did discover that its movements could themselves form the action of a novel – and not just serve as the means to other ends in the development of a plot or a character" (*Challenge*, 6).

25 In commenting on *The Sacred Fount*, Carolyn Porter has pointed out how the deficiencies of this method of observation result when "the contemplative posture of the observer becomes so entrenched as to seem to constitute his identity" and the act of observation becomes a process of self-validation. "When observation is carried to this point," as it is by the text's nameless narrator, "reified consciousness behaves as if it were a disembodied eye, only to be faced with its own presence in the world it presumes to observe" (*Seeing and Being*, 35).

26 Paul Armstrong sums up the dialectic between the reader's understanding of Strether's experiences and Strether's own in his *Challenge of Bewilderment*. "The reader's challenge," Armstrong explains, "is not only to know Strether's world better than he does by taking fuller, more considered advantage of available clues. James also asks us to understand *how* Strether understands more acutely than he himself can – to develop a more sophisticated self-consciousness about the process of interpretation which his groping quest for knowledge dramatizes than even this extraordinarily reflective character can, given his many pressing involvements" (77).

27 The full quote from Gadamer's "On the Problem of Self Understanding" is relevant here, given the interpretive disputes James's texts often evoke. In Gadamer's analysis, the "understanding of a text has not begun at all as long as the text remains mute … When it does begin to

speak, however, it does not simply speak its word, always the same, in lifeless rigidity, but it gives ever new answers to the person who questions it and poses ever new questions to him who answers it. To understand a text is to come to understand oneself in a kind of dialogue" (57).

28 In examining this scene John Carlos Rowe makes a point that applies to *The Ambassadors* as a whole. Rowe suggests the country scene is "a metaliterary moment not only for James's novel, but more important, for Strether's own composition of self, which is made up as much by the characters with whom he is involved and defined as of 'himself': the unbounded, liberated 'observer.' In order to compose himself, Strether must construct his relations with others" (*Theoretical Dimensions*, 198–99).

29 Paul Ricoeur, *Hermeneutics and the Human Sciences*, 32–40.

30 In following Strether's and James's logic here I am aligning myself with what Edwin Fussell has referred to as the "Protestant prejudice," which leads Strether to misunderstand Marie de Vionnet's "presence in church," along the following lines: since she is a Catholic "she must be innocent because sinners don't go near churches, they take right hold of themselves and amend their lives" (*Catholic Side*, 152).

31 William's comment is worth considering for its similarity to Henry's project in *The Ambassadors*. "Visible nature," according to William, "is all plasticity and indifference, – a moral multiverse, as one might call it, not a moral universe" (*Will to Believe*, 43–44).

32 Jim Pocock alerts Strether to the deceptive quality of the Newsome women when he first meets Strether in Paris. When Strether notes his surprise to Jim that Sarah did not show claws, Jim informs Strether that "you don't know her well enough ... to have noticed that she never gives herself away, any more than her mother ever does ... They wear their fur smooth side out – the warm side in ... They don't lash about and shake the cage ... and it is at feeding-time that they're quietest" (22:86–87).

5 RECOVERY AND REVELATION: THE EXPERIENCE OF SELF-EXPOSURE IN JAMES'S AUTOBIOGRAPHY

1 Ross Posnock makes the point even more forcefully by pointing out how critics have persisted in segregating James's later work such as *The American Scene* from the fiction so as to obscure or even omit the cultural and political aspects of James's hermeneutics. According to Posnock, "[t]his segregation had muffled the subtle power of James's historical imagination, ensuring that his identity would remain more or less that of a genteel aesthete" (*Trial of Curiosity*, vii).

2 In a rather ironical way this process of "living over the spent experience" of childhood took on a nasty literalness for James. As he began to create the autobiography James was struck with a reoccurrence of a

childhood illness. As Fred Kaplan explains in his recent biography of the author, James "become painfully ill with 'a most violent and vicious' attack of shingles, 'herpes zonalis,' . . . an inflammation of the nervous system by the reactivated long-dormant virus from childhood chicken pox" (*Henry James*, 544).

3 In his examination of James's autobiography, William R. Goetz also notes how James's reconstruction of his memories is, in its way, a demonstration of Jamesian consciousness: "In the autobiography this means that the older James's reconstruction of the young boy's experience, his reading into it and finding appropriate language for it, is not a violation of that earlier experience but is the only adequate way of expressing it, of developing its potential content" (*Darkest Abyss*, 40).

4 See also Goetz: James's "autobiography is explicitly predicated on a postromantic belief in the genetics of the individual soul, on the belief that the child is father to the man. James writes with an implicit teleology as he traces the seeds of himself as a mature imaginative artist back to their origin. The entire story, like Hegelian history, is written in a future anterior tense" (*ibid.*, 36).

5 See also James's notable statement on the artist's mind in "The Art of Fiction." For James, how an author produces "the illusion of life," forms "the beginning and the end of the art of the novelist" (53).

6 Cameron argues that the mastery "lies in determining the rules which govern the power behind consciousness's transformative procedures . . . Mastery lies not only in investigating the phenomenology of the domination, on the one hand, and that conversion, on the other, but finally, . . . in attempting to master consciousness itself, to rethink or to revise what thinking is" (*Thinking*, 20).

7 Goetz makes a similar point about this aspect of James's autobiography. Goetz argues James's foregrounding of the elapsed time between his conceived idea and the discovery that he was the "ultimate theme shows the autobiography to be in a sense the culmination of James's entire career" (*Darkest Abyss*, 10).

8 That James was acutely conscious of the difficulty such a narrative act would present is evidenced by his immediately following his surprise discovery of the long-sought topic with the following caveat: "It wasn't what I should have preferred, yet it was after all the example I knew best and should feel most at home with – granting always that objectivity, the prize to be won, shouldn't just be frightened away by the odd terms of the affair" (*Autobiography*, 455).

9 James's so obvious breaching of this line in his characterization of himself as a "man of imagination" has led Ross Posnock to read this passage as an act of "autogenesis" by which "James turns himself 'inside out'." and becomes "subject and object of his passion, or rather 'subject and victim'" (*Trial of Curiosity*, 178).

10 I find myself in agreement with Paul Armstrong who argues that the

"incompleteness" in James's endings "challenges the reader's desire for closure in order to suggest that interpretation is never final and that meaning begins only to begin again, without transcendental origin or determinate end" (*Challenge*, 22).

11 Gadamer makes a point about the aesthetic experience which can help illuminate my argument about the supposed tension between the aesthetic and the human experience. He says "we learn to understand ourselves" through the aesthetic experience and that if we want the knowledge to be lasting we must not allow the "experience of art ... to be side-tracked into the uncommittedness of the aesthetic awareness" (*Truth and Method*, 86, 87). James would agree.

Bibliography

Armstrong, Paul, "Art and the Construction of Community in 'The Death of the Lion'," *The Henry James Review* 17 (1996), 99–108.

    The Challenge of Bewilderment: Understanding and Representation in James, Conrad, and Ford (Ithaca: Cornell University Press, 1987).

    The Phenomenology of Henry James (Chapel Hill: University of North Carolina Press, 1983).

Bakhtin, M.M., *The Dialogic Imagination*, ed. Michael Holquist, trans. Caryl Emerson and Michael Holquist (Austin: University of Texas Press, 1981).

Bell, Millicent, "Henry James and the Fiction of Autobiography," *The Southern Review* 18 (1982), 463–79.

    Meaning in Henry James (Cambridge: Harvard University Press, 1991).

Benjamin, Walter, *Illuminations*, ed. Hannah Arendt, trans. Harry Zorn (New York: Shocken Books, 1969).

Berland, Alwyn, *Culture and Conduct in the Novels of Henry James*, (New York: Cambridge University Press, 1981).

Bruns, Gerald L., *Hermeneutics Ancient and Modern* (New Haven: Yale University Press, 1992).

Butterfield, R.W., *"The American," The Air of Reality: New Essays on Henry James*, ed. John Goode (London: Methuen & Co. Ltd., 1972), 5–31.

Cameron, Sharon, *Thinking in Henry James* (Chicago: University of Chicago Press, 1989).

Casey, Edward, *Imagining: A Phenomenological Study* (Bloomington: University of Indiana Press, 1976).

Cervantes, Miguel de, *The Ingenious Gentleman Don Quixote de la Mancha*, trans. Samuel Putnam (New York: The Modern Library, 1949).

Collecott, Diana, "Framing *The Portrait of a Lady*: Henry James and Isabel Archer," *The Magic Circle of Henry James: Essays in Honour of Darshan Singh Maini*, eds. Amritjit Singh and K. Ayyappa Paniker (India: Sterling Publishers Private Limited, 1989), 41–72.

Dawidoff, Robert, *The Genteel Tradition and the Sacred Rage: High Culture vs. Democracy in Adams, James, and Santayana* (Chapel Hill: University of North Carolina Press, 1992).

Dietrichson, Jan, *The American Novel of the Gilded Age* (New York: The Humanities Press, 1969).

Donadio, Stephen, *Nietzsche, Henry James, and the Artistic Will* (New York: Oxford University Press, 1978).

Dupee, Frederick W., "Introduction," *Henry James, Autobiography*, (New York: Criterion, 1956).

Eakin, John Paul, *Fictions in Autobiography: Studies in the Art of Self-Invention* (Princeton: Princeton University Press, 1985).

Edel, Leon, *Henry James, The Conquest of London. 1870–1881* (New York: J.B. Lippincott, 1962).

The Master (New York: J.B. Lippincott, 1972).

Ellmann, Maud, " 'The Intimate Difference': Power and Representation in *The Ambassadors*," *Henry James: Fiction as History*, ed. Ian F. Bell (London: Vision Press, 1984), 98– 113.

Ellmann, Richard, *Oscar Wilde* (New York: Alfred A. Knopf, 1988).

Ermarth, Elizabeth Deeds, *Realism and Consensus in the English Novel* (Princeton: Princeton University Press, 1983).

Feidelson, Charles, "James and the 'Man of the Imagination'," *Literary Theory and Structure: Essays in Honor of William K. Wimsatt* (New Haven: Yale University Press, 1973), 331–52.

Fogel, Daniel Mark, "Framing James's *Portrait*: An Introduction," *The Henry James Review* 7 (1986), 1–6.

Henry James and the Structure of the Romantic Imagination (Baton Rouge: Louisiana State University Press, 1981).

Foucault, Michel, *The Use of Pleasure: Volume 2 of the History of Sexuality*, trans. Robert Hurley (New York: Vintage, 1986).

Freedman, Jonathan, *Professions of Taste: Henry James, British Aestheticism, and Commodity Culture* (Stanford: Stanford University Press, 1990).

Fussell, Edwin, *The Catholic Side of Henry James* (Cambridge: Cambridge University Press, 1993).

Gadamer, Hans-Georg, "On the Problem of Self Understanding," *Philosophical Hermeneutics*, trans. David E. Linge (Berkeley: University of California Press, 1976).

Truth and Method, trans. Garrett Barden and John Cumming (Crossroads: New York, 1985).

Gallagher, Catherine, *The Industrial Reformation of English Fiction: 1832–1867* (Chicago: University of Chicago Press, 1985).

Gass, William H., "The High Brutality of Good Intentions," *Fiction and the Figures of Life* (New York: Knopf, 1970).

Goetz, William R., *Henry James and the Darkest Abyss of Romance* (Baton Rouge: Louisiana State University Press, 1986).

Gramsci, Antonio, *Selections from the Prison Notebooks of Antonio Gramsci*, ed. and trans. Quintin Hoare and Geoffrey Nowell Smith (New York: International Publishers, 1971).

Griffin, Susan, *The Historical Eye: The Texture of the Visual in Late James* (Boston: Northeastern University Press, 1991).

Habermas, Jurgen, "A Review of Gadamer's *Truth and Method,*" *Understanding and Social Inquiry,* eds. Fred R. Dallmayr and Thomas A. McCarthy (Notre Dame: Notre Dame University Press, 1977).

Heidegger, Martin, *Being and Time,* trans. John Macquarrie and Edward Robinson (New York: Harper and Row, 1962).

Holland, Laurence B., *The Expense of Vision: Essays on the Craft of Henry James* (Princeton: Princeton University Press, 1964).

Iser, Wolfgang, *The Act of Reading: A Theory of Aesthetic Response* (Baltimore: Johns Hopkins University Press, 1980).

The Implied Reader: Patterns of Communication in Prose Fiction from Bunyan to Beckett (Baltimore: Johns Hopkins University Press, 1978).

James, Henry, *The American* (Boston: Houghton Mifflin, 1962).

The American Scene (Bloomington: Indiana University Press, 1968).

"Americans Abroad," *The Nation,* October 3, 1878, 208–9.

Autobiography, ed. Frederick Dupee (New York: Criterion Books, 1956).

The Complete Tales, ed. Leon Edel, 12 vols. (New York: J.B. Lippincott, 1964).

Henry James Letters, ed. Leon Edel, 4 vols. (Cambridge: Harvard University Press, 1974–84).

Italian Hours (New York: Grove Press, 1909).

Italian Hours, ed. John Auchard (University Park: Penn State University Press, 1992).

The Letters of Henry James, ed. Percy Lubbock, 2 vols. (New York: Octagon Books, 1970).

Literary Criticism: Essays, American and English Writers, Vol. 1, (New York: Library of America, 1984).

Literary Criticism: European Writers and the Prefaces, Vol. 2 (New York: Library of America, 1984).

The Notebooks of Henry James, eds. F.O. Matthiessen and Kenneth B. Murdock (New York: Oxford University Press, 1947).

The Novels and Tales of Henry James, 26 vols. (New York: Charles Scribner's Sons, 1909).

"Project of Novel," *The Ambassadors* (Boston: Houghton Mifflin, 1960).

The Sacred Fount (New York: Grove Press, 1953).

James, William, *Pragmatism: A New Name for Some Old Ways of Thinking. The Meaning of Truth: A Sequel to Pragmatism,* 1907, 1909, (Cambridge: Harvard University Press, 1978).

The Principles of Psychology, general ed. Frederick Burkhardt, *et al.,* 3 vols. (Cambridge: Harvard University Press, 1981).

The Will to Believe and Other Essays in Popular Philosophy (New York: Dover, 1956).

Kaplan, Fred, *Henry James. The Imagination of Genius: A Biography* (New York: William Morrow and Company, 1992).

Kaston, Carren, *Imagination and Desire in the Novels of Henry James* (New Brunswick: Rutgers University Press, 1984).

Krook, Dorothea, *The Ordeal of Consciousness in Henry James* (Cambridge: Cambridge University Press, 1962).

Lewis, R.W.B., *The Jameses: A Family Narrative* (New York: Farrar, Straus and Giroux, 1991).

Malraux, Andre, *The Psychology of Art. The Creative Act*, trans. Stuart Gilbert (New York: Pantheon Books, 1949).

Matthiessen, F.O., *Henry James: The Major Phase* (New York: Oxford University Press, 1944).

The James Family (New York: A.A. Knopf, 1948).

McCormack, Peggy, *The Rule of Money: Gender, Class, and Exchange Economics in the Fiction of Henry James* (Ann Arbor: UMI Research Press, 1990).

Moody, A.D., "James's Portrait of an Ideal," *The Magic Circle of Henry James: Essays in Honour of Darshan Singh Maini*, eds. Amritjit Singh and K. Ayyappa Paniker (India: Sterling Publishers Private Limited, 1989). 21–40.

Nussbaum, Martha, *The Fragility of Goodness* (Cambridge: Cambridge University Press, 1986).

"Perception and Revolution: *The Princess Casamassima* and the Political Imagination," *Love's Knowledge* (New York: Oxford University Press, 1990).

"Perceptive Equilibrium: Literary Theory and Ethical Theory," *The Future of Literary Theory*, ed. Ralph Cohen (New York: Routledge, 1989), 58–85.

Pater, Walter, "Conclusion," *The Renaissance. Studies in Art and Poetry*, ed. Donald Hill (Berkeley: University of California Press, 1980).

"Wordsworth," *Essays From The Guardian* (London: MacMillan and Co., Ltd., 1918), 89–104.

Porter, Carolyn, "Gender and Value in *The American*," *New Essays on The American*, ed. Martha Banta (Cambridge: Cambridge University Press, 1987), 99–129.

Seeing and Being: The Plight of the Participant Observer in Emerson, James, Adams, and Faulkner (Middletown: Wesleyan University Press, 1981).

Posnock, Ross, *The Trial of Curiosity: Henry James, William James, and the Challenge of Modernity* (New York: Oxford University Press, 1991).

Ricoeur, Paul, *Hermeneutics and the Human Sciences*, ed. and trans. John B. Thompson (Cambridge: Cambridge University Press, 1981).

Rivkin, Julie, "The Logic of Delegation in *The Ambassadors*," *PMLA* 101:5 (1986), 819–31.

Rowe, John Carlos, "The Politics of the Uncanny: Newman's Fate in *The American*," *The Henry James Review* 8 (1987) 79–90.

The Theoretical Dimensions of Henry James (Madison: University of Wisconsin Press, 1984).

Said, Edward. *Orientalism* (New York: Vintage Books/Random House, 1979).

Scott, Joan, "Experience," *Feminists Theorize the Political*, eds. Judith Butler and Joan Scott (New York: Routledge, 1992), 22–40.

Seltzer, Mark *Henry James and the Art of Power* (Ithaca: Cornell University Press, 1984).

Simmel Georg. *The Philosophy of Money*, 2nd enlarged edition, ed. David Frisby, trans. Tom Bottomore and David Frisby from a first draft by Kaethe Mengelberg (New York: Routledge, 1990).

Stevens, Wallace, "The Idea of Order at Key West," *The Palm at the End of the Mind: Selected Poems and a Play by Wallace Stevens* (Vintage: New York, 1972).

Stowe, William, *Balzac, James, and the Realistic Novel* (Princeton: Princeton University Press, 1983).

Strouse, Jean, *Alice James: A Biography* (Boston: Houghton Mifflin, 1980).

Tanner, Tony, "The Fearful Self," *Twentieth-Century Interpretations of* The Portrait of a Lady, ed. Peter Buitenhuis (Englewood Cliffs: Prentice Hall, 1968), 67–82.

Teahan, Sheila, *The Rhetorical Logic of Henry James* (Baton Rouge: Louisiana State University Press, 1995).

Thackeray, William, *Vanity Fair* (Boston: Houghton Mifflin Co., 1963).

Todorov, Tzvetan, *The Conquest of America: The Question of the Other*, trans. Richard Howard (New York: Harper and Row, 1984).

Torgovnick, Marianna, *Closure in the Novel*, (Princeton: Princeton University Press, 1981).

Trilling, Lionel, "The Princess Casamassima," *The Liberal Imagination* (New York: Anchor Books, 1953).

Walton, Priscilla, *The Disruption of the Feminine in Henry James* (Toronto: University of Toronto Press, 1992).

Wutz, Michael, "The Word and the Self in *The Ambassadors*," *Style* 25:1 (1991), 89–103.

Index